You

B·e·l·o·n·g

✦ Sayeh Dashti ✦

Library of Congress Control Number: 2016908641

ISBN: Softcover   978-1-5245-0505-9
         Hardcover   978-1-5245-0506-6
         EBook   978-1-5245-0504-2

Print information available on the last page

Rev. date: 10/26/2016

To order additional copies of this book, contact:
Xlibris
1-888-795-4274
www.Xlibris.com
Orders@Xlibris.com

To our children around the world

You Belong

◆ Sayeh Dashti

Illustration by Nooshin Razani

The never-ending line
this line is yours,
it came from your ancestors and to
this
very moment…
every generation
has one
but once…
we shared
one.
This is about our never-ending line to find a connection to others.

Darya Morshed (at age 8)

Through the generations, I am here to tell you my story.

 Kea Morshed (at age 9)

Contents

Preface

You Belong is a book of oral history, human anthropology, and memoir inspired by a recorded cassette tape of my mother (Bibi Sediqeh). Listening to my mother's recorded voice and subsequently transcribing her words now as a mature person is enabling me to appreciate the magnitude of each event and fills me with the deepest regret for losing the precious moments when she was alive and present and eager to talk. The stories my mother told over and over were pieces of history—pieces of the history of our family, our country, and the world.

The first part of this book is a transcription and translation of the recorded voice of my mother talking about historical events that took place in the southern region of Iran near the Persian Gulf in the early twentieth century. Her father, her uncles, and her husband (my father) were the decision makers of that era—we read about them and those events in history books; she puts us there.

The second part of this book consists of stories of myself and my siblings growing up in Tehran in the 1950s and 1960s. It describes our social customs, the music we listened to, the movies we watched, our schools, the books we read, the food we ate, etc.

I was born and raised in Iran. At the age of twenty, I got married and moved to the United States, where I experienced college life during the early 1970s, gave birth and raised three children during the 1980s and the early 1990s. After the Iran-Iraq war, we left America and moved to Iran with our two sons, leaving our daughter in college in the United States. When each of our sons reached the age of military draft (sixteen), we sent them back to the United States under the supervision of their young sister, who was in medical school at the time.

In the last twenty years, like millions of Iranian parents and grandparents, we have lived up in the air between Iran and other countries, where we have left our children with the hope of a more prosperous life for them.

Our international children are now having their own children, born and raised in various countries. Their grandparents come from Iran to visit them every year and return. They have no idea who we are! These stories are to introduce us to our children and their children; they belong to them.

One
Welcome

A caravan came to a halt at my grandfather's house in the city of Borazjan in Bushehr Province in the south of Iran not far from the Persian Gulf. It was close to midnight, but everyone knew that household never actually slept. The residents had just finished cleaning up after many guests who had stayed with them for the last few days. They were ready to retire when they got the call.

Sultan,[1] who was the right-hand man of Aqa ye Bozorg (my grandfather), ran to him with an alarmed voice to report that they were out of firewood (*hizum*) with which to prepare food and *qalyan* (hookah or water pipes) for the caravan that had just arrived.

This was the house where Bibi, my mother, was born in 1917 and grew up in the 1920s. She told us many stories about events that took place in that house, a lot of which were later recorded in history books.[2] The way in which Bibi told us the details of the stories created lasting images in our minds—as if we had actually experienced the events ourselves. She took us behind the scenes of the history of our country and our family. She especially talked about how the structure and the system of their domestic quarters (*andarooni*) operated—the section of their house where most of the preparations for guests took place. She described the storerooms for supplies such as firewood, bedding, hookahs, and meal ingredients such as wheat, rice, sugar, flour, etc., in detail and created a vivid image of how their establishment accommodated numerous visitors who arrived, most of the time, unannounced.

The service quarters, which consisted of the kitchen, the maids' rooms, and the storerooms, were arranged around a rectangular, open courtyard about two thousand square feet in area. The large copper pots of food were prepared outdoors in the middle of the yard on several brick rocket stoves built on the ground. The stoves were heated using firewood that was hard to find in the hot and humid climate of Borazjan.

"Even though our family had several palm tree groves, with a large number of palm trees, we would never consider sacrificing them for firewood. My father did not allow killing the palm trees. In our family, cutting a palm tree was considered an act of homicide, spilling blood," Bibi told us.

The firewood came from different types of trees and from other cities and was stored in a large storeroom raised off the ground to protect the wood from getting damp.

According to Bibi, the most essential cooking ingredients were stored in a row of enclosed bins with small valves at the bottom and sliding wooden doors on top. The food supplies were brought straight into the andarooni yard by horses, camels, and mules. From the top they filled the storage bins with supplies of food up to their full capacity and, as needed, they turned the valves on the outside to get certain quantities (*kail*) of rice or other items.

Rice was brought from a village in Fars Province called Faryab. Bibi believed that Faryab had the best rice in the country with the most distinguished aroma. Bibi always regretted that her family had owned a rice farm in that region for some years, but later on they either sold it or somehow lost its ownership.

As in most Iranian households, bedding had its own separate storeroom. We had the same type of room in our house when we were growing up in Tehran. Individual sets of bedding for each guest were folded and wrapped in a square piece of fabric (*chador shab*), stacked all the way to the ceiling. Each set consisted of a hand-sewn, cotton-filled mattress, a quilt, and a large cylindrical pillow filled with cotton.[3] The mattresses, the quilts, and the pillows were covered with fresh linen either sewn on or pinned on using very large safety pins.

Once a year a cotton bower (*panbeh-zan*) came by to treat the cotton and to redo the beddings.[4] He had a wooden instrument with a string plus a club. He first took the flattened cotton out of the bedding sets and fluffed them up. He performed his job like a skillful musician, an artist. To prepare for his performance, he first spread out a large piece of fabric in a corner of the yard, separated all the covers from the cotton, and then took his instrument, tuned it, and began fluffing the cotton with a certain rhythm one could dance to: "*pip pip panbeh, pip pip panbeh.*" As his work progressed, a mound of refreshed white cotton was created which made him invisible to the eyes of the children who sat in a row to watch him perform. Even though he was hidden for a while, his exhilarating music continued. He reappeared as he filled the new covers with fluffed-up cotton. Fresh colorful mattresses, quilts, and pillows in bright colors—pink, blue, yellow, and green—were arranged on the ground like spring flowers. He then kneeled on the ground and created incredible designs on each piece, by running a large needle and thread through the satin and the cotton, making individual knots and creating a variety of designs. And he was done!

The bluish-white linens were replaced for each new guest. The sheets covered the underside and part of the front of the quilts, leaving only a small piece of the colorful satin showing, sacrificing the glamor of colors for clean hospitality.

Cotton-beater (*hallaje*). A wall painting on the northeast side of the Grand Bazaar, Tehran. Photo: Sayeh Dashti, 2011.

Before the invention of electric washing machines, laundering was a full-time job for one of the maids (*rakhtshoor*). She washed the sheets, the clothes, the cloth diapers, and most everything else in the house that was made of fabric. She sat in a squatting position all day long, washing things in a couple of metal basins placed on the ground. Her daily challenge was to wave away the crows trying to steal her soap with their beaks. Dried herbs called *chubak* (soapwort (*saponaria officinalis*)) were used as soap. For the white fabrics they added a natural whitener, a rich ultramarine powder called *lajvard* (lapis lazuli); it gave the white fabrics a bluish tone as bright as moonlight. *Lajvard* was handled carefully because it was rare. It came from mines in the Kohrud Mountains near Kashan and Qom in central Iran.[5] The powder, wrapped in a cone-shaped white paper, was laid next to a large, round tray of washed clothes that were ready for the final rinse. When the wash was done, the laundress squeezed the clothes using both of her strong hands to twist them in a spiraling movement to make a swirl. She put some of the more delicate fabrics on top of her head in a large pile of swirls. "The piles never fell off even when she rocked back and forth rubbing the fabrics between her two pale, pink hands," Bibi still marveled.

For elongated fabrics such as linens or turbans—belonging to some of the holy guests—another woman came to help. Ceremoniously, the two women stood at a calculated distance as they whirled, twisted, and spun the cloths. They came closer together, one step at a time. With each step, they made a fold, and when they got to an arm's length from each other, the helper was handed the cloth and walked away, avoiding any splash of water.

The cook was in charge of washing the dishes as well as cooking. He or she used leftover ash from the stove, and mud, to clean the greasy dishes. The clean dishes and the pots and pans were turned upside down to dry over large brown straw baskets inside the kitchen.

Our mother, Bibi, smoked from an early age. Most of the stories she told us highlighted the significance and the widespread habit of smoking while she was growing up. As a child, she had smoked a qalyan and then switched to cigarettes in her adult life. Apparently the most critical, an absolutely essential item—something no household and its guests could survive without—was a qalyan. A solid supply of qalyan and its elements (tobacco and charcoal) was without a doubt a nonnegotiable necessity for the majority of the residents—men, women, and even some children. Some visitors had their personal qalyan and their personal assistants who carried the qalyan for them (*qalyan kesh*). However, the firewood and a good supply of treated tobacco was a must.[6]

"In this house, one would never get bored. Aqa had made four buildings for the guests. They are still there. Now one is a school in his name, one is the Census Bureau, another is a military office, and the other one, I do not know," Bibi tried to recall.

The ruins of the house in Borazjan still stand. Photo: Abbas Dashti, 2014.

4

People came to Aqa ye Bozorg's house for a variety of reasons and from different walks of life—peasants to royalty. They came for jobs, for food, for blessing, to resolve a dispute, to make a political decision, to plan a strategy to defend the region, to campaign, to receive a fair judgment, or simply to rest before they went abroad.

At times people of different tribes, diverse religions, opposing political views, or with wounds from deep animosity arrived at Aqa ye Bozorg's house simultaneously.

"It was well understood that all people who arrived in our house had to leave their arms and their differences by the entrance; to enter as friends. They were equally treated as friends once they were inside. The animosity waited until after they left," Bibi clarified, and we witnessed it at her own memorial service in Borazjan.

The horsemen were opening the gates for the approaching caravan. Sultan stared at Aqa ye Bozorg, waiting for his orders. My grandfather ordered Sultan to tear down a large wooden gate and burn it for firewood.

"Of course!" Sultan responded, impressed by his master's problem-solving ability. "He should have known that the large wooden door, or any other object for that matter, was of no value as long as our guests were treated right," Bibi said.

Notes

1 See Story 7, "Black Members of Our Family," in this volume.

2 Mohammad Javad Fakhra'i. *Dashtestan dar gozar e tarikh* (Shiraz: Entesharat e Navid, 1383 [1994]).

3 Some households used a carpeted wrap (*rakhtekhab peech*) with leather straps securing it.

4 Hans E. Wulff, *The Traditional Crafts of Persia: Their Development, Technology, and Influence on Eastern and Western Civilizations* (Cambridge, MA: MIT Press, 1966): 180–81. Wulff describes the tools of the cotton bower or *panbeh-zan* as follows: "The tools of the bower are a rod for a preliminary beating of the fibers, the bow, and a mallet. The bow consists of a round bow shaft that is made up of laminations of poplar wood or willow wood glued together with a fish glue popularly called *jid*. The top of the bow is shaped like the neck of a harp, the foot is formed by a board that is inserted into the slot of a round board carrier, and the whole is attached to the shaft by four gut strings. The tightening is achieved by inserting two wedges. A strong bowstring prepared from four individual guts runs from the bow top to the end of the footboard of the bow. At the top it is attached to a peg, runs over strips of soft leather, and around the corner of the square footboard, where it divides into two guts on each side and is wound around the foot of the bow shaft. Rough tightening is achieved by twisting a toggle peg through the strings. Final adjustment is made by pushing a block made from a roll of hard leather between string and footboard. A smaller tightening string wound by a peg provides the proper tension. The bower usually carries a spare string wound around the shaft. A bundle of cotton yarn is fastened to the bow shaft near its center of gravity. In operation the bower passes one hand through this sling, which at the same time protects his hand. The bow is then placed over the fibers and is beaten with a round mallet made from ash wood. The ridge at the end of the mallet grips the bowstring, and when the latter's tension becomes too high it slips off the ridge, causing a strong vibration. As the string is kept in contact with the fibers these vibrations loosen them and throw them away from the bower. To take the weight off the bow it is either suspended from the ceiling by a string or, when bowing in the open, the bower places a thick cushion between the bow-holding arm and his knee. After the bowing the cotton is rolled into large balls."

5 Wulff, *The Traditional Crafts of Persia*: 147, 148, 163.

6 The tobacco from the south is very strong. The leaves are separated from their stems (*khash kardan*) and are soaked in water overnight.

Two
Our Ancestors—The Four Brothers; Sanctuary (*Bastkhaneh*)

One evening in 1987 in my sister Nafiseh's home in Leeds, England, we gathered around Bibi and listened to her stories. The young people present were the descendants of four of the eleven brothers who had migrated from Bahrain to the southern part of Iran.

The four brothers were the sons of a prominent family in Mahouz, an area in Bahrain.[7] Our family was in conflict with the government of the time in Bahrain. They were Shiites, and the Sunni ruler of Bahrain was a tyrant. Our family had always opposed their barbaric reign and their abuses. Of course the rulers of the region felt threatened by our family's devotion to Iran and their influence amongst the people and aimed to get rid of them. They had gone so far as ordering their execution. It was at this point that the brothers migrated to Bushehr, a port city in the south of Iran. They settled in various regions of Bushehr Province and Fars Province: Borazjan, Kolol, Ahram, and Kazeroon.[8]

This basic drawing of the map of the Persian Gulf shows the position of the island of Bahrain in relation to the southern Iranian cities and towns of Bushehr, Borazjan, and Shiraz that are mentioned in Bibi's stories. Drawing by Sayeh Dashti.

A story narrated by Bibi:

All of the brothers like their fathers before them were leaders of their communities. They were statesmen, scholars, and had written many important books. Some of the books they had written are still being taught in the University of Tehran, especially the book by our ancestor, Sheikh Solaiman, entitled *The Laws and Documentation of Will*. He was a scholar of the highest order.[9]

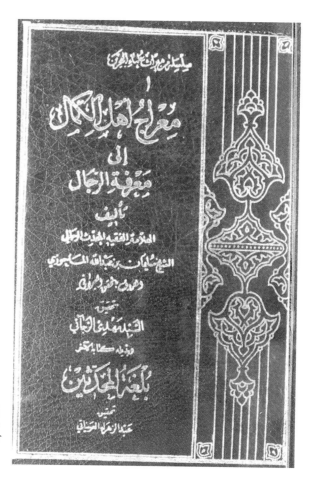

One of the books written by our ancestor Sheikh Solaiman Ibn 'Abd Allah al Mahouzi Bahrani, known as Mohaqqiq al Bahrani (scholar of Bahrain), *The ascendance of the nobles towards the knowledge of hagiography*, 1687 CE. Photo: Sayeh Dashti, 2011.

Khaleh Robabeh (Bibi's oldest sister) married the descendant of the brother in Ahram [A'Mehdi, A'Sadri, and their siblings' ancestors]. Khaleh Abibi (Bibi's older sister) married the descendant of the brother in Kazeroon [A'Borhan and his siblings' ancestors], and I married your father [Abdollah Dashti] who comes from the family of our ancestors in Kolol.

The brother in Borazjan was the grandfather of my father, Mohammad Hossain Borazjani Mojahed [Aqa ye Bozorg]. He was the son of Sheikh Najaf Ali, who was the son of Sheikh Davood, one of the four brothers.

Along with the khans, he ruled and managed the whole region of Dashti. The khans did their own things, they collected taxes—they acted much like mayors and sheriffs—policing the region and keeping order. Their decisions though had to be in accordance with our father's.

This is how our house in Borazjan became a sanctuary [*bastkhaneh*]. *Bastkhaneh* implies that if anyone gets to the shadow of the walls of that house, he will be safe; a refuge—no one could get close to them or shoot at them. This did not mean that one could get away from the law. First they were given security and protection and then, according to the laws, my father decided what the fair judgment should be—even if that meant going to jail.

One time a few prisoners who had stolen things on their way back from the public bath, in the middle of the city, with prison guards, managed to run towards our house. Our security guards had seen how the prisoners tricked their guards and escaped. They ran to our house and leaned against the walls saying, "If you are men enough, come and get us!"

Notes

[1] Mehdi Mahouzi, "Ebne Maitham Bahrani va maratib e elmi, adabi va ensani ye vei," *Pajouheshnameh e farhang va adab* (Research & scientific journal of culture and literature), No. 4, Spring and summer of 1386 (2007) (Tehran, Azad University Publishers, Roud e hen branch, 1386 [2007]), 36. A quotation from Seyyed Mohsen Amin al Hossaini al Ameli, *Aayan al Shieh, Vol. 35:* "The rural district of Mahouz included three villages: Dawnaj, Helta, and Alghurayfah. These three villages, specifically Dawnaj and Helta, were the most prominent areas of Mahouz in Bahrain and most of the prominent learned men, scholars, rulers, literary and business men have come from these area."

[2] Ahmad Eqtedari, *Asar e shahr ha ye* bastani e savahel va jazayer e khalij e Fars va darya ye Oman (The antiquities of the ancient cities of the ports and islands of the Persian Gulf and Oman Sea) (Tehran, Anjoman e Asar e Melli, 1348): 206: "From Choghadak, to the left of the Shiraz-Bushehr road, the area of Tangestan starts. The towns of Boneh Gaz, Tol Siah, Chah Peer, Gandom Reez, Bolfariz, Golgoon, Semel, Shavah, Abad, Mahmood Ahmadi, Ahram, Khaveez, Ali Sini, Golki, Sadini, Anbarak, Maymand Hassani, Souraki, Khiaraki, Qab Kalki, Baghak, Shamshiri, Ali Changi, Zarbarimi, Gar Kour, Gourak, Chah Tol, Pahlevan Keshi, Gainak, Korri, Bashi, Tadoumari, Boulkheir, Rostami, Delvar, Khour Shahaub are in the district of Tangestan. Ahram is the center of Tangestan and the towns of Korri, Bashi, Tadoumari, Boulkheir, Rostami, Delvar, Khour Shahaub are some of the ports of the Persian Gulf."

[3] Sheikh Solaiman ibn 'Abd Allah al-Mahuzi al-Bahrani was born in AH 1075 in the village of Dawnaj in the Mahouz area of Bahrain. Since his ancestors were from the mainland of Iran (Setrah) they were also known as Setravi. Sheikh Solaiman was highly educated and is believed to have known the Koran by heart by the age of seven and at ten years of age he studied jurisprudence in Hajr near Yamameh. By the time he was twenty-four, he had written many valuable books and, with the highest religious rank, he became the religious leader of Bahrain. As was the custom of the time in Bahrain, as a leader, he moved to the center of the religious leaders and the business leaders in Bahrain, Bilad Al Qadim. Sheikh Solaiman is known as a researcher, scholar, and a rarity of his time (*Mohaqqiq nadirat al-asr wa zaman*). There are more than one hundred publications left by him. Most of them show his courage in discussing controversial issues against the popular belief. He was also a poet. A collection of his poetry was compiled by his student, Seyyed Ali Ibn Ibrahim ale Abi Shababeh.

Sources:

√-Muhammad Muhsin Agha Buzurg al-Tihrani, *al-Dhari'ah ila tasanif al-shi'ah* (Beirut: Monzavi Printing, 1403 [1983]).

√-Muhsin al-Husayni 'Amili, *A'yan al-shi'ah* (Beirut: Dar al-Ta'aruf, 1403 [1983]): 7, 302–7.

√-Sulayman al-Mahuzi al-Bahrani, *Fihrist al-babawayh wa-'ulama al-Bahrayn* (Qom: Ahmad Hossaini Press, 1404).

√-'Ali ibn Hasan al-Bahrani, *Anwar al-badrayn fi tarajim 'ulama' al-Qatif wa-al-Ihsa' wa-al-Bahrayn* (Najaf: Matba'at al-Nu'man, 1377).

√-Yusuf ibn Ahmad al-Bahrani, *Lu'lu'at al-Bahrayn* (Qom: Entesharat e Mohammad Sadeq Bahr al Uloom.)

√-Isma'il Baghdadi, *Hidayat al-'arifin* (Beirut, 1410 [1990]): vol. 1.

-Muhammad Baqir ibn Muhammad Akmal Bahbahani, *Ta'liqat rejalieh: al ta'liqat alal monhaj almeghal Astarabadi* (Tehran, 1307).

-'Abd Allah Jaza'iri, *Al-ijazah al-kabirah* (Qom, 1409): 44.

-Muhammad al-Baqir ibn 'Ali Zayn al-Abidin Khonsari, *Rowzat al jannat fi ahwal al ulama wa al sadat* (Qom: Asadollah Esma'ilian Publishing, 1390–92).

-Kheiraldin Zarkoli, *Al alam* (Beirut, 1986): vol. 3, p. 128.

-'Abd Allah ibn Salih Samahiji, *Maniat al momaresin*, 1018 shamsi. Manuscript in Ayatollah Mara'shi Najafi' Library, Qom.

-Hossain Taqi al-Nuri Tabarsi, *Mustadrak al-wasa'il* (Tehran: Mohammad Reza Nouri Najafi, 1321).

-www.wikifeqh.ir

-Ali al-Oraibi, "Rationalism in the School of Bahrain: A Historical Perspective." In *Shiite Heritage: Essays on Classical and Modern Traditions*. Edited and translated by Lynda Clarke (Binghamton, NY: Global Academic Publishing 2001): 331.

-www.encyclopaediaislamica.com

Three

German Consul Wassmuss and British Political Agent Cox

A few framed telegrams hung on our living room wall for years. We asked Bibi to tell us the story one more time so we could tape her voice. She began by criticizing an Iranian film director, Homayoun Shahnavaz: "How could a director alter what is written in history books? The television series *Daliran e Tangestan* is not accurate. What they show is completely inconsistent with what actually took place,"[1] she said and then continued to give us the history relating to the telegrams.

Dashtestan refers to Borazjan and small towns surrounding it. Dalaki, Kolol, Bagh e Hesar, Ab Pakhsh, Sa'd Abad, Shabankareh, Manizak, and Tang e Eram are all part of Dashtestan. Tangestan includes Ahram, which is the center of Tangestan, and the small towns around it such as Baghak, Mahmood Ahmadi, Shamshiri, Delvar, etc.[2]

It is hard to describe the reality of that region. You go for miles and it is all plains; flat land with only a few trees. Then you get to some tents, or a couple of mudbrick huts, called *khaki*. In them you find people who are so superb, so dignified, with such high moral values [*ma'refat*].

When the British arrived in Bushehr in 1915, it was their intention to start a war. Aqa ye Bozorg found out about that and immediately let the entire region, especially the khans, know that there was going to be a war.[3]

When they received the message, the heads of all tribes came to our *birooni* and had a meeting with Aqa. Aqa ye Bozorg relayed the order of *jihad* against the intruders, the British. All of Dashti's prominent people had come to participate in the meeting in defense of the region. Khaloo Hossain[4] and his five sons, Chahkootahis, Nasser Khan e Qashqai, Masal Khan, Ghazanfar al Saltaneh all had come to our house. Asheikh Ja'far, father of Asheikh Bahaedin from Khooti, also tried to come.[5]

This is when Aqa ye Bozorg was given the title *mojahed*.[6] His order was according to the *sharia*, under the order of Akhoond e Mullah Mohammad Kazem Khorasani in Najaf.[7]

11

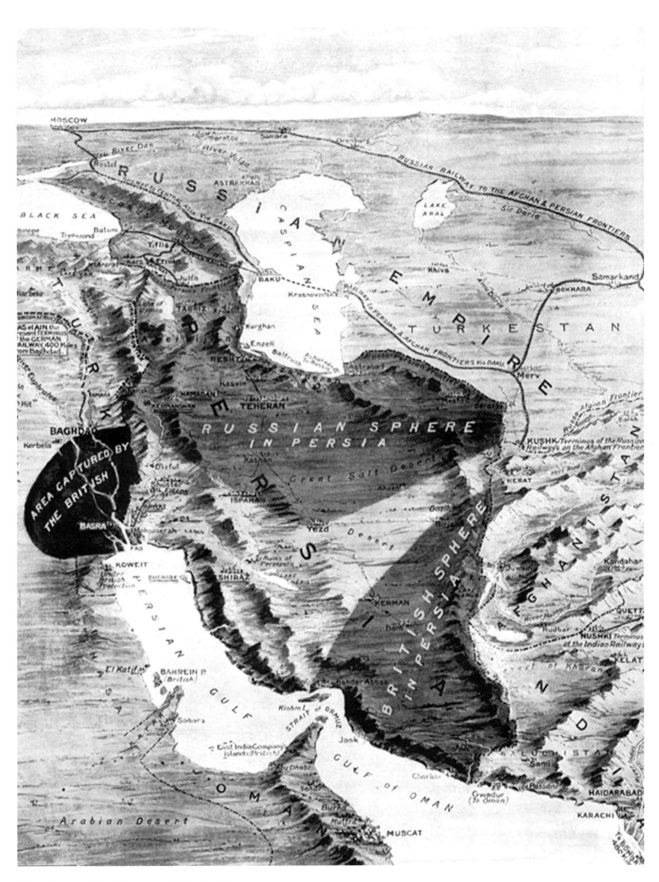

Map of Persia, 1900s. Photo provided by Noel Siver.

There is a good-sized square near Borazjan called Bast e Choghadak; that square had become the battleground.[8] The British army was on one side of the square and the Dashtestanis were on the other side. Dashtestanis only had bravery and were armed with regular, outdated rifles. The British however had everything—they were well equipped; they had come with what Dashtestanis called *paltan,* meaning a well-equipped army. They had guns, shrapnel, pounders, airplanes, etc. They had even constructed a railroad to bring their supplies from a short distance!

I had pointed out all these facts to the director of the television series. One of the misleading messages of the series *Daliran e Tangestan* is that it highlights the involvement of Tangestanis, whereas the Dashtestanis were more involved and sustained more casualties. Khaloo Hossain and one of his sons died in that war. They did everything to defeat England and they did. Most history books have recorded it. I believe the history book written by Davani is a valid book; it has all of these facts in detail.[9]

Yes, the television series was right to make a hero out of Ra'is Ali Delvari.[10] He was such a brave general. The British had gone to the small port of Delvar by way of the sea, which goes to Bikheh e Dashti and then to Delvar. The British had come with a small ship to fight Ra'is Ali. Ra'is Ali had said to a British general, "We will toss you all in the sea so far that you will have to swim back to London!" He defeated them in Delvar. Yes, Ra'is Ali Tangestani was the bravest one. Unfortunately, an Iranian traitor assassinated him.[11] Aqa ye Bozorg went to Delvar to personally give his condolences to Ra'is Ali's father, Zayer Mohammad. My father wrote a telegram to the religious leaders in Shiraz to make sure they supported Ra'is Ali's family and he ordered that Ra'is Ali's brother, Abdol Hossain, be decorated with a medal and then he had a very dignified funeral ceremony for him in his home in Borazjan.[12] The history books say that Sheikh Mohammad Hossain had learned to use a gun too; he was fighting on the front. It was not as though he just relayed the order of *jihad* and stayed home in safety; he was on the front line, the books say.

We won the war; however, I assume that British soldiers had orders to take it easy on us. That is a fact! They came and attacked us a few days, and then again they would leave. Then they came back again! If they really wanted to, they could eliminate the whole region in no time.

The German consul happened to be in Bushehr at the time all this was going on. His name was Wassmuss.[13] He had been in Iran for a long time. He could speak, read, and write Farsi perfectly. He even dressed like a southern Iranian tribesman. When the British came, he went on the run.[14]

He came by way of the island of Sheef, a shortcut. He had first come on a donkey to Shabankareh. From there, it took him twenty-four hours to get to Borazjan on foot; he even had to crawl at some points. It was about twelve miles distance.

He knew that if the British found him, they would tear him to pieces. That is why, when the British came, he went on the run. First he escaped to Shabankareh. He went to Malek Mansour Khan and his father, Mam Ali Khan [Mohammad Ali Khan]. They took him to their tent. They were afraid of the British too, so they told him, "You need to leave. If the British look for you here, they will kill you and kill us all too. The only place you can go, your only chance is to the house of Sheikh Mohammad Hossain, Aqa ye Bozorg; his house is a *bastkhaneh*." And he agreed.

Wassmuss took off the very same night. He got the directions to our house; streets had no names then. He was told to go left and then go right. People crossing his path assisted him on the way until he finally made it to our house in the middle of the night.

He stayed with our family for a long time. If the British had ever found out, they would have certainly destroyed our house—they did not care about any *bastkhaneh*.

Wassmuss made it to the house and our guards carried his body inside. Aqa ye Bozorg put him in his library first. He then noticed that the man was seriously injured from the roughness of the road. There were thorns stuck in his body. He sent Sultan and one of our guards on a horse to take Wassmuss to Dalaki to be treated by a man called Kal Esma'il [Karbalaii Esma'il].

Kal Esma'il had a reputation for knowing how to treat gunshot wounds. This was because he was wounded once and had treated himself with certain natural substances [*marham*] that grew in the mountains. So now he was thought of as the *hakim* of the area! There were no doctors there.

He wrapped the consul's entire body with the *marham*. They nursed him for four days, gave him good food, and sheltered him before bringing him back to our house. Sultan stayed with him the entire time.

Aqa ye Bozorg hid him in the *sardab e sen* [a cavernous basement]. This basement was very deep; more than sixty steps down. There was no electricity then. In summertime the heat gets unbearable in Borazjan. The basement was in two levels, *sen* and *nim-sen*. *Sen* was sixty steps deep; we used it to store our food such as meat and watermelon, etc., like a refrigerator. The *nim-sen* was only twenty-five stairs deep. It was painted white and always very clean. That is where we slept in the afternoons to escape the heat.

Eventually, after weeks, he sent Wassmuss to Shiraz, to return home.

There were no cars then, only *qafeleh*s, a caravan of mules. The head of the caravan [*charvedar*] was Mish Esma'il [Mashhadi Esma'il]. My father sent for Mish Esma'il and told him to reserve one side of his saddlebag for him, but he did not say for what. He simply said, "We have a delicate cargo to send to Shiraz." When it was time for the *qafeleh* to leave, Aqa ye Bozorg went in person to hide Wassmuss in the saddlebag. Wassmuss curled up in the bag. They covered him up completely and made some holes in the saddlebag to let in some air to breathe. They put in a canteen of water and some food.

The roads from Borazjan to Shiraz were dirt roads, usable for animal transport. Interestingly, the British had built those roads too. The mountainous, narrow dirt roads in that area were extremely dangerous; they were rough and bumpy with sharp *kotal*s [bends]—Kotal e Dokhtar, Kotal e Malu, Kotal e Pir e Zan were frightening places for anyone crossing them.

The dangerous nature of the mountain passes between Shiraz and Bushehr is seen in this photograph taken from a bus. Photo: Fahim Fahimi, January 1970.

Remains of the old track between Kazeroon and Shiraz were still visible in 1970. Photo: Noel Siver, May 5, 1970.

Wassmuss made it to Kazeroon and then to Shiraz safely. In Shiraz, he sent a telegram to Germany and a copy in Farsi to Aqa ye Bozorg with the consulate's stamp on it.

The telegram reads:

Let it be known that I have survived because of the sacrifices Sheikh Mohammad Hossain Borazjani made. Anytime, anywhere, any member of his family crosses Germany and needs our help, you are obliged to assist them; they saved my life with grace.

The other telegrams that hung on the wall of our home were the original telegram from the British consul to Sheikh Mohammad Hossain Borazjani and Aqa ye Bozorg's reply (see below). Bibi believed that this document was what our family was most proud of. She said, "Our family does not need a promise from Wassmuss, but the fact that we are still here and we have a country we call Iran is due to the courage of these few great men who did not sell themselves and gave their lives to protect Iran."

Our father, Abdollah Dashti, wrote in his journal:[15]

The British forces, who had occupied the area of the Persian Gulf since 1856 (The Anglo-Persian War 1856–57) and again in 1915, were getting nervous about the conditions in Dashtestan. They were exerting pressure, as much as they could, but it had not changed anything—the people were resisting them very firmly.

Portrait of Wilhelm Wassmuss, 1880–1931.
Drawing by Maryam Shirvanian, 2016.

The British were trying to seek Sheikh Mohammad Hossain Borazjani's support as a powerful man in the region to do something about all this! One of the communications was sent by Sir Percy Cox,[16] the Consul General and the political ruler in the region. The telegram was endorsed by George V, King of the United Kingdom and Emperor of India, asking Sheikh Mohammad Hossain Borazjani to go to Bushehr and from there to Karbala and reside there—not to mention that the whole region including Iraq was ruled by the British—a man from Bushehr (Khan Bahador) was appointed by the British to govern Karbala. Sheikh Mohammad Hossain wrote a courageous telegram back to him:

> "I am a citizen of Iran and a member of Iranian society. If there is a message of any order or request, it should come from the Iranian king, not a king of a foreign country! I am a Moslem and live under the sky of my God and no one has the right or permission to tell me where I should live. When you contemplate to appoint me to go to the holy cities of Karbala, Najaf, and Baghdad, even though it is my wish to live the rest of my life next to the holy shrines, but coming from you as an order it is against my will and my God's will. It is impossible that I do a thing like that based on your decision. The fact that you mention that you will pay for my expenses and are actually trying to bribe me, you must know that never ever in my entire life have I gone to sleep or woken up with a *shahi* [about a penny] left in my pocket. Therefore, my daily living and that of my family comes from God and not from a blasphemer, an intruder."

Seyyed Qasem Yahossaini, in his book *Ra'is Ali Delvari tahajom e Britania va moqavemat e janoob* (Ra'is Ali Delvari: The British military transgressions and the resistance of the south), quotes Ra'is Ali:[17]

On April 26, 1915, Ra'is Ali wrote a letter to Sheikh Mohammad Hossain Borazjani. This letter stands out as what we could call Ra'is Ali Delvari's manifesto:

> May my life be sacrificed upon your enlightened existence. May I sacrifice my life for your courage and your patriotism. The British have created a rumor that "I have been supporting the German Consul!" God is my witness and I have no fear of anyone else; they cannot threaten me with these rumors. I know that they have also sent you a threatening telegram. In fact I was so thrilled by the telegram Your Excellency sent in their reply; only God knows the extent of my joy when they read it to me from the newspapers.

> *Afarin* [Bravo!] Bravo! Bravo! God is sending you his blessings. It is appropriate to say that the entire people of Fars and the Persian Gulf are proud of and boast about the official and very strong telegram you sent them. May God protect you at all times. Please do not be disappointed if all people are not supportive at this time. If you allow me, I will be at your service with my life.

> I would like to come and pay my respect, I just do not know how.

> Ali Delvari.

Here follows the exchange of telegrams between British consul Sir Percy Cox and Sheikh Mohammad Hossain Borazjani that took place in 1915:

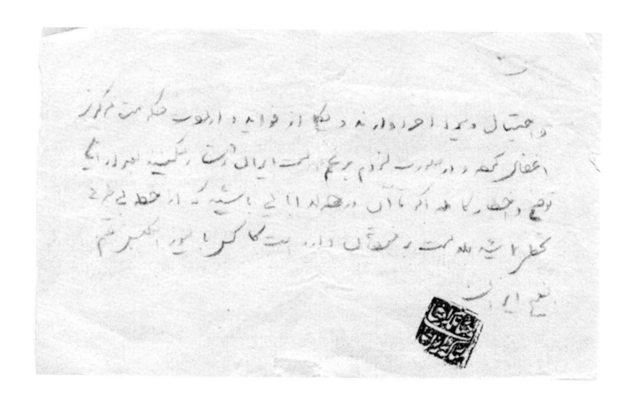

The British consul's telegram to Sheikh Mohammad Hossain Borazjani in three pages. Dashti family history material.

Translation of the telegram sent by British consul Sir Percy Cox to Sheikh Mohammad Hossain Borazjani:[18]

Bushehr 575-6154-22

The Honorable, the Learned Scholar, Sheikh Mohammad Hossain:

Since I am certain of the fact that you are a righteous citizen of Iran, I feel obliged to inform you of some facts and information I have on this very important occasion; facts which you may not know and I like to inform you as a friend.

The British government has been a sincere ally of Iran from the past, has supported Iran during times of difficulties and challenges, and has always assisted the Iranian government financially and otherwise. At the present time regarding the European war, as you are aware, the British government is at war with Germany. Germany, on the other hand, for its own selfish purposes has involved the Ottoman Empire in the war. Clearly it was not at all necessary for the countries of Great Britain and the Ottoman Empire to be involved in the war with each other. But, since it is apparent that Great Britain is the largest country governing Moslems, repeatedly and for its obvious commitments it has shown that it has respected and safeguarded the holy places of the Hejaz and Iraq. As a gesture of good will it has provided food at its own expense for the Hajjis and the people of Jeddah and the holy shrines, just to show that it has no intention to engage in war with the Moslems.

Our friend, the Iranian government, has made a serious effort to remain neutral up to this point, but now it is becoming apparent that the German and Ottoman governments, due to the difficulties they are now facing, are using Iran's neutrality as their *mal al-mosaleheh* [indemnity] and are dragging Iran into the war as well.

A few days ago it was brought to light that the German Consul is busy in Bushehr provoking the people of Tangestan to attack Bushehr. It is absolutely necessary that he be expelled from Bushehr. The existing papers and evidences are indicating that the German Consul with the cooperation of the Swedish agents of the Gendarmerie Nationale, without the knowledge of the Iranian government, are plotting to provoke the dignitaries and the rulers of the south to engage in a hostility against the British. Moreover we are informed that the heads of the gendarmerie are creating false rumors about the factual events of the war and are trying to mislead prominent people such as yourself to trick you into cooperating with them and the Ottomans and the Germans in an attempt to attack Great Britain. Of course, dear friend, you are not that naïve to be misled by these means, knowing that animosity towards the British government, which has no purpose or feeling of unfriendliness towards you, is nothing but ignorant. Not only will you cause problems for yourself, but you will endanger the people and the government of your country. The Iranian government is not aware of any of these plots and certainly does not mean to follow the Ottomans as a model and become Germany's toy, since it is most obvious that if they do, they will be ruined.

The healthiest thing for you, friend, is to firmly resist the manipulations and the provocations of these foreign violators. Their past history should clearly show you that it is the government of Germany that has made them deliver its evil plans and is completely removed from the will of the central government and if necessary will act against the central government. No other way to explain and warn you that if you be that benighted to the level to cross the line of neutrality, you yourself are to blame.

Cox

Consul of Great Britain in the Persian Gulf

As soon as this telegram was received by Sheikh Mohammad Hossain Borazjani, he sent an unyielding reply to the consul.

Sheikh Mohammad Hossain Borazjani's reply to Sir Percy Cox, printed on July 12, 1915. Dashti family history material.

Translation of the telegram sent by Sheikh Mohammad Hossain Borazjani to British consul Sir Percy Cox:

Borazjan [printed on 29 Sha'ban 1333 [July 12, 1915], Bushehr

The Honorable Mr. Cox, *baliyuz* [consul general][19] of Great Britain residing in Bushehr:

Your telegraph has arrived, even though due to my righteousness and my devotion to my beloved country, I should have replied to your letter through my government, not to forget that your communication to me also should have come to me via the Iranian government, but, since you have acted illegally and have sent me the letter directly, I am forced to answer you directly.

Regarding the World War, it is obvious that the great government of Iran has chosen to stay neutral, and so far Iran has completely followed the rules of neutrality without any errors. If you take a fair look at the situation, you will see that the agitation of Iranian people against your government is only due to your esteemed government and the Russians' interference in the Persian Gulf area, the southern and the northern parts of Iran. You have both acted against Iran's neutral policy whenever you had a chance. If, as you claim, the Germans are provoking the Iranian *ashayer*, you have no strong evidence to support such accusation. Suppose this is as you say, you are the ones who have taught them such misbehavior and I am so sorry that you have chosen our country as the battleground for your benefit and those of other foreigners and because of this, you have forced the dignified people of Iran to react, whereas you are well aware that each individual of the prestigious Iranian population has made an effort to support its government's policy of neutrality.

Regarding the Swedish authorities: Our gendarmerie knows very well that the office of gendarmerie is a government-run office and follows the rules of the central government. They have never, not one of many employees nor the officers, acted outside of the lines of their duties and that of their nationalism.

The fact that you name your esteemed government as the ruler of some of the Islamic countries, be most certain that governing on the surface is not due to your knowledge or wisdom and this shall disturb the feeling and the emotions of Christian society. Deep down all the Moslems of the world are looking up to the honorable governments of Iran and the Ottomans and await the *fatwa* of the religious leaders of these two countries.

You have pointed out the cooperation of the British government with the Iranian government. This is also a matter that is unclear. The Iranian people believe that all the damages we have suffered in the North are all planned with your approval and support. Disrespecting the holy grounds of Khorasan, where your government stayed inactive, also supports my point. In fact you know too well that the Iranian people, after their religion, they value their government and their independence and avoid opposing their own government. By all means, when the religious leaders issue an order from Iraq, the people will give their wealth and their lives. You should know that during this time, if it were not for my efforts to keep peace, the patriotic *ashayer*s of the South would have reacted by now, since the British government has repeatedly and purposely acted in spite of its promises and has attacked Basra which is the gate to Iraq and has no borders with England, and has created chaos within the Moslem countries and these days the religious leaders of Iraq with the cooperation of the Ottoman government have engaged in war with you. Myself, in time, have been able to prevent the agitation of our people, but I am sorry to inform you that your recent actions in the Gulf and Nasseri and Mohamareh (Khorramshahr) and taking the consul general of Germany who has no opposition to Iranian neutrality, have disturbed our minds and today almost one thousand [*lak*] Dashti, Dashtestani, and Tangestani gunmen insist on discontinuing friendly relations with you, especially when we hear that you have disembarked an army in Bushehr and have prepared to attack the Iranian people, all these have created hatred in us. To sum it up, basically, the people of Iran have always tried to keep peace and to avoid war and disturbance and continue to do so. It is up to you now to stop violating our cities, return the consul general of Germany, secure boundless peace and our relationship.

I now remind you of this important point. If your aggression continues, control of the people's reaction becomes improbable; the responsibility and the blame is upon you and your thoughtless acts, which have crossed the line of neutrality and not mine. "One who finds no logic resorts to excuses [*Leghad a'zar men anzar*]."

The server of my people—Mohammad Hossain Borazjani

Sir Percy Cox. Photo: Licensed by Imperial War Museum, England.

Notes

[1] Bibi is referring to the television series, *Daliran e Tangestan* directed by Shahnavaz. In 1976 his crew came to our house to interview her. According to http://iranian.com/main/blog/darius-kadivar/pictory-daliran-tangestan-old-iranian-tv-series.html, *Daliran e Tangestan* (The brave of Tangestan) was an Iranian television series (1973) that narrated the story of the Iranian revolt in Bushehr (southern Iran) against UK imperialism in the 1920s.

[2] Soroosh Atabak'zadeh, *Jaygah ye Dashtestan dar sarzamin e Iran* (The position of Dashtestan in the land of Iran) (Shiraz: Entesherat e Navid, 1373 [1994]). Map of Dashtestan following title page.

[3] Hamid Algar, "Religious Forces in Twentieth-Century Iran," in P. Avery et al. (eds.), *The Cambridge History of Iran, VII: From Nadir Shah to the Islamic Republic* (Cambridge: Cambridge University Press, 1991): 732–64. Abd al-Reza Hooshang Mahdavi, *Tarikh e ravabet e khareji ye Iran* (History of Iranian foreign affairs) (Tehran: Entesharat e Amir Kabir, 1349 [1972]): chapter 6.

[4] Khaloo Hossain is mentioned in the following newspaper article: Afshin Parto, "Goosheh'i az hamaseh ye Ra'is Ali Delvari va yaranash," *Nasim e Janoob* (A breath from the South) 786 (15 Shahrivar 1394 [September 6, 2015]): 4.

[5] "Sheikh Ja'far Mahallati decided to go to Borazjan. I sent a messenger to ask him to change his mind; the messenger asked me to do this directly. I sent the head of my cabinet to warn him of the dangers, but he did not listen." Quoted from Mehdi Qoli Hedayat (Mokhber al Saltaneh), *Khaterat va khatarat* (Memories and the dangers) 5th ed. (Tehran: Entesharat e Zavvar, 1375 [1996]): 271.

[6] *Mojahed* means having the characteristics of someone who fights for a non-personal and humanitarian goal such as freedom. Hasan Anvari-Sokhan, *Farhang e bozorg e sokhan*, vol. 7 (Tehran: 1381 [2002]).

[7] Ali Morad Farrashbandi, *Goosheh'i az tarikh e enqelab e mosallahaneh ye mardom e mobarez e Tangestan, Dashti va Dashtestan alaihe este'mar* (A view of an angle of history of the armed resistance of the people of Tangestan, Dashti and Dashtestan against exploitation) (Tehran: Sherkat e Sahami ye Entesher, 1362 [1983]): 41. Akhoond e Mullah Mohammad Kazem's telegrams to various parts of the country are published in Nazem al-Eslam Kermani, *Tarikh e bidari ye Iranian* (The history of Iranians awakening) compiled by Ali Akbar Sa'idi Sirjani. 7th ed. (Tehran: Entesharat e Paykan, 1392 [2013]): vol. 2, 515–668.

[8] Choghadak is five farsakh (one farsakh equals 6.23 kilometers) from Bushehr, seven farsakh from Borazjan, two farsakh from Ahmadi, one and a half farsakh from Chahkootah, four farsakh from Ahram. This small city is twenty-four kilometers southeast of Bushehr, on the way to the main road from Bushehr to Borazjan and the beginning of the belt road to the ports of Bushehr and Hormozgan. Choghadak was a place of resistance of the people of the south against the British army in AH 1273 and 1333: Seyyed Ja'far Hamidi, *Farhang'nameh ye Bushehr* (An encyclopedic dictionary of Bushehr) (Tehran: Sazman e Chap va Entesharat, Vezarat e Farhang ve Ershad e Islami, 1380 [2001]): 244.

[9] Ali Davani, *Nahzat e ruhaniyun e Iran* (The movement of the Iranian holy men) (Tehran: Bonyad e farhangi ye Imam Reza, 1360? [1981?]): vol. 1, 254–76.

[10] Seyyed Qasem Yahossaini, *Ra'is Ali Delvari tajavoz e nezami ye Britania va moqavemat e janoob* (Ra'is Ali Delvari: The British military transgressions and the resistance of the south) (Tehran: Pardis e Danesh, 1391 [2012]): 171–74.

[11] According to Yahossaini there are four versions as to who was behind the death of Ra'is Ali Delvari:

[1]- A British high official paid one hundred *lireh* to a man called Gholam Hossain Tangaki to kill Ra'is Ali. Yahossaini quotes Rokn'zadeh-Adamiyat, *Daliran e Tangestani* (The brave of Tangestan), 185, regarding this theory.

[2]- Some sources, such as Farrashbandi, *Janoob e Iran dar mobarezat e zed e este'mari* (The south of Iran in the battles against exploitation), 60, believe that Gholam Hossain Tangaki invited Ra'is Ali to his house, yet when he arrived, he refused to receive him. There was a shooting and Ra'is Ali was killed in that shooting.

[3]- Abdolmajid Jamali published an article, "Zendegi ye Ra'is Ali Delvari" (The life of Ra'is Ali Delvari), *Rooznamah ye Jomhoori ye Islami ye Iran* (Islamic Republic of Iran newspaper) No. 3457, 24 Ordibehesht 1370 (May 14, 1991), p. 9. In this article he also reported that Hossain Khan e Chahkootahi and Zayer Khan Chahkootahi killed Ra'is Ali out of jealousy.

[4]- Foreign publications such as the Annual Report of the British Consulate in Bushehr by General Cox have reported his death as accidental: The First World War in the south of Iran, annual reports of the British Con–sulate in Bushehr, translated by Kaveh Bayat, Bushehr: Congress on the eightieth anniversary of the martyrdom of Ra'is Ali Delvari, 1373 (1994), pp. 41–42.

[12] *Adl* newspaper, Shiraz, published this telegram. Ahmad Akhgar, *Zendegi ye man dar tul e haftad sal e tarikh e mo'aser e Iran* (My life during the 70 years of Iran's contemporary history) 1st ed. (Tehran: Akhgar, 1366 [1987]): 157. Abol Hassan Hossaini, *Naqsh e Ayatollah Mojahed Borazjani dar qiam e shahid Ra'is Ali Delvari* (Role of Ayatollah Mojahed Borazjani

in the insurrection of Ra'is Ali Delvari the martyr) (Tehran: Entesharat e Aineh ye Janoob, 1388): 51. The telegram from Sheikh Mohammad Hossain Borazjani to Aqa Mirza Ebrahim Mahallati in Shiraz: "Shiraz, The Honorable Aqa Mirza Ebrahim, the Blessed . . . Ra'is Ali Khan Delbari [Delvari] has been martyred; but this atrocity has cost us desperation and his loss is effecting the Moslem world; telegraph his father Zayer Mohammad to honor him for having a son like that and he has a child with the name of Abdol Hossain, decorate him with a medal of honor. Send instant reply please. Mohammad Hossain Borazjani."

13   Wilhelm Wassmuss (February 14, 1880 – November 29, 1931) was a German diplomat, known as "Lawrence of Persia." Quoted from Oliver Bast, *Les Allemands en Perse pendant la Première Guerre mondiale d'après les sources diplomatiques françaises*, Travaux et mémoires de l'Institut d'études Iraniennes 2, Paris, 1997; trans. by Hossain Bani Ahmad as *Ālmānīhā dar Īrān: Negāh-ī be taavvolāt e Īrān dar jang e jahānī e avval bar asās e manābe e dīplomātīk e Farānseh* (Tehran: Pardis e Danesh, 1392 [2013]): 28, 30, 37, 42, 45, 46, 59, 71, 74, 100, 102, 153–55.

14   Wipert von Blücher, *Zeitenwende in Iran: Erlebnisse und Beobachtungen* (Biberach an der Riss, Germany: Koehler und Voigtländer, 1949). Trans. by Kaykavoos Jahandari as *Safar'nāmahi Blushir, gardish-i rūzigār dar Īrān* (Tehran: Entesharat e Kharazmi, 1369 [1990]): 102–3. "After Wassmuss left his post as the head of the German group in Afghanistan, he made a decision to come to Iran and block one of the most strategically important roads in the south of Iran. He was probably the only one who was qualified to do such an incredible act. He was previously the consul at Bushehr and knew the region very well. He knew their language and customs and deep in his heart, he had an undeniable passion towards Iran and the Iranian race. He expressed his love to the untamed children of a region who lived in the most remote areas of Iran. He risked his life and singlehandedly took on this mission, went to Dashtestan and Tangestan and lived there for years. Wassmuss was a man from [Ohlendorf], Germany, with blond hair and a big skull. He had blue eyes and a strong body. His most outstanding characteristic was his very kind heart, a childlike innocence, and an unbelievable persistence in achieving his goal. It was through his strong personality and originality that the Dashtestanis trusted him. Through his efforts, an important chapter was written in the history of WWI. Maybe the only thing similar to it is Lawrence of Arabia. Dashtestanis and the Tangestanis resisted the British invasion fighting hard and Wassmuss was able to block the British transportation from the south to Shiraz."

15   Abdollah Dashti, *Az Jam/Reez ta Tabriz* (From Jam/Riz to Tabriz) Compiled and edited by Badieh Dashti. (Tehran: Farhang e Hezareh e Sevvom, 1385 [2006]): 114.

16   www.britannica.com/biography/Percy-Cox: "Sir Percy Cox, in full Sir Percy Zachariah Cox (born November 20, 1864, Herongate, Essex, England—died February 20, 1937, Melchbourne, Bedfordshire). . . . Educated at the Royal Military Academy, Sandhurst, he served in the army in India from 1884 to 1890, when he joined the Indian political service. From 1893 to 1914 he held various political posts in the Persian Gulf area and Persia. He was knighted in 1911. During World War I, as chief political officer of the Indian Expeditionary Force, Cox was responsible for all relations with local authorities in British-occupied Iraq. From 1918 to 1920 he acted as British minister to Persia." Cyrus Ghani, *Iran and the Rise of Reza Shah: From Qajar Collapse to Pahlavi Rule* (London and New York: I.B. Tauris Publishers, 1998): 28. "After Harrow and Sandhurst Cox had begun his career as an India Office civil servant and in 1899 Curzon had appointed him Consul in Muscat. In 1903 he and his wife had travelled by boat with Curzon, who was then Viceroy of India (1899–1905), and Sir Arthur Hardinge, British Minister in Tehran (1900–1905), up the Persian Gulf on a leisurely inspection trip and had gained the further confidence of Curzon. Cox had been appointed in 1915 Britain's Resident in the Persian Gulf, a post he held until his appointment to Tehran. The Resident was in effect the supreme authority concerning British interests in the Gulf region including all the Sheikhdoms. The Resident's seat was in Bushehr in southern Iran which flew the British flag and was treated by Britain as part of her territory. Cox had extensive dealings with Iranian officials during this period and was regarded as an expert in Iranian affairs."

17   Seyyed Qasem Yahossaini, *Ra'is Ali Delvari tahajom e Britania va moqavemat e janoob* (Ra'is Ali Delvari: The British military transgressions and the resistance of the south) (Tehran: Pardis e Danesh, 1391 [2012]): 112–21.

18   Mohammad Hossain Rokn'zadeh-Adamiyat, *Fars va jang e bain al-melal* (Fars and the World War): 273–74. Hossaini, *Naqsh e Ayatollah Mojahed Borazjani dar qiam e shahid Ra'is Ali Delvari* (Ayatollah Mojahed Borazjani's role in the resistance movement of Ra'is Ali Delvari the martyr): 27–32.

19   *Baliyuz* means the political representative of a country in another country. This term comes from the Middle French word *baillir* meaning to govern: Dehkhoda et al., *Loghatnameh Dehkhoda* (dictionary); *Tarikh e Yamini* (Tehran, 1272 [1893]): 356; Hamidi, *Farhang'nameh ye Bushehr* (An encyclopedic dictionary of Bushehr): 121.

Four

Disarming the Khans: Sheikh Mohammad Hossain Borazjani

Bibi answers our questions regarding the historical event of disarming the khans:

It was at the beginning of Reza Shah's reign [1925]. He had disarmed the khans of the whole country except the region of Dashti. The province of Dashti is a combination of plains and high mountains. The mountainous area is labyrinthine—even the planes that drop bombs cannot get to it. Reza Shah went to our mother's brother, Ali Dashti [known in the family as Aqda'i], who was in Parliament at that time and said, "We have achieved the disarming of the tribes throughout the entire country, except your hometown. Would you please do something; they trust you. Give them reassurance on my behalf, so they will give up their guns."

Aqda'i said, "It is not my job. This is a job for Sheikh Mohammad Hossain Borazjani. They respect him. You should write to him yourself if you want him to do that."

I remember this. It was the month of Ramadan when my father got the telegram from Reza Shah. I was about six years old and very sick that day. My chest was wheezing; I guess I had pneumonia. I was in bed with fever when my father came to my bedside and put his hand on my forehead. He kissed my forehead for the first time. I never forget it. He told me, "Look Baba, I have to go. I would not leave you like this if I did not have to. The lives of the people are in danger. If I do not go, hundreds of people will lose their lives. I am leaving you in the hands of God."

All the tribesmen [*ashayer*] of Dashti, with their guns, had fled to the mountains and the army of the Shah was chasing them. My father went unarmed. He went with Sultan, his right-hand man, who also got to carry his water pipe [*qalyan dar*]. Two other men accompanied them: his secretaries, Seyyed Mam Reza and another man (Bibi could not remember his name). They first rode on their horses to Khormooj, the center of Dashti, and then to the foot of the mountains.

Sultan swore so we could believe him as he said, "As soon as we got to Khormooj, the news of our arrival went from the tower of Khormooj to the *ashayer* [tribesmen] that Sheikh Mohammad Hossain had come to see them. The next morning all came down from the mountains! As they came, one by one, they laid down their rifles, bowed to him, and kissed his hand."

28

The *ashayer* love their guns. "Yes of course when you come we trust you," the chief told Aqa. 'Without our guns we are like women. But we are putting our trust in you.'

Aqa ye Bozorg was telling them, "Look, this country is being fixed. Shah has asked me to reassure you. Hopefully this country will no longer be a country of bandits. The Shah has promised, you will be saved. This is not a life. How long are you going to be on the run? You have had to go to the mountains every time something has happened." They honored his request.

Then from Khormooj a telegram was sent to Borazjan for the head of the military to come and collect the weapons. They loaded many four-horse carriages and took them away. "The pile of rifles was so high that Aqa became invisible; we could not see him anymore," Sultan reported. He stayed for twenty days to complete his mission.

Sheikh Mohammad Hossain then returned to Borazjan. When he was coming back, there was an incredible crowd waiting to welcome him. There were so many. After a week, Khaloo Hossain, the big chief of Dashti, came to visit him. He brought along a caravan of camels with boxes of sugar cubes and tea. We had a big room; we closed the room and filled it up with tea and sugar boxes. He had said, "I know you do not accept gifts, but this is only a sweet [*shirini*]."

So they came. Even Jamal Khan, the great khan of Borazjan, came to our house to greet Aqa. Yes, this is how it was.

Tribal men with rifles. Photo source unknown.

Sheikh Mohammad Hossain Borazjani.
Photo: Dashti family album.

Even after the government was centralized, Shah had ordered his army to still abide by the rules of Sheikh Mohammad Hossain and our house continued to be a sanctuary for people who sought refuge.

The following passage was translated from the book by Seyyed Abol Hassan Hossaini, *Naqsh e Ayatollah Mojahed Borazjani dar qiam e shahid Ra'is Ali Delvari* [The role of Ayatollah Mojahed Borazjani in the insurgency of Ra'is Ali Delvari the martyr] (Tehran: Entesharat e Aineh ye Janoob, 1388): 21–22.

Sheikh Mohammad Hossain Borazjani

"Sheikh Mohammad Hossain was the son of Najaf Ali, son of Sheikh Davood, son of Sheikh Yousef.[1] Because he had pronounced a decree urging resistance against British dominance in Iran, he was given the title *mojahed* [which means 'soldier of the holy war']. He was a prominent leader not only in the south but in the entire country of Iran. We must admit that after Allameh Sheikh Solaiman Mahouzi, he is the most distinguished member of the Mahouzi family to this date.[2]

He was born in 1249 shamsi [1870] in Borazjan. We do not know much about his early years, however we can guess that at a very early age he decided to study in Najaf. He has had his own classroom in Qavam School and was the most distinguished student.

Sheikh Mohammad Hossain had two brothers, Mirza Mohammad Hassan and Sheikh Hassan. Abdollah Dashti who was a member of parliament for several terms was the son of Sheikh Mohammad Hassan and also the son-in-law of Sheikh Mohammad Hossain. He was also educated in Najaf and resided in Borazjan. Sheikh Hassan also completed his education in Najaf and came to live in Tehran. He travelled to India, but returned to Tehran and remained there.

After completing his education, Sheikh Mohammad Hossain settled in Borazjan. His house was open to everyone and people had sincere devotion to him and his family. People from all walks of life filled his house at all times. His influence amongst the people had resulted in his ability to resolve most of the problems of the people who came to his door. His knowledge, open-mindedness, and his ability to reason soon attracted all the people. He was a competent authority and the chief of Borazjan and Dashtestan. His presence in Borazjan coincided with World War One, for that reason most historians and researchers begin writing about him at about this period of his life."[3]

At the end of his life, 1308 [1929], he was exiled to Tehran and passed away in 1319 [1940]. He is buried in Imamzadeh Abdollah.

His tombstone reads:

Hazrat Ayatollah Ozma Sheikh Mohammad Hossain Borazjani farzand e rezwan aramgah Haj Sheikh Najaf Ali keh naslan bad e nasl aleih e kofoor e dinieh boodeh va dar rah e esteqlal va azemat e Iran masaf kardeh va dar saf e mojahedan masaf dadeh va dar sal e 1310 shamsi az Dashtestan mooled e asli ye khod be Tehran amadeh va panjshanbeh dovom e khordad 1319 da'vat e labeik gofteh va jan be jan afarin sepordeh shodeh ast (dar al rezwan).

[His excellency, the great Ayatollah Sheikh Mohammad Hossain Borazjani, son of heavenly (paradise) Haj Sheikh Najaf Ali, who generation after generation has fought against the country's enemies and has battled for the glory of Iran and been on the line of fire in these battles. In 1310 shamsi (1931) has come to Tehran from Dashtestan, his original home, and on Thursday, Khordad 2, 1319 [May 23, 1940] has accepted the invitation of death and has freed his soul (may he reside in heaven).]

Sheikh Mohammad Hossain Borazjani's tombstone on the grounds of Imamzadeh Abdollah, south of Tehran. Photo: Mohsen Jazayeri, 2015.

There is a boulevard in Borazjan now called Sheikh Mohammad Hossain Mojahed Borazjani. His statue is in the middle of the boulevard. Photo: Abbas Dashti, 2015.

Notes

1   Abol Hassan Shams al Din Sheikh Solaiman ebne Abdollah ebne Ali ebne Hassan ebne Ahmad ebne Yousef ebne Ammar ebne Ali ebne Solaiman ebne Davood ebne Ammar Mahouzi Bahrani was born in 1075 Hijri in Mahouz. He was a prominent *mojtahed* of the Safavid era and in his time he was the ruler of Bahrain. He passed away in 1121 Hijri and is buried in Dawnaj, Bahrain in the shrine of Maitham Mahouzi. From Seyyed Ja'far Hamidi, *Farhang'nameh ye Bushehr* (An encyclopedic dictionary of Bushehr) (Tehran: Sazman e Chap va Entesharat, Vezarat e Farhang ve Ershad e Islami, 1380 [2001]): 585.

2   Hojat al-Eslam Seyyed Mohammad Hassan Nabavi, *Yadgarnameh*. Edited by Seyyed Qasem Yahossaini and Abdol Karim Mashayekhi. (Bushehr: Entesharat e Bushehr, 1382 [2003]): 59.

3   Mohammad Hossain Rokn'zadeh-Adamiyat, *Daneshmandan va sokhansarayan e Fars* (The scholars and the orators of Fars) (Tehran: Kitabforoushiha ye Islamiyeh va Khayyam, 1337 [1958]): vol. 2, p. 258.

Five

Noosh Afarin: The Royalty in Us

For each story, Bibi chose a target among her audience. This one was directed at me. She had so artfully created those images in my mind that, after so many years, it is in fact hard to differentiate whether I heard the story from her or I was there to witness it myself—I can close my eyes and see it all, vividly.

Bibi stood up with a magnificent smile and narrated the story of Noosh Afarin,[1] as she moved around and acted out the scenes: "Akh, you should have been there," she said. "The caravan of horses had stopped by the gate of the andarooni. We had all gone to the yard to greet her," Bibi continued. "She was so gorgeous. Her beautiful green eyes looked straight at me. She had come to have lunch with us from Dashti on an Arabian horse accompanied by at least ten other bibis (*khatoons*),[2] their maids (*qalyan dar ha*), and many bodyguards.

She was wearing a *shalvar* (skirt) of at least thirty to forty meters of handmade silk, folded in the most artistic style, with amazing combinations of colors, in many layers; layer over layer. On top of her skirt, she was wearing a shiny *shaliteh* (a short tunic) open on both sides from her waist, allowing the folds of the skirt to flow as she moved. She gently yet skillfully dismounted from her horse and walked so elegantly into our house. Her manners and her style mesmerized me. She was my idol," said Bibi. "Her name was Noosh Afarin. She was the daughter of a khan of Dashti, a princess, and a khan herself."

"Noosh Afarin was a skilled horse rider. She went from village to village to visit the families and give them all kinds of assistance. She was so brave, so powerful, and so feminine and kind. When she passed through a village, men and women respectfully bowed to her and her group." At this point, Bibi would look at me and say, "When you have a daughter, make certain you name her Noosh Afarin." Bibi demanded this of me, and I received her request honorably.[3]

With her unmistakable modesty, there was something very royal about Bibi—she admired beauty, elegance, and she herself was so dignified. One could wonder, how could a person be so humble yet so exquisite? There was an innate capacity in Bibi to cover the whole spectrum of humanity. In fact, the history of our ancestors shows that they have gone up and down this spectrum fluently: down to earth as nomads, so familiar with rough surroundings and most comfortable with earth, and then again delicate and formal as nobles.

Our blood is a mixture of royalty and piety! Generation after generation, our ancestors have married into the families of khans and our khans have married into the families of our humble religious leaders. Together they have created exclusive blood, multidimensional personalities.

The royalty in our blood comes from the khans. *Khan* means king or a ruler who controls a state or a region (a khanate or a *khan neshin*). The khans were the prominent rulers of various regions of Iran. Before they had to integrate with the central government, they governed and protected their territories with their own military. Most of them lived luxurious lives—fancy houses, imported furniture, fine jewelry and clothes, Arabian horses, and many servants.

The other part of our blood comes from the sheikhs (leaders of righteousness) and the most devout nationalists. Material or personal ownership did not mean much to them—what they owned was there to serve, and what was theirs belonged to everyone—it was there only to share and to serve.

The intermarriages between the khans and the religious leaders continued in our family generation after generation: Fatemeh, our father's grandmother, was the daughter of the prominent khan of the Kolol khanate in Bushehr.[4] She married our great-grandfather, son of Mohammad Hassan, a jurisprudent.

The great-grandfather of Ali Dashti (Bibi's uncle) was the great khan of Dashti. When one of his sons (Abbas) got very ill, the father made a vow—pledging to God that if his son recovered from the illness, he would send him to Karbala to study the *sharia*. Abbas recovered from his illness, and his father sent him to Karbala and Najaf, just as he had promised God. He studied jurisprudence, stayed in Najaf, and married an Iranian woman from the family of a khan from Dashti. They only had one son, Abdol Hossain, a sheikh.

Sheikh Abdol Hossain also married a woman from Dashti named Maryam and had three sons and two daughters.[5] One of the daughters, Zahra, married a khan from Jam. (Masood Khan is the grandson of Ali Dashti's sister.) The other sister, Fatemeh (Bibi's mother), the great-granddaughter of the chief khan of Dashti, a noblewoman, married Sheikh Mohammad Hossain Borazjani, a holy man, a dervish.

Ammeh ye Bozorg, our great-grandaunt, a saintly woman herself, married twice—each time to one of the richest khans of Dashti.

The late Zan Aqa, Bibi Amineh (Abaj's mother), whom Sheikh Mohammad Hossain (Aqa ye Bozorg) a holy man, married after the death of Bibi's mother (daughter of a khan), was the first cousin of Bibi Fatemeh, a noblewoman.

Both the khans and the holy people, our ancestors, were fundamentally tribal people—very much in touch with both the simplicity and the glory of humanity.

Bibi continued with the following story:

> Once upon a time, there was a young man who was in search of the truth. One day he packed his small bag, kissed his mother's forehead and left the house to find the greatest dervish of the time and request the receipt of his mentorship. He wanted to travel the deserts and the mountains, seeking freedom of soul and longing to become a true dervish.

He travelled from village to village, city to city, inquiring for the renowned dervish. Most people knew about the great man and directed him to the right location. Eventually he reached the bottom of a hill decorated with tall trees, rows of fragrant flowers and narrow streams of fresh water running throughout the well-manicured garden. On top of the hill there stood a beautiful large mansion. The young man seemed confused, "Why did people direct me to this lush place instead?" "I was looking for a true dervish, not a nobleman!" he thought to himself. He was certain he had gotten lost. However, he was very tired from the long trip and soon he fell asleep under one of the trees in the garden. Hours later he woke up as the shadow of a man fell across his face. He jumped up with fear and said, "I am sorry if I stepped on this ground. Wrong directions misled me. I was led here by mistake!"

The man helped him to his feet and asked: "Who are you looking for?"

"I am looking for the greatest dervish of all times!" the young man said.

"What do you want to learn from him?" The man asks.

"I want to find the truth of life. I want to learn to be modest and carefree, like he is known to be. I am seeking his apprenticeship," he boasted.

"Follow me," the man instructed him. He got up and followed him up the hill and to the entrance of the glorious and vast house; ever more astonished, he started objecting: "Where are you taking me? I am not a thief. Please believe me. I am a seeker and want to follow the great dervish on the path to righteousness."

The old man gently put his hand on his shoulder and smiled peacefully. "Let go of your pack and we shall go."

"No," he said. "This is very important to me; all I own is in here."

"As you wish!" said the old man.

"What about you? Are you leaving all this behind?" the young man asked.

"We are seeking the truth, are we not? It is time to go!"

He knew then. The rich man was indeed the renowned dervish.

"How easy it was for the true dervish to let go of all material belongings," Bibi would conclude her story, and always followed it with a couple of poems from Sa'di and Molana.

From the *Golestan* of Sa'di, she recited:

> Of what avail is frock, or rosary,
> Or clouted garment?
> Keep thyself but free

From evil deeds.
It will not need for thee to wear the cap of felt,
A dervish be in heart and wear the cap of Tartary.[6]

And from Molana's *Mathnavi*, she recited:

Water that's poured inside will sink the boat
While water underneath keeps it afloat.
Driving wealth from his heart to keep it pure
King Solomon preferred the title 'Poor'
That sealed jar in the stormy sea out there
Floats on the waves because it's full of air,
When you have the air of dervishood inside
You'll float above the world and there abide . . .[7]

"It is our duty to value beauty and to use and appreciate what God has given us," Bibi would say. "God wants us to have good things, beautiful things; he wants us to not waste. Not keeping our things in good shape is being unthankful (*na shokri*). But know that they are there to serve us; we are not their slaves; that is the art of all elite human beings who are thankful [*bandeh ye shaker*]," Bibi always said.

Notes

1   "Noosh Afarin was herself the Khatoon of Zirah after her father Esma'il Khan passed away. Esma'il Khan, the great Khan of Zirah, had two sons (Mohammad Ali Khan and Lotf Ali Khan) and five daughters. One of the daughters was Noosh Afarin who became the great Khan of Zirah after her father. Noosh Afarin never married and ruled over more than half of Zirah. In the year 1921 C.E. there was a riot orchestrated by the governor of Borazjan, Asef al Molk, against her family and as a result the khanship was given to Sohrab Khan.

In the year 1929, Noosh Afarin was infected by tuberculosis and passed away in Shiraz. She was extremely popular and her death as a young woman still brings tears to the eyes of the people of that region." Quoted from Abdollah Dashti's journal *Az Jam/Reez ta Tabriz* (From Jam/Reez to Tabriz) Compiled and edited by Badieh Dashti. (Tehran: Farhang e Hezareh e Sevom, 1385 [2006]): 124.

*"Zir Rah or Zirah is an ancient rural district to the northwest of Borazjan. This district used to be the most prosperous before Islam and a city called Tavaj or Tavaz was situated in this region. Tavaz was known as a center of trade and for the art of weaving. This large and well-developed city, in a prominent location by the sea, at the time of the Achaemenid Empire, is believed to have been completely destroyed by an earthquake in the sixth or seventh century Hejira." From the book by Soroush Atabak'zadeh, *Jaygah e Dashtestan dar sarzamin e Iran* (Place of Dashtestan in the land of Iran) (Shiraz: Entesharat e Navid, 1373 [1994]): 60, 96, 97.

2   A woman khan is called a *khatoon*. However, in the south the word *khatoon* was never used; instead a noblewoman was called a *bibi*.

3   Bibi was so very pleased when I named my daughter Nooshin.

4   The father of Fatemeh was the ruler of the khanate of Kolol in Bushehr where one of the four brothers, our ancestors, had settled.

5   Except for Ali, the Dashti brothers are called khans: Mohammad Khan, Abdollah Khan. Ali Dashti was referred to as Sheikh Ali because he had had an Islamic education in Najaf.

6   The story of the dervish is in *Golestan,* chapter 2, story 16.

7   Molana Jalal al-Din Rumi, *The Mathnavi: Book One.* Translated by Jawid Mojaddedi. Oxford World's Classics Series. (Oxford: Oxford University Press, 2004): 63.

Six
The Year of Ravage (*Sal e Gharati*)

Prior to the reign of the Pahlavi Dynasty (1925–1979), most provinces of Iran were controlled by the khans of each region. The khans were armed and had incredible influence in their communities. The khans collected taxes and had the means to guard the territory against any threats. Throughout Iranian history, there have been constant battles between the court of the king of the time and the local khans. When Reza Shah came to power, he made an attempt to centralize the government and the army, and to collect taxes from all over the country. In order to succeed, he needed to weaken the khans by initially disarming them. Being an oil-rich area and a free port, the province of Bushehr on the Persian Gulf has always been one of the wealthiest regions of Iran. The town of Borazjan had also become significant because my grandfather Sheikh Mohammad Hossain Borazjani, who was a major influence in the state of Bushehr, lived there.

In the early 1920s, the country had become an insecure place. After the Russians left Iran, people feared another war. The southern khans had managed to arm themselves again. Their relationship with Sheikh Mohammad Hossain Borazjani was changing. It had reached a point where, if the decisions he made did not agree with their wishes, they considered it a threat and a personal attack. For instance, during one of the elections, when Sheikh Mohammad Hossain did not recommend one of the main khans of Chahkootah for the House of Parliament, this khan and his tribe became his enemies.

Typical clothing worn by men in the Bushehr and Persian Gulf region. Ra'is Ali Delvari Ethnological Museum, Delvar, Iran. Photo: Abbas Dashti, 2010.

Changes in the country had begun to take place rapidly. In August 1927 one of the more unconventional orders from Tehran had come by telegram (*bakhshnameh*) ordering all men (except the clergy) in the country to wear a uniform consisting of a European-style suit and headgear called a *kolah Pahlavi* (Pahlavi cap).[1] Most tribesmen considered this order to be a true insult—king or no king, the man was allowing himself to tell them what to wear!

Southern men used to wear a long shirt (*qaba*), a pair of pleated pants that narrowed at the ankles, and a large shawl they wrapped around their waist. Over the shawl, most khans wore a wide leather belt to hold their bullets (*qatar e feshang*) and hung a rifle from their shoulders. The shoes were handmade of cotton with leather soles (*giveh*), and over their clothing some wore an *aba*. Head cover was just as important for men as it was for women—one would never see a man without a hat, a turban, or a head covering—determined according to their family tradition, custom, rank, climate, and so on.

This new law and other changes in the political scene in the capital had made the khans lose trust in their best supporter, Sheikh Mohammad Hossain Borazjani. They had made plans to regain power. This event that took place in July of 1929 is known in our family as *Sal e Gharati* (the Year of Ravage).

A story narrated by Bibi:

> This time, Reza Shah came in person. He arrived in Bushehr to meet with my father. My father also went to the port of Bushehr, but he stayed at the Treasury Building and waited. He owned the building but he had rented it to the Treasury. He said, "If the Shah asks for me directly, I will go; otherwise I will not."
>
> Reza Shah waited in his car in the main square in Bushehr for twenty minutes. Finally he got out of the car to greet the people who had come to the square to welcome him. "Where is Aqa Sheikh Mohammad Hossain?" he inquired.
>
> Poor Seyyed Molk (the governor of Bushehr)! He got the order to go get Aqa. We heard that he was running with his big belly moving from side to side; hitting himself on the head in fear, all the way to the Treasury Building.
>
> Aqa then walked back with him to see the Shah and to describe the situation of the region to him. He told the Shah that the khans have been the protectors of the region because they have guns and because they know the area centimeter by centimeter. "Their power protects our region against any intruders. Taking away their rifles would be like taking away their identity. They did give up their arms once, but we did not get protection in return," Aqa told Reza Shah.
>
> Reza Shah replied, "Yes, Sheikh, I realize that. However the country is torn into pieces and you and your family and the entire region live in fear all the time. The country must be united and be governed by a central government. The army of the government will protect the entire country and not just a region. There is always the threat of other tribes attacking your people, as it has been for years."

This made sense to my father and he began to trust Reza Shah and promised to cooperate with him. He asked the Shah to give his word that he will protect the tribesmen and the local people. Shah gave his word.

The khans all suspected that to be Aqa ye Bozorg's plan. As soon as Shah went back to Tehran, they sat around to make a decision about this situation. Their decision was to remove Sheikh Mohammad Hossain and his son Najaf Ali [Aqa ye Koochik].[2]

The government's army [*nezami*] in Borazjan was very small and on that day most of them had gone to Mamasani, Bakhtiari, and to the road to Mashhad, to watch out for Qashqais and bandits on the roads. Only about thirty soldiers were left in Borazjan at the time of ravage.

That night, about nine o'clock, a workman came in and told my father that Seyyed Baqer, a relative from Kolol, has come and wants to see him with some confidential news. We were having dinner in the *andarooni*. My father left to receive him in the *birooni*.

On his way to our house, Baqer had crossed paths with the army of Ebrahim Khan (Ghazanfar al Saltaneh's son) and Aqa Khan's brothers, who now had joined forces (five hundred gunmen) in a base near Borazjan. He had found out that they were about to attack our house and take our father and brother. Sheikh Khaza'l, one of the major khans,[3] had concluded that Aqa was responsible for allowing Reza Shah to take over their territory and their freedom.

"Aqa, you should leave Borazjan immediately. They are after you and your son, five hundred of them. They think you are behind all of this," Baqer was shaking as he was reporting this.

Aqa told Baqer, "Go have dinner and do not worry. The khans are my friends and even if they do come, they have come for *bastkhaneh*, to seek refuge, and not to attack!"

Aqa returned to the *andarooni* and finished his dinner with us. He told one of the maids to go serve Seyyed Baqer a good dinner and prepare a place for him to sleep. He seemed very calm and did not share with us the news he had heard.

The khans and their men had come with their horses and their guns to surround our house, but they would not dare walk inside. They were shouting from a distance, "Tell us where he is. We are only after him and his son. We are not going to bother anyone else," they reassured the guards on the rooftop. My father had ordered our gunmen not to shoot until they get orders from his daughters.

We slept on the rooftop of the *andarooni* and my father slept on the higher level of the roof. We were all asleep when we heard the gunshots. Aqa ran to the lower rooftop to announce, "I suppose the gentlemen are here [*hazaraat amadehand*]!" Robabeh (Bibi's oldest sister) was there too with her daughter Vajiheh. He woke us up gently and told my sister, "Collect all the women's clothes and drop them in the well." We all realized that getting hold of a woman's clothes by a stranger was the ultimate insult to a family's pride. To really hurt a family, they might put a piece of woman's clothing on the tip of a rifle for all to see. My father could never tolerate that. So the first thing he demanded was that we collect our things, wrap them up in a *boqcheh* and throw them in the twelve-meters-deep well in our yard, and we did.[4]

I was about nine years old and my *shalvar* [skirt] was fourteen meters already. My sisters had forty-meter-wide *shalvar*. It was heartbreaking to let go of our beautiful clothes. He then ordered us, "If they actually come to the *andarooni*, jump in the well, all of you." His face looked numb as he uttered these words, preparing to leave. My sisters and the other women were indeed ready and willing to obey him, never considering an alternate option. I knew I was not going to jump! I knew it! I have kept this secret all this time, now I want you to know that I was not going to do it, even though it was an order from my father.

Then the gunfire escalated; it was already reaching our house. They had come right next to the building. They came close to the house and close to the *andarooni*. Some of them were already under the bridge [*dalan*] that connected the *birooni* and the *andarooni*.

We normally had four gunmen who protected the house from burglars. They were like security guards—most of the time they announced visitors and messengers. All four men had incredible Arabian horses. They were on top of the stable, where they could actually shoot many gunmen on the ground, but Aqa had ordered, "Make sure not to spill a drop of blood!"

That night, out of our four gunmen, two had disabled guns; the bullets were stuck in the guns! Actually, if they were allowed to shoot, the two rifles could have taken out most of the khans' army from the top of the *dalan*. Aqa insisted that they wait to first see what they were after—he never imagined they actually wanted him and his son. He had always been their strongest supporter.

It was not too long ago that in defense of three of the khans, who had been taken to Shiraz to be interrogated by the government, he went out of his way to be there for them. He personally went to Shiraz to secure their safe return. I remember that day too. Sultan ran inside the *birooni* in the middle of the night. His eyes were red like bloody lights on his dark face. "Aqa! Get up, Aqa! There is someone here saying that three khans have been taken to Shiraz." My brother and I were with our father all the time. Even though I was a girl, he would let me sleep in the *birooni* so I didn't feel unloved. I was a baby when we lost our mother, and he protected us with so much compassion so as not to feel that loss.

He carried me to the *andarooni* to my sisters, whispering, "Baba, I have promised some people that I would support them and now I cannot leave them. What kind of person would I be if I did not keep my word?" he said before he left us that day.

He first ordered the government agents in Borazjan to go and bring the khans back right away. They had excused themselves for not having a car, which was unacceptable to my father. He arranged for a car, made one of the soldiers sit and drive, as he himself sat in the car to go to Shiraz. He stayed for months until he was able to release the khans and bring them back to Borazjan safe. That is the kind of history he had with the khans. Of course he could never believe that they wanted to attack his family, to kill him and his son.

On that devastating night of ravage, one of our men, a relative, came in the middle of the house to call Sultan to go talk to the messenger of the khans. The messenger told Sultan, "Hey, come bring your ears here. Go tell your master we are here to take him and his son. Don't you say that they are here for any other reason. Tell him what we are telling you. It does not seem like anyone is getting our message right!"

Aqa ye Bozorg's first reaction was, "All right! Go bring my *qalyoon*." First Sultan hurried in with a regular *qalyan* from the *andarooni*, but Aqa sent him back ordering him to "bring my own *qalyoon*." My sister Robabeh was so annoyed with him that she said, "This is no time to ask for your own *qalyoon*, Aqa!"

"I want my own *qalyoon*!" he insisted.

Now you know where I have come from! Do not ask me why I smoke!

I remember the exchange of brave words between our gunmen and the khans' gunmen: "Kal Sheikh Hassan, move out of the way! I am going to hit you no matter who you are; even if you are the father of Abu Taleb (the father of Prophet Mohammad) [*zaanoot o bebar ooval. Be khoda agar baboy e Abi Taleb bashi, joori mizanamet ke agar babay e Abi Taleb bashi . . .*]." Our gunman said, "You can never do that, never [*Nemitooni ah Sheikh Mahsen! Nemitooni!*]"

Finally Aqa and our brother, Seyyed Mohammad Reza Siasi, his secretary, and Sultan left from the rear of the house. Meanwhile, our friends, a very loyal tribe, the Paparis (Karballa Abbas Papari and his son Mohammad Ali), helped them get away. They went to the deep basement and by means of a pathway came out of a neighbor's house, far away.

The tunnel must have been very dark and the small doorways, very short. Aqa hit his head on one of the lintels and lost the sight in one of his eyes. With the help of neighbors, they made it. From there, friends took them to Shiraz and they were able to escape the ravage.

Aqa knew that his family would not rest until they had been reassured that he and their brother were safe. He had a special key to a small wooden box where he kept his documents. One of the Paparis volunteered to deliver the key back to his daughters as a sign that they had reached their destination.

We saw a man approaching our house. It was very difficult to distinguish him from the army of the khans. But we soon trusted him to be a friend, as he had come straight to the family quarters and had given a small handkerchief with a key inside to one of the maids. He was then let in for protection.

Once my sisters received the key, they sent a message to the gunmen on the rooftop to allow the khans' men into the *birooni* to see for themselves that the men of the house were not there. The khan's army searched the entire *birooni* and of course did not find them.

When we heard their voices by the *andarooni*, my sister Abibi went out of the room, grabbed the barrels of five guns, all at once hollering at the gunmen: "Dare to come into our private quarters? When I tell you they are not here, that means they are not here." And she pushed them away so hard that they started running! That is how brave Abibi was.

Meanwhile my father arrived in Gandom Reez and from there he went to Samal to the house of Ra'is Ali Samali and from there to Ahram and from Ahram he took a car to Bushehr. Sardar Entesar and the entire population welcomed him and his companions and showed them sympathy. Reza Shah then ordered General Habibolah Sheibani, the head of the Army of the South, to take Sheikh Mohammad Hossain to Shiraz by means of a small German-made plane called a Junkers.

While my father and brother were in Shiraz, they got a message from Aqda'i and Reza Shah. Reza Shah asked him to go to Tehran to avoid having to support the khans. "You realize that your house cannot be disrespected by us once the khans take refuge there," Reza Shah had said.

My father was an amazing man. After all this, he stayed in Shiraz until one of the khans, Ghazanfar al Saltaneh, who was still in the custody of the government, was released.

My sisters stayed in Shiraz with their husbands and children. Our father, my brother, Sultan's family, and Sheikh Abdollah went along with him to Tehran and stayed at Aqda'i's house on Sa'di Street before they returned to Borazjan.[5]

After my father escaped, Ebrahim Khan (Ghazanfar's son) and Aqa Khan's brothers and their followers entered our house and sent the women and children out to a relative and then from there we went to Bushehr. They looted our house and took everything—everything.

Either as a request or a polite order, our family was later [in 1931] exiled to the capital city, Tehran, under the watchful eyes of the king.

Sheikh Mohammad Hossain's wooden safe or documents chest.
Photo: Mohsen Jazayeri, 2014.

Notes

1   en.wikipedia.org/wiki/Pahlavi_hat, accessed August 20, 2014.

2   Young Master refers to Sheikh Mohammad Hossain's son, Najaf Ali.

3   Khan of Khuzestan.

4   *Chah e davazdah qaddi,* also known as *chah e vale,* is a well about 10 meters deep.

5   Abdollah Dashti, *Az Jam/Reez ta Tabriz* (From Jam/Reez to Tabriz) Compiled and edited by Badieh Dashti. (Tehran: Farhang e Hezareh e Sevom, 1385 [2006]): 147. Reza Shah arranged for Sheikh Mohammad Hossain Borazjani to have his eyes treated before he returned to Borazjan. Dr. Nejat, the only eye specialist in Tehran, was chosen to perform the operation.

Seven

Black Members of Our Family

Sheikh Mohammad Hossain Borazjani and his right-hand man, Sultan. Tehran, 1930s. Photo: Dashti family album.

Bibi embarrassed me every time we were in Bullock's Department Store in Los Angeles, and she stopped an African American woman shopper telling her that she loved her. She insisted that I translate her message, "We love our blacks." She literally followed them around and continued to say:

> Tell her that we are mad at America for having had slavery. Shame on them! They can never clean this stain off their history. Our blacks are members of our families; never slaves, not in our family nor in the history of our country.

Obviously, I could not convey such an inherently prejudiced message. Instead, I would try to compliment the ladies, as they could not understand why my mother was holding on to their arms and smiling at them so compassionately. "She says you are so beautiful and she loves your elegant blouse," I would say. I could tell, however, that they knew there was much more to it than what I was saying.

The history of the blacks in our family traces back to our great-aunt. We had never met Bibi's aunt, and Bibi herself was a young child when her aunt passed away. As one of the pivotal people in Bibi's life, however, we heard so much about her. Every time Bibi looked at her own rough and cracked feet, for instance, she commented on Ammeh, "Do you believe that the soles of her feet were as soft and clean as a newborn baby's? When she was up the ladder reaching out for something, I would notice how clean they were," she would say. Then that memory led her to paying respect to her aunt by adding a few more sentences about her:

> She was immaculate, generous, and so close to God. She was known to have owned a bottomless pot. Like magic, she made food in a pot, served the entire family, the workers, and after all that, she would go to the *birooni* wall and pass the pot of food to the poor with plenty of food still left in it. There were always people who waited for the food on the other side of the wall, not knowing who was giving it. Bless her soul.[1]

Ammeh's measuring cup. Photo: Mohsen Jazayeri, 2015.

I have interviewed many family members who are old enough to know or to remember the stories told. None can match Bibi's precision of course. Storytelling was a rare gift Bibi had; she had everyone's trust to talk about the real people. She had an innate talent to create a very clear image of what she wanted to tell. Sometimes she got up and acted out the stories. She gave details, described the settings, and gave the background of the events with thoroughness. She gave the dates, the hours, and the entire background when she talked about a person or an event. I wish I had paid more attention to every word she had said about the history of the black members of our family. For now, these are the bits of information I could gather. The most willing to tell these stories was Bibi Batool, our cousin (Khaleh Robabeh's daughter). I checked her stories with the information I collected from a few more cousins. This is what they unanimously had to say about the black members of our family:

It all started when our great-aunt (Ammeh ye Bozorg) married the khan of Dashti. Together they had two children, a boy and a girl. When the children were still toddlers, a cholera epidemic hit the south and killed both babies. The khan, Ammeh's husband, did not survive the horrendous loss and a few months after losing his children, he died in grief.

Ammeh was a very beautiful woman and had many suitors. She refused to remarry and remained in mourning for years. Eventually her brother, Sheikh Mohammad Hossain Borazjani, convinced her to marry a prominent man from Dashti, another khan.

This khan brought all his wealth to Ammeh, including two African children he owned. He put the children in Ammeh's "papers" (dowry).[3]

Successive epidemic of cholera killed hundreds in the south of Iran. People of all ages lost their lives, specially the very young white children—most black children survived.

Ammeh had a son with her second husband. Once again she lost her son and her husband to cholera; she and her two black children survived. She decided to devote the rest of her life to serving God and serving her black children. She was at her prayer mat most of the day, praying to God.

When Bibi's mother passed away, Ammeh rolled up her prayer mat, put it aside, and said, "The real prayer, my obvious mission in serving God, is to raise my brother's children." She took her chest of clothes, grabbed the hands of her two adopted African children, Sultan and Samanber, and came to live with Aqa ye Bozorg and his four children.

Aqa ye Bozorg was very grateful to her. He was especially impressed when he learned that she had left all her material goods behind.[4]

She took extraordinary care of her nieces and nephew. "Khaleh (Bibi) was still a baby when she lost her mother, she washed your mother's hair with rose water," Bibi Batool said.

Ammeh passed away a few years later. When they told Aqa ye Bozorg that Ammeh had passed away, he was devastated and had said, "Do not tell me my sister has passed away; tell me that my home is destroyed (*khoonam kharab avideh*)."

Sultan and Samanbar were raised in Sheikh Mohammad Hossain Borazjani's house.

Sultan, a young free man, married a black woman, the very beautiful and graceful Narges who lived in the household of a khan from Dorooga. They had a very respectful and fancy wedding. There was a male professional cook in the kitchen, which was a sign of a real fancy ceremony. "I had seen Narges, Fezeh's mother. She was the most graceful woman. Her *shalvar*s were as wide as ninety meters; all hand embroidered,"[5] Bibi Batool said.

Sultan and Narges lived in a house next to Aqa ye Bozorg. "The house was given to them by your father's father," Attieh, my other cousin, said. Together, they had five children, three sons and two daughters: Sa'id, Qanbar, Fezeh, Zarafshan, and Jamshid.

Every story Bibi told included the name of Sultan and his family. She never mentioned her father without mentioning Sultan at his side. She never talked about herself without including Fezeh as part of her soul.

The following is a quotation from Bibi's recorded voice relating to the black members of our family:

> There were no garages or hotels in Dashtestan or Borazjan. Dashtestan was on the way to Shiraz and Bushehr. There were many travelers. It was also a road to Karbala. The daughter of Nasser al Din Shah, the aunt of Ahmad Shah Qajar, with her husband and their many companions, came from Tehran to go by ship to Karbala.
>
> I remember the time they came to our house. Oooo there were so many people. I was a child, but I remember it well. Ahmad Shah was in power then. His daughter was in her fifties. Aqa ye Bozorg gave the order to hide our blacks. He was worried that if the princess, the sister of the Shah, liked them, she would take them. Sa'id (Fezeh's older brother) was only eight years old and stunningly good-looking. Aqa hid all the black children.

When Sheikh Mohammad Hossain was exiled to Tehran in 1931, Sultan and his family accompanied him. They lived in the same house with Sheikh Mohammad Hossain and his family.

When birth certificates were issued in Iran, Aqa ye Bozorg got them for his family and for Sultan and his entire family at the same time. Sultan chose the last name *Sa'idi* after his oldest son Sa'id.

Written in his will, Sheikh Mohammad Hossain has ordered that Sultan and his entire family were to live as free people and always be supported by our family. Sultan was one of his heirs. He was given a house and monthly retirement allowance as long as he lived.

Translation of our grandfather's last will and testament:

> In the name of God
>
> I hereby testify to the oneness of God Almighty and to the prophecy of Mohammad and his family. On this seventh day of Rajab 1358, 31st of Mordad 1318 [August 23, 1939] I, this

humble man of God, Mohammad Hossain Borazjani, son of the late Najaf Ali Borazjani, make public all my assets and money to all and everyone.

Once my debts are paid, what remains should be divided amongst my heirs who I am designating here and what God Almighty has assigned as our religious duties: they are my four daughters and my wife, and what should be given on my behalf to the poor and the needy without hesitation and waste. What I owe are as follows: About three hundred *tuman*s to Mr. Mohammad Hassan Khan Behbahani and two hundred *tuman*s to Mr. Hajj Abdolnabi Tahim and the amount of two hundred *tuman*s to the heirs of Hajji Seyyed Baqer.

Any outstanding taxes on past earnings, three hundred and forty *tuman*s, and any related outstanding bills must be paid in full. Shafi' Abad and Shal properties and the two lands bordering them on the north (bought or exchanged) one and a half shares of sixth part of real estate [*dang*] from the village of Koloocheh are exclusively my properties and no one else has claim to them. The property of Dokhtarak (in the process of exchange) belongs to my nephew Sheikh Abdollah [Dashti] and my other heirs have no claim in that, of which the amount of four thousand *tuman*s should be given to the sheikhs of Ahram and to my daughter Robabeh. The cost of burial of the young master [his son Najaf Ali] and my own burial place next to my unfortunate son, in our family cemetery, amount of one thousand *tuman*s should be considered and must come from my own earnings before it is divided amongst my heirs. Amount of two thousand *tuman*s to be set aside for the poor who depend on my support, from Ahram to Borazjan (five hundred *tuman*s a year for four years and according to their needs and merit). Two hundred *tuman*s for a period of one year for every night of Friday prayers, including reading the Koran, the expenses of the cemetery, including the lights they use to light the family cemetery, giving away food, etc. One hundred *tuman*s for ten years, or as long as they shall live, goes for the expenses of my sisters. The property in Cyrous Street in Tehran [*Khaneh ye Shahr*] should be maintained and kept up from the general budget and my daughters should keep it as their own property.[6] Five hundred *tuman*s extra from my wages should be given to support Tahereh [*Abaj*]. Before any division, two hundred *tuman*s marriage-portion [*mehrieh*] to Tahereh's mother [*Zan Aqa*] that I owe her and must be settled. And one thousand *tuman*s to Sultan to buy a house and his other expenses must be paid from all my heirs' shares so he will never be dependent or in need.

I name Sheikh Abdollah and my three daughters Robabeh, Abibi, and Sediqeh as the executors of my will.

There are a few other things that I will write on a separate page as I remember them:

The salary that I get from the government should be claimed by Sultan's son.

Mohammad Hossain Borazjani

Notary public endorsement:

On this night of Thursday, last day of Mordad and the first day of Shahrivar month, one thousand and three hundred and eighteen I have had the honor to be in the presence of Sir Sheikh Mohammad Hossain Borazjani and he had ordered me to notarize the will he has written in his own handwriting. The will written on this and the other page is confirmed and correct.

Abu Torab

In the early 1800s the Europeans were still smuggling slaves from various parts of Africa. They loaded them on ships and took them to different parts of the free sea for sale.[7] They separated the children from their families, young girls, young boys, whoever seemed worthy of a sale. We sadly learned that many families in Africa disfigured their children in order to avoid losing them to slavery.

On a trip to East Africa with my daughter and her family, we stood at the very port where shiploads of human children were taken away as goods. Some of the ships had come to the port of Bushehr. Sultan and Samanbar, a brother and a sister, were most probably aboard one of those ships.

The dearest, most trustworthy, and most humble man in the history of my family had once been torn apart from his family, right there, where I was standing with my children and grandchildren. It made me shiver to my core.

The last will and testament of Sheikh Mohammad Hossain Borazjani, pages 1 and 2 (original).

The seal of Aqa ye Bozorg.
Photo: Mohsen Jazayeri, 2015.

Notes

[1] Bibi had a similar virtue. Who remembers the pot of rice she made for lunch? Even though the bottom of the rice burned every time, it still fed all of us, our children, our workers, and there was always enough left for the street cleaners.

[2] Bibi Batool tried to explain that a woman's papers were different from her dowry. What she tried to say sounded more like adoption papers even though government birth certificates did not exist in Iran at that time. The names of the two black children were written on the first page of Ammeh's Koran, an indication that she was their lawful mother.

[3] Women's clothing was very sacred and private in the south of Iran.

[4] A sign of ladyship.

[5] Each of Bibi's sisters sold their share to Bibi and our father and bought other properties for themselves.

[6] Gholam Hossain Moqtader, *Kelid e khalij e Fars* (The key to the Persian Gulf) (Tehran: Entesharat e Amir Kabir, 1333 [1954]): 59–68.

Eight
The Four Sisters

Khaleh Robabeh. Drawing by Ahmad (Abaj's son), Tehran, 1989.

Khaleh Abibi, about 1957, in Shiraz. Photo: Dashti family album.

Bibi Sediqeh (our mother), about 1952, at Darband Hotel, Shemiran, north of Tehran. Photo: Dashti family album.

Abaj wearing aba, about 1955. Photo: Dashti family album.

Khaleh Robabeh

By means of a special ceremony, Khaleh Robabeh was wedded to a palm tree! The palm tree was chosen to absorb the force of evil that took her first two fiancés. The evil of illness had claimed the lives of the two older brothers of our father, the most precious eligible young men of the family who were suitable for the first daughter of Aqa ye Bozorg. This could not be tolerated a third time. The belief was that the evil was transferred to a palm tree. "If you must strike a third time, as is your custom, hit the tree" was the message they sent to the evil force.

She was only sixteen when her mother passed away. She is the only sister who experienced her mother's presence throughout her childhood. When she lost her mother, she assumed that role and mothered her sisters and brother. She herself froze in the mentality of her teenage years for the rest of her life. With that mentality, she could see right through the naked reality. She only accepted what was true and detected all pretenses. She openly, however quietly, reflected upon the fake and the unnecessary actions of those around her. She herself was so direct and pure. She was completely undisguised.

She was a keeper of a responsibility, carrying out her mother's mission silently and with contentment.

Khaleh Robabeh was a villager in the true sense. Her life was defined within the matters of the andarooni (the private quarters of a home). She was extremely feminine, delicate, and immaculate, and had incredible taste in beautifying her surroundings. She had been educated at home by a private tutor, being able to read the Koran. She had married the son of her aunt, one of Aqa ye Bozorg's sisters from Ahram, and stayed in Ahram and Borazjan except for those times when she travelled to Tehran to be with Bibi. She had six children: Vajiheh, Batool, Mehdi, Sadraldin, Kheiri, and Nuraldin. She was the mother-in-law of her two nieces, Nafiseh and Attieh.

When Sheikh Mohammad Hossain Borazjani passed away, the four sisters made a vow to name one of their sons *Mohammad Hossain* after their father's name. While three of the sisters did that, Khaleh Robabeh refused, saying, "None will ever be big enough to carry that name."

Khaleh Robabeh was about twelve years older than Bibi. She was born in Karbala in 1905, at the time that her father, Aqa ye Bozorg, was a student of theology, lived in Ahram, and passed away in Tehran on April 24, 1990.

Khaleh Abibi (Ma'soomeh)

Khaleh Abibi was the second child of Aqa ye Bozorg. Known for her bravery and outspokenness, she was an educated and eloquent woman who led many gatherings of men and women who were initially decision makers of the country. She married her distant cousin, Zia al Din Hadaeq Ebne Yousef, a literary man with over forty publications, who later became the main Ayatollah of Shiraz. She managed a large home for her six children, Fatemeh, Borhan, Hamideh, Attieh, Mohammad Hossain, Yousef, and many of their relatives who lived with them. In the exacting society of Shiraz, where she lived most of her adult life, similar to the courts of the ancient kings, she was shoulder to shoulder with men on social issues and ethics.

The famous story of "Year of Ravage" reminds us of her bravery. She was the one who grabbed the barrels of many rifles, not allowing the khan's gunmen to get into their andarooni. She was the Joan of Arc, the heroine of the south.

She mostly lived in the big cities of Iran (Tehran and Shiraz) and led a large social group. Whenever she visited us in Tehran, our house was filled with visitors who came to pay their respects to her. The mayor of Tehran and other prominent politicians and their families were her closest friends.

Khaleh Abibi was efficient, pragmatic, and an absolutely committed individual who never ever complained. She devoted the last years of her life to nursing her ill husband with compassion and with an open heart. She believed that commitment is meant to be absolute, something no one else could replace.

It was my turn to clean the room I shared with my sisters. I wrapped up the work and came to the living room to sit with everyone else. Khaleh Abibi called me back into my room and said to me privately, "When you do a job, do it in a way so when you leave, people say with confidence, 'Sayeh has been here.'"

She was in complete control of her life and death. At the age of seventy-eight, in good health, she travelled to Tehran to be with Bibi and told everyone, "I have come here to die." She had decided when and where. She just died one day (August 19, 1993).

Her name Abibi (Aqa Bibi) means, Sir Bibi.

Bibi Sediqeh

Bibi's birth certificate indicates the date of her birth as 1296 (1917). She, however, took pride in saying she was born the same year as the Shah (1919). She was about three years old when her mother passed away shortly after giving birth to her only son. Bibi and her brother were raised together like two delicate flowers. Her superior character and her delicate nature endeared her to everyone around her.

When Bibi was about ten years old, our father was sent to his uncle, Sheikh Mohammad Hossain to be raised by him. His father, Aqa ye Bozorg's brother, Sheikh Mohammad Hassan, having lost his other sons, had asked his brother to look after his remaining son.

Bibi was wedded to our Baba twice, first at the age of about twelve and then in her early twenties when they were formally married. The first ceremony was a real marriage and not the Islamic temporary marriage (*sigheh*) and the second one was a ceremonial wedding when Bibi had reached a suitable age.

Bibi gave birth to ten children, two of whom did not survive infancy, a boy and a girl. She was only fifty-two years old when our Baba passed away. Bibi passed away on April 5, 1997 at the age of seventy-nine. She was ill for a short while. She was taken care of at home with all her children with her. She was taken to the hospital for the last few days of her life.

Bibi was one of the fittest individuals who had survived many illnesses and hardships. She was in great health all her life. She hated being sick and hated being old or needy. She showed no will to fight for her life once she did get ill and was getting old.

Bibi was a birooni person. Like most male leaders of her family, almost everyone depended on her care and wisdom. She loved beauty and justice equally.

Our protagonist, Bibi Sediqeh, was the kingmaker herself.

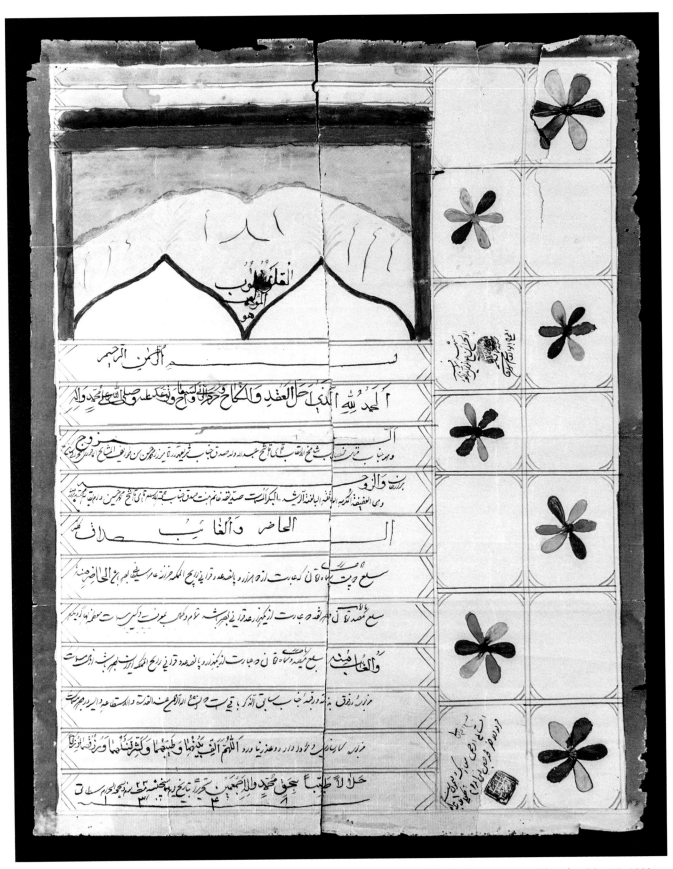

The front page of the marriage certificate for the first marriage of Bibi Sediqeh to Abdollah Dashti, written on Thursday, May 22, 1930. Photos: Dashti family album.

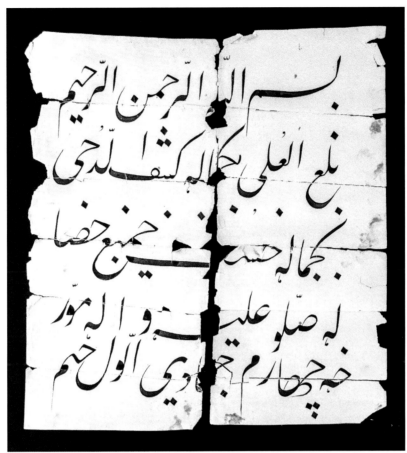

A second page of the marriage certificate for the first marriage of Bibi Sediqeh to Abdollah Dashti, written on Thursday, May 22, 1930. Photo: Dashti family album.

Abaj (Bibi Tahereh)

My cousin Amir was telling us about a dream he recently had. He dreamt that he was asking Bibi to tell him about his mother, Abaj:

I dreamt that I was asking *khaleh* (Bibi) about my mother. It was elusive and I could not see or hear her at first. Then suddenly, from behind a thick and enormous crystal wall, *khaleh*'s face appeared. It was obvious that she could not get through that shield of clear crystal, but her face, like the engraved shape of a goddess, spoke to me, 'Your mother is the first woman I ever met.'

As young girls, one of our fears was: What if Abaj gets old? What happens to all her beauty? Our prayer was answered. She is now in her early eighties, looking more gorgeous than any woman, ever. Her manners are classy and delicate. She is tall with a perfect woman's shape. People used to say that she looked very much like Ava Gardner or Queen Soraya. We didn't like that at all. In our view, she is more beautiful and more graceful than either one.

Abaj is the youngest and the only surviving sister of the four sisters. She is the only child of Zan e Aqa (Aqa ye Bozorg's wife after Bibi's mother).[1] Born in 1934 in Tehran, Abaj was only twelve years old when her mother died of typhus.

The three older sisters took care of her like their own daughter. That is why we call her *Abaj*. The word *abaj* comes from *abji*, meaning sister. *Abaj* means the older sister. She called her sisters *Abji*.

She had her own room in the house before she married. When she married and left the house, the room was still called *Abaj's room*. Her clothes, her doll, her way of taking care of herself, and the way she loved us and Bibi was something no one could ever match.

Her doll's name was Lili. The way I remember Lili is as a hairless plastic doll, the size of a newborn baby. I remember seeing it years later, at the bottom of a closet, all pale and naked.

The dolls that her generation used to play with were mostly make-believe dolls. For example a pillow wrapped in a cloth diaper became a baby, a coin wrapped in a piece of cloth with sticks to shape a person was a scarcity; the coin was not lying out there to be used by a kid! At the very most, someone made a doll out of remnant fabrics only if there was ever the luxury of time.

Lili was brought from Europe for Abaj and was the most luxurious object in the house. Abaj named her Lili after a girl in the neighborhood (the Norouzis' daughter). Lili got so much respect; no one could touch her or play with her except Abaj and my sister Talieh sometimes. No one could remove her from the glass showcase in Abaj's room. Abaj says:

Lili helped treat so many children! If a child got sick in our house and would refuse to take the bitter medication, all they needed to do was to ask me to allow that child to hold Lili for a minute. The kid took the medication gladly every time. Lili and Giti (Talieh's doll) were playmates.

Everything about Abaj was magical, even the way she got mad and then laughed at herself for it. People behaved themselves when she was around; even people in the bus! All she had to do was to look at them the way she does! It was indeed magic. Abaj's laughter brings tears of joy to her eyes as she tells us the story of mischiefs. "I swear I didn't say anything to the whining children in the bus; I just looked at them, and they immediately stopped!"

She carried out Bibi's wishes and was able to confront people in style. Her son Amir most appropriately called her "a silk rock."[2]

We bragged about her beauty at school. We loved it when our friends came over so we could show off our incredibly gorgeous aunt.

She used to make her own dresses. I have never seen a more stunning dress than the dark gold chiffon she made in the shape of a mermaid. Whatever she wore looked beautiful on her. Her black and silver sari gave elegance to the Indian tradition.

Her dressmaking was an expression of her art. She says she used to create a design in her mind and think about the design night after night. "It had become a ritual before I went to sleep," she says.

"In the morning, I laid everything on the floor and started creating. I created my clothes with what was available. None of the designs came from any magazines; they were all my own ideas. There are people who still talk about them and have asked me about the dresses and where I got them from."

Out of a light green moiré blanket with yellow silk backing, left by her mother, she created the most stylish overcoat. Even the spots chewed by moths were arranged into a beautiful design. Everyone thought they had brought it for her from Paris.

Looking at her glamor, most everyone assumed she came from a rich family. What she was brought up with, in fact, was not money but an endless source of appreciating beauty in every aspect of life.

"Our family never had anything extra to put aside, including money. What we had was there because it had a function or even many functions. Nothing existed in our household because it was expensive. Khaleh Abibi got a pair of scissors and cut a large Persian carpet about half a meter to fit the room! A curtain would turn into pajamas for kids and later into a potholder. There was never any waste," Abaj remembers.

The evenings in the living room of *Khaneh ye Shahr*, where all our life's essential elements such as Bibi, Khaleh Zakieh, Fezeh, Zarafshan, Banafsheh, and us were present, the sound of the sewing machine, sharp and expert comments by Bibi supervising the designs to proper perfection, the sensation of a new creation in the making, fresh tea, and the silence in awe as our Abaj created a dress and tried it out, ought to be what magic is made of. Her head covering was like Bibi's. She wore the same *aba* with golden tassels. When Bibi and Abaj wore their *aba*s and walked toward something, the ground shook under their feet; their pyramid was completed when Khaleh Zakieh joined them!

Our Abaj married the son of the leading Ayatollah of Shiraz and moved to Qom, and then to Shiraz. She left home on May 1, 1951, the night my sister Sepideh was born. Every time she came to visit counted as the sweetest moments in our lives. Her children were siblings to us and children to Bibi.

She has four children, Amir (Mohammad Ja'far), Mohammad Hossain, Amineh, and Ahmad. Her husband has passed away and now she is in charge of the most enormous public service in Shiraz.

My son and I visited her and her daughter in their home in Shiraz a few years ago. My son could not help but say, "Wow! Did we not visit a bunch of queens just now?"

Notes

1   Bibi had told everyone not to refer to Abaj's mother as Zan e Aqa (Aqa's wife): "She should be called *marhoom e Bibi*" (the late Bibi).

2   Amir has created a website about his family: http://www.majdnaameh.com.

Nine
Eulogy

The word "brother" was a forbidden noun, a taboo, in our home. The horror of losing young boys of our family, however, resided among us like a living being. We grew up with it, were heedful and even respectful of it. We were considerate of its boundaries, and were consciously aware of its power. We knew when to stop the conversation, when not to allow ourselves to contemplate facing such a monster.

Even though as children we had some sensory attachment to mourning for the loss of loved ones, we still grew up without being properly introduced to the concept of death.

In general, our adults somehow tampered with the reality of death. They decided who was dead and gone and who was to be eternal. There were people such as Aqa ye Bozorg, Bibi's father, who had passed away before any of us were born, yet his presence was preserved in such a way as if he had never died. Bibi talked about her father with such incredible admiration and reverence that we could actually feel his presence and felt obliged to obey his rules. When Bibi said, "My father has willed . . ." (*Aqam vasiat kardehand keh . . .*), the order was unbendable. She lived by her father's principles and expected the same from everyone else. She kept many great people of our family alive by talking about them all the time and by telling us stories about the details of their lives.

Grief for her losses did come to her in occasional waves and was usually accompanied by a deep sigh and a stare into oblivion (her head turned to the right as her eyes went to the left). To come back to present time, she performed a ritual of rubbing her eyes with the bottoms of the palms of her hands, a few rounds to the right and then a few rounds to the left, followed by a specific movement to bring her eyeballs back into place. "What if her eyes never return to normal?" I remember how we protested with laughter and tried to not let her do that. I also do remember that we welcomed it knowing that this was a way to set her mind straight about some complications—a ritual to get back to normal. Shortly after, she seemed capable of riding on those waves by sending her blessing to the soul of the deceased and continued on.

Most gracefully, she dealt with the death of our father, her uncle, Aqda'i, her sisters, and many of her friends and family members. She talked about them freely and told stories about them. She kept their principles alive while accepting their physical deaths.

An occasion of quality interaction between Bibi and our Baba was when they commemorated a dear friend or relative who had passed away, a high regard to honor the dead person. Our Baba usually uttered with condolence, "Ay! Ay! Ay! Ay!" And then Bibi told him the details of what had happened and how the person had passed away, a beautiful, honorable, and spiritual way of dealing with death. They gave the matter proper time, attention, and respect. Our father made it a duty to attend funerals and weddings as equally important moments of one's life. It had also become a principle to inform the close relatives of the news of the death of their loved ones, immediately and as soon as it happened. They considered the information as a privilege a person should have; a human right to be informed about the death of his or her loved ones. Always a trusted relative was chosen to bring the news in person, never by phone or letter.

In January of 1971, when my father died, Dr. Mohammad Khalil Hodjat, Abaj's cousin, was designated to come to Philadelphia to bring me the news of my father's passing. Our Baba had lung cancer and was very ill for months after I had left Iran. It never occurred to me that the talk of illness is about my father and that death could be attached to him. I must have been told in so many ways that he had cancer. I do not recall ever hearing it or thinking about it. The notion was immediately dismissed from my brain. Weren't my parents supposed to be immortal?

When our cousin came to bring me the news, I felt the strongest urge to be held tight, as if the pieces of my body and brain were about to fall apart with the incredible speed of a wheel turning within me, while the centrifugal force wanted to throw everything to the farthest point out of sight and mind. I fell asleep. For the first time I experienced waking up in the morning and felt the darkness, not light. And then a remarkable desperation that only lasted a few minutes or hours, I cannot remember. Then I knew what to do: I will put the monster in a dark room and I will not allow myself near it! I never displayed my father's photograph and I resented—really hated—when someone referred to my father as the late (*marhoom e*) Sheikh Abdollah, I did wish they were dead instead; well for that moment anyways, and I continued on.

Bibi had lost her only brother at the peak of his youth, at the age of eighteen. He had died of a simple disease, misdiagnosed and mistreated by wrong medication. His death marks the most devastating event in the history of our family, our extended family, and their related communities. His death was considered an assault on the life of such a pure superior being. His death threatened Bibi's mental health, a tragedy that had caused great fear and anxiety and most probably a fear or a loss of trust in God. Her fear turned to superstition at times, worrying that God might demand a sacrifice when things are just right.

People who were present when Aqa ye Bozorg received the news of his son's death testify that they heard the sound of his back breaking. He also lost his eyesight completely.[1] He announced that he is indeed dead but will continue to live until he completes building the house for his daughters.[2]

The death of Bibi's brother was above and beyond any horror—it was the deepest, an absolute and ultimate darkness, a forbidden space, outside any imagery. If accidentally and for a short moment it manifested itself, the world we stood on collapsed. His death was our mother's deadly and incurable illness, a dangerous tumor no one could trust.

Psychology speaks of different stages of grief, denial being the first stage. Not facing the death of her brother was not Bibi's ignorant denial; it was a responsibility to life. In many ways it was her undeniable strength, a powerful control of an inevitable evil. She knew that if she looked at it, she would lose trust in the universal justice; she would have to denounce God, or she could die. She could not afford any of that;

she could not even give herself to any physical or mental illnesses. She had to maintain her sanity, no matter what the challenge; she was in charge of life; so many people depended on her.

A few days before Bibi died, she lost control of the monstrous reality of her brother's death. She stood in the middle of her room in the dark of night and talked about her brother. She had no guards and no means of protection. Her illness was catching up with her—swallowing her. Once she surrendered, she died.

When Bibi passed away, we went to Borazjan for her funeral ceremonies. Her death had given permission to the people of that town to talk about the death of Aqa ye Koochik (young master). It sounded as if it had just happened even though fifty-eight years had passed. Their friends and neighbors had started mourning the death of the most precious young man. They were chanting in the streets, hitting their heads and chests, "This is the day of Ashura." "This is the day that the most righteous Son of God Najaf Ali dies. Alas Bibi! Alas Bibi! (*Heif e* Bibi, *yad e* Bibi)."

Left to right: Bibi Sediqeh, Aqa ye Koochik, and Khaleh Abibi, mid-1930s.

Najaf Ali Borazjani and his cousin Abdollah Dashti, 1930s.

Najaf Ali passed away in the spring of 1939 at the age of eighteen. He is buried in our family cemetery in Imamzadeh Abdollah south of Tehran. A friend of the family, Mr. Zendehnam, wrote a poem that is engraved on his tombstone:

Spring was here,
so were the abundance of flowers and rapture.
Every which way you turned,
you could see a bird reuniting, romancing a flower.

Succeeding the hardship of a winter,
we too were bestowed a gift; the universe gave us a new life!
Celebrating, the birds assembled around him.
Each and everyone, indebted, gave their hearts and souls in return.

Alas the monster of autumn had set an ambush.
Such atrocity was to come.
The demon was going to take his life.
The celebration felt in peace; it was springtime after all!

Nourishing him with all they had to give,
reassured he is there to stay,
they helped him grow tall.

Wishing, dreaming,

may be some day soon he will join a perfect mate; make a nest of his own,

and they dreamed on.

The hands of death took him one early spring morning,

The garden swallowed its rage; the birds ran around mute,

only the sound of old trees, bending; breaking dry:

Damn you monster, how cruel could you be?

Have you ever filled a heart with joy as you go around?

You broke my back, you took my youth from my arms. Why? Have you no wisdom, God?

Did my garden have one too many? Uprooting a young palm? Have you no mercy, God?

Oh my beloved son, I had hoped for so much,

Now, I cannot tolerate this horrendous loss.

Yes God, maybe you are right,

For a free soul, this prison was too tight!

Tell us,

Did you envy us?

You wanted him for your own garden?

Is that why?

Young master Najaf Ali's tombstone in Imamzadeh Abdollah, south Tehran. Photo: Mohsen Jazayeri, 2015.

Notes

1   Story 6, "The Year of Ravage" (*Sal e Gharati*), in this volume.
2   Story 11, "*Khaneh ye Shahr*" (City Home), in this volume.

Ten
Zarafshan Remembers Bibi's Wedding

At the age of eighty-four, she looks as beautiful as ever. She is Fezeh's younger and only sister. Fezeh was much older than Zarafshan, about eighteen years older, and from the same parents, Sultan and Narges.

When Sheikh Mohammad Hossain Borazjani was ordered to leave Borazjan for Tehran in 1931, baby Zarafshan (her name means spreading gold) came along with them. Aqa ye Bozorg and his second wife (Zan Aqa), Bibi, Najaf Ali (Aqa ye Koochik), Sultan, Fezeh, and Zarafshan moved to Tehran. Bibi's older sisters were already married, so they stayed in Fars with their own families. They first rented a house in Tehran from a family friend, the Kazemis. This was a massive house with a large garden in downtown Tehran (Eyn al Dowleh).

My sister Nafiseh called me this morning. "If you want a story, come here now; Zari is here," she told me.

I dropped everything, grabbed my laptop and cell phone, and got to her house in less than three minutes. It was a little awkward since any time my sister calls me to go for tea or something, I bring up many reasons why I cannot go or that I cannot stay long. Zarafshan, however, was a valuable source for *You Belong* stories and I did not want to miss that opportunity.

She was happy to see me, and I was overly excited to see her.

Noticing how she was guarding herself, I realized that it was a little too obvious that I had rushed there just for the sake of asking her questions. I reassured her that I did not want any sad stories, realizing that she was avoiding many of the devastations our families had endured in the past.

Ironically, most of the stories, which could have been priceless for our future generations, are either gone with the people who lived them, or buried in the hearts of the older people who are now too fragile and vulnerable to want to recall them. Bibi, I believe, was an exception. She felt obliged to keep the memories alive; everyone else is avoiding them! Some believe that it is a disservice to our youth to involve them with the pain of the past or rather make them believe that it was all fun and joy.

Zarafshan objected to my request to hear a memory of her childhood very determinedly at first: "*Hilat az dor e aval khalas shodim* (It took many tricks to survive the first round of life)," she said helplessly, sensing that I was also determined to make her talk.

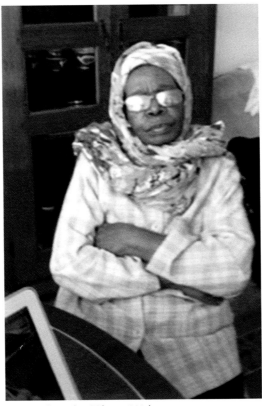

Zarafshan at the time of the interview. Photo: Sayeh Dashti, Tehran, 2014.

"Zarafshoon," I began, "I promise, I just want to tell the story of Bibi to my children and their children," I said sincerely.

"*Mikhaii qeseh barashoon begi?* (You want to tell them tales?)" she led up guardedly. "Yes, of course, stories are so good for children," she continued—whether she was dismissing me or she was making fun of me, I am not sure.

"Zari jan, I want them to see what it was like when you were their age. I want them to know that they belong to a grand family with such honorable people like yourself, like Bibi and your families. It is so important that they know what high values they come from," I started cautiously.

"*Baleh Sayeh khanoom,* you should know that Bibi Sediqeh always consulted with my mother on important decisions," she told me quickly as if having said that she does not need to say anything else. But her own statement was taking her to the past. I saw her gaze changing gradually from paranoia to a warm and kind trust. She needed more reassurance though. She looked at Nafiseh for support, wanting someone to save her from all this.

Nafiseh came to my rescue, "*Zari baba, inn mikhad dou kalemeh bara ye bachehash ke inja nistand qeseh begeh* (She wants some stories for her kids who live abroad.)" She made it sound like I was a naïve and harmless foreigner. I played along.

"Zarafshoon, tell me a happy memory you have from Bibi," I tried once more, almost begging.

"I remember Bibi's wedding," she was testing. I suddenly jumped up to run to my car to get my tape recorder. "Zari stop! Stop right there," I said as I was running. "Oh my God. This is a gem. Aqa Mohammad, hurry up, bring her tea." My excitement almost blew it! I could not help it though. I had found the jewel of the jewels. Bibi's wedding? Are you kidding me? Zarafshan was probably the only surviving individual who was present at our parents' wedding.

I got back and took a deep breath. I put the tape recorder (my iPhone) next to her and asked her permission if I may tape her voice. She seemed flattered and pulled herself together.

"But I was only about four years old and I don't remember much!" she said timidly. (She was actually nine years old at the time.)

"It is totally all right. Anything you remember, anything," I begged.

The wedding of Bibi and your father was in the house that they had rented from the Kazemis.

Bibi was wearing a light blue satin dress with a long white lace veil. Bibi and her sisters did not wear white wedding gowns. One of them wore pink, one green, and Bibi Sediqeh's was blue. She looked like the most beautiful princess, like an angel.

There was a large table with so much pastry and fancy fruits, she started unexpectedly.

I was going around and around that table, staring at the pastries. Aqda'i (Ali Dashti) was walking around the garden, checking everything for perfection. He usually had a cane in his hand. He was still young. His cane was not like the one I am using now to help me walk (she uses crutches to walk). Most gentlemen had a hat and a cane. He lifted his cane and pointed it at a pastry on the table. He then ordered me to pick one up and give it to him. (Zarafshan was acting out the scene.)

I thought he wanted it for himself. That is how I allowed myself to pick a big one. Then he softly told me to go ahead and eat it.

I deeply appreciated what he did for me that day. There was no way I would have dared to touch anything.

Yes, Sayeh *khanoom*, Bibi was a mother to us. Bibi was dearer to me than my own mother. She bought me beautiful dresses and took me with her to visit her friends. I got a lot of attention from her friends too.

I walked close to her during her wedding. I dared not touch her dress; it was so elegant. She gave me the same dress to wear on my own wedding day. Imagine, I wore her dress at my own wedding; that is how kind she was. Bibi Sediqeh's wedding was very formal. There was no music and no dancing at her wedding. Even when Fezeh did her *killllllllleeeee* [*kel mizad*][1] she was told to stop. She did it anyways of course every few minutes!

Zarafshan stopped herself here. "Do you remember my father at his wedding?" I asked. "No, I don't. I was only four years old." She wanted to dismiss my questions.

"Zari *loos nasho. Bishtar begoo* (Do not be so spoiled, tell her more)," Nafiseh said as she brought us tea and waved to me not to give up.

"Your father was wearing a suit and a starched formal white shirt and black-and-white tie." She warmed up once more.

There were so many people working in the house that day, mostly men working in the kitchen. I still remember the aroma of food coming from the kitchen. None of us were allowed in the kitchen, except Fezeh who managed everything. The dinner table was better than in the king's palace; I am sure of that.

Then the bride and groom went by car to Ali Dashti's house in the Mokhber al Dowleh neighborhood in downtown Tehran [Ali Dashti used to live there before he moved to Elahieh] and they returned in the morning.

"Who else was there at the wedding?" I asked.

"Aqa ye Bozorg was there, so was Zan Aqa (Abaj's mother), Bibi's sisters, and their families. Arganis, Kazemis, the senators and ministers (*vazir vozara*)," she continued.

What a woman she was, Zan Aqa. I was the same age as Bibi Tahereh (Abaj). Zan Aqa personally took both of us to Bersabeh Nursery School with a one-horse carriage [*doroshkeh*] every morning. She prepared our lunches herself and put them in lunch boxes with four compartments. Then again in the afternoon she came with a carriage to pick us up. Bibi Tahereh and I were very close. I could not sleep until I put my head right next to her head. Then when I fell asleep, they took me to my room.

Zarafshan. Photo: Dashti family album (about 1945).

As young girls, we were well protected from the outside world. The concept of romantic love between a man and a woman was taboo and it was talked about for the first time in our household (not in a good way) because of Zarafshan. Her love for the son of my nanny, a white boy, had become a huge scandal and made Zarafshan a pivotal person in our lives.

Hassan and Zarafshan loved each other and wanted to get married.

All the women we knew loved their husbands, and their husbands loved them; that was a given. However, their love was usually formed or revealed after they got married. The marriages were mostly a stronger tie of the two families; a renewed vow, their love for each other was a holy responsibility. "Thou shalt love thy spouse." In most cases the love was formed by a commitment to each other, which usually led to a respect for each other and then liking each other and hopefully to a private romance.

Falling in love first, as Zarafshan did, was like catching an incurable disease. "Zarafshoon *ashoq shodeh, karish nemishe kard*" (Zarafshan has fallen in love, there is nothing we can do) is what we heard.

So Bibi got to work and arranged for Hassan to marry Zarafshan.

My nanny hated Zarafshan and her entire family. Now we were introduced to the hostile nature of racial prejudice.

My sweet nanny, the small round person from Dulab (a village near Tehran), a person so loving was now looking for any opportunity to express her hatred.

Nanneh ye Hassan was the most compassionate person I had known. She loved the babies she was hired to take care of, Dadashi (my brother) and me. She also always expressed her love openly. For instance, she would wake me up in the middle of the night and feed me sweet and thick date syrup. When my mother objected to this, she would simply reply: "But my baby gets bored sleeping so long (*naneh rula delash sar mireh bacham*)." She took the best care of Dadashi too. He was always well groomed, well fed, and loved by her.

As babies, we were fed and cleaned up before Nanneh took us to Bibi's room in the morning. With open arms, in her bed, Bibi used to say "*Gonjishkham amadand*" (Here come my little birds). We stayed a few minutes and then ran out to play.

The usual scene for Nanneh ye Hassan was to sit on the floor with her legs crossed and a baby on her lap, rocking. She was also a very caring mother to her own two children Hassan and Sara. She constantly talked about them to every one—asking questions, looking for guidance, even taking her own share of things for them. Her children were adults when she came to us. Sara was married and had her own children but Hassan was still single.

This lovable woman with half a nose and a round face, her half-white, half-copper hair sticking out of her white scarf, sat at her daily prayer carpet any opportunity she found: "*Anah o ackbar*" (*Allah o*

Akbar, or "God is great") was the only part of the prayer she performed in her own primitive way and her Dulabi accent. The rest was merely and purely profanity—begging God to cause pain, suffering, death, destruction . . . to this black family. Her arms stretched to the heavens like two minarets of an ancient mosque; her head as a dome and her call to God, loud and clear.

When she was done, she would kiss the prayer stone (*mohr*) and get back to her own sweet, motherly duties. Blasphemy started when Zarafshan got pregnant with her first son and her craving was to chew on Nanneh's prayer stone.

Nanneh ye Hassan at Nafiseh's wedding, Tehran, 23 Shahrivar 1346 (September 14, 1967). Photo: Dashti family album.

What an unusual circumstance it all seemed: members of a family not loving each other! Bibi was caught in the middle.

Hassan was gone most of the time. We witnessed heartbreak when Zarafshan found out that Hassan had married a white girl as his second wife, arranged by Nanneh.

Zarafshan never stopped loving Hassan. They never got a divorce, but Hassan lived with his second wife. When he came to visit, she fell for him each and every time. The result was usually another baby. They have five children.

I remember the times when Hassan came to visit. He would stand next to his white three-wheeler (auto rickshaw) with a guilty smile. He always had this smile on his face. With his hands folded in front and his head bent to one side, he came to ask Bibi's permission to enter.

Bibi finished her cigarette by skillfully separating the lit part from the filter, extinguishing it. Then she told Fezeh to let him in. Escorted by Fezeh, he would walk in and stand by the door of her room still with the same smile and folded hands mumbling some words of apology.

Bibi's first words were "*Gandet begiran*, Hassan. *Khejalat nemikeshi*?" (Damn you, Hassan. You should be ashamed of yourself.

Then with her own smile, knowing how desperately everyone was waiting for their reunion, she would dismiss him to go to Zarafshan, even though that meant a huge insurrection between Fezeh, Nanneh ye Hassan, and Zarafshan.

As young girls, we followed their love story and our brothers experienced adventure by driving Hassan's three-wheeler; they called it *copcopi*.

Besides being introduced to the emotional novelties she brought into our world, Zarafshan was the first woman we knew who worked outside of the house.

Our father found her a job as a custodian at an elementary school. She had sixth-grade education and was very socially and politically aware. She read the newspapers and followed the political events closely. She is still devoted to the Shah and speaks her mind freely about the new government.

She is now following Syria's political stories in detail. She believes if Assad leaves, our government is next! She cannot wait for that to happen.

In later years, with financial support from our family she got a small house near Tehran. She left our house and raised her children as a single mother. Three of her boys, all university graduates, have their practices near Tehran. Her youngest son is a medical doctor, and one of her sons, an engineer, has moved to America with his wife and children. Her daughter, a mother herself, and a real lady, lives close to her mother in the same city.

Hassan's second wife died young, and Hassan passed away a few years ago after years of being handicapped with Alzheimer's. Zarafshan is still very much in love with him.

Similar to Hassan's three-wheeler. Photo: Sayeh Dashti, Mumbai (Bombay) India, 2004.

78

Notes

1 http://en.wikipedia.org/wiki/Ululation. "Ululation . . . is a long, wavering, high–pitched vocal sound resembling a howl with a trilling quality. It is produced by emitting a high-pitched loud voice accompanied with a rapid movement of the tongue and the uvula." The term ululation is an onomatopoetic word derived from Latin. It is produced by moving the tongue rapidly back and forth repetitively in the mouth while producing a sharp sound. Ululation is practiced in certain styles of singing as well as in communal ritual events used to express strong emotion. In Middle Eastern countries ululation is commonly used to express celebration, especially at weddings.

Eleven
Khaneh ye Shahr (City Home)

Khaneh ye Shahr
16 Borazjan Koucheh[1]
Cyrous Street
Sarcheshmeh, Tehran
Tel : 5123

The entrance of Khaneh ye Shahr. Photo: Shawhin Roudbari, 2010.

The small door on one side of the large iron gate finally opened. The sleepy head of a young male workman appeared; we had woken him up from his Friday afternoon nap. His condition was seemingly oblivion as the four of us howled, "Where were you? We were ringing and banging on this door for so long? God damn it. Don't you know the door to this house should never be closed? Ever!" we barked at him. We could have easily given him a heart attack; that is how loud we were, and how odd we might have come across!

He could not speak for a moment; he was stuttering and was trying to defend himself, "I . . . I . . . did not hear. I didn't know. We were working all night; we slept late," he was trying to find excuses. We just brushed him off and went right into the warehouse. The warehouse appeared like a temporary stage set in an abandoned playhouse. We felt stuck. We desperately needed it to move, to make way for the images of our childhood home.

My sister Sepideh, my cousin Amir, and I were quickly being sucked into the memories of our childhood home as we ran from one corner of the building to the other, in tears. My husband, who was accompanying us, gently explained to the young man, "Please forgive them, this was their childhood home. They were born in this house more than sixty years ago." He then added in a whisper, "They have lived in America." Everything seemed fine after that piece of information; as foreigners, specifically Americans, we were allowed to innocently act weird!

The young workman seemed hesitantly convinced and possibly a little flattered to be our tour guide, yet he remained suspicious, not taking his eyes off us until we actually left. He walked close to us as we went wild over each hidden emblem of our past life, being careless how we bumped into the expensive machinery, making him more nervous.

Now we were standing in the middle of a printing press house, what was once our yard.

The unsightly warehouse with monstrous printing machines, the piles of cardboard boxes, the toxic smell of chemicals, and the metal roof hiding the blue sky were soon swept aside as we reengaged with the vivid imagery of our childhood imprinted in our souls.

"Where is the swimming pool?" I asked frantically. "This is it, we are standing on it." My sister was warming up to her memories:

"*Bacheh ha holeh be doosh*!" (Towels on shoulders, kids!) Standing on the greasy tiles of the warehouse, she started chanting the slogan that evoked the most nostalgic memories.

Oh my god. The voices of my older sisters running down the stairs declaring, "*Bacheh ha holeh be doosh*," echoed in my mind. That meant permission was given to us to go in the water. It also meant that people were waking up from their afternoon naps. When that treaty was announced, from each room a restless kid confined in a room with a parent, forced to be quiet while all the grown-ups were sleep, was set free; released. We would all run out with a towel.

What we called a pool was not actually a pool. It was a small hexagonal container of water—the size of a Jacuzzi. The edge was the safe place for the smaller kids like myself. The middle part was probably about three feet, too deep for most of us.

There was a metal mesh covering the water for our protection. We held on to the edge of that metal net while our father pulled it gently to the middle as we bravely kicked and splashed, still holding on. The younger ones always wore a cork belt like miniature soldiers. The older and braver kids like Nafiseh would run from the stairs inside the house directly to the middle of the pool and slam into the water like a cannonball. Our father was the one who had taught all of us how to swim. It was impossible not to trust him; he was one hundred percent focused. He stood in the middle of the pool with his distinguished bearded face, very white body, and maroon color swim trunks, holding us under our tummies and gently turning around and around as we kicked and paddled.

◆ ◆ ◆

When Sheikh Mohammad Hossain Borazjani was exiled to Tehran in 1931, he rented a house from his friend Mr. Kazemi in Eyn al Dowleh, a prominent neighborhood in the center of Tehran.[2] This is the house where his son, Najaf Ali, got sick and passed away in the spring of 1939.

Even though the death of his son had rocked him to his core, literally breaking his back, Aqa ye Bozorg was determined to stay alive until he completed building the house he intended to leave to his daughters. "Now that there will be no men left, my daughters should have their hands in their own pockets. I will not rest until I build a house for them. My daughters should be financially independent," Aqa ye Bozorg had been quoted as saying following the death of his son.

Reza Shah bought Aqa ye Bozorg's land in Borazjan and gave him some lands in Tehran in return! In the year 1931, Aqa ye Bozorg exchanged some of that land and bought a plot (about two thousand square meters) in the neighborhood of Udlajan located in the center of Tehran. He built three structures on that land.[3]

Within walking distance to the north of the property is the House of Parliament in Baharestan Square; to the south is the Grand Bazaar of Tehran; to the northwest are the Russian embassy and the British embassy, to the west is the neighborhood of Pamenar.

A recent aerial view showing Borazjan Alley and Khaneh ye Shahr. The metal roof was erected when the property became a printing plant. The open space to the left is a schoolyard. Photo: ICT Organization Municipality of Tehran, map.Tehran.ir.

Façade of Khaneh ye Shahr. Photo: Shawhin Roudbari, 2010.

There were three separate buildings erected on that plot of land: the main house, the house to the west (known to us as *Khaneh ye Zereshki*), and a small house to its north (known to us as *khaneh koochikeh*). The western building was a one-story house Aqa had built for his second wife, Zan e Aqa. Ever since I can remember, that house was rented to a family from Rasht, called Zereshki. He had a trucking company. There was a door from our yard to their yard (usually open) and another door from their yard to one of the rooms in our basement (closed but unlocked). Mr. Zereshki and his wife had two sons, Nader and Nasser, our playmates, born about 1948 and 1950.

The little house consisted of one room on top of another room. It was usually used by one of Fezeh's relatives, extra guests, or was rented out. Some of its inhabitants were a single man named Sedarati (known to us as *Sedarati kaleh shekasteh,* because he had broken his head at some point!), two women Banoo and Farideh, etc. . .

We lived in the main house that was a two-story structure with five rooms on the upper floor and four rooms on the lower level.

The large beige wooden door to the house was two steps from street level. It opened into a foyer where flights of stairs led to the hallways upstairs, downstairs, and the front yard.

Aqa ye Bozorg lived to complete the houses and lived in *Khaneh ye Shahr* before he passed away on May 23, 1940. He observed the same lifestyle in Tehran—the house was always open and the kitchen always serving. When people from the south arrived at the bus terminal on Sa'di Street, they took a carriage or a taxi that took them straight to *Khooneh ye Shahr*. They used to say, *"Yek Tehran, yek manzel e Aqa"* (One Tehran, one house of the master).

After Aqa ye Bozorg passed away, our parents bought the shares of the main house from Bibi's sisters and left the doors open and the kitchen serving; *"Yek Tehran, yek khooneh e Sheikh Abdollah va Bibi Sediqeh"* (One Tehran, one house of Sheikh Abdollah and Bibi Sediqeh).

◆ ◆ ◆

The water in the pool came from the Qanat e Hajj Alireza (a subterranean canal) in the Udlajan neighborhood. Once a week, on Wednesdays, a *mir-ab* (water keeper) came with his long metal pole to turn the bolt on the side of the pool to allow the water to drain into our yard. He appeared like a Robin Hood opening the safe to a treasure for the poor. The water sprang out like a dome of crystal. The clean, icy sweet water came in and refilled the pool, went around the box trees (*shemshad*) and then into the water-storage tank in the cellar. Once every couple of weeks another man with a different social standing came to clean the pool (*ab-hozi*). He had the reputation of being a thief and a child kidnapper. With his pants rolled above his knees and his two metal buckets that smelled like stagnant water, he came around the neighborhood and chanted, "*Ab hozi, Ab hozieh, Ab e hoze mikeshim*" (We are the pool cleaners. This is the pool cleaner). He repeated this until someone let him in to clean the pool of greenish water.

Even though the pool was now covered over with many layers of concrete, the faucet next to the edge of the pool was still there, sticking out of the tiles. This faucet belonged to Fezeh. No matter where I am in the world, when I hear the *azan* (call to prayer), I picture Fezeh running from the kitchen with a large colander of rice as the *azan* on the radio called for noon prayers. She washed the rice under the water coming from the faucet—the pot of rice was too large to be handled inside the kitchen. No one dared be in the water when Fezeh wanted to rinse her rice; feeding so many people was a serious matter after all.

The cellar was still there—the cool dark stairs led to a water-storage tank. That was where we kept some food for refrigeration; tons of watermelons and wooden boxes of some other fruit brought to us from our farm in Shahriar (mostly grapes, apples, and pears) that were kept in the cellar.

Sepideh continued as she moved a few feet from the pool, "Here was the apricot tree." She helped me recall the blossoms and the games we played. We ate the apricots mainly because we wanted the pits. By rubbing the pits of the apricots on the tile of the yard for hours and hours, there appeared a hole in each side of the pits. We then emptied the kernel with a needle and made a whistle out of the apricot pits.

"You see that wall?" I said, pointing to the south side of the warehouse. "There was the grape arbor. We could never reach the rambling grapes, but felt lucky when a bunch of dusty sour grapes fell to the ground for us to eat, unwashed! We made mudbricks underneath that arbor; rows and rows of bricks and then we made dollhouses with them; two- or three-story structures, then we used the red wild cherries for the chandeliers. We also made a simpler structure called Arabi house. We used actual bricks for it. "One brick on the right, one brick on the left, and one brick on top for its ceiling," I said. I was trying to include my husband and the workman by sharing what we were recalling from our memories.

At that point, my sister and I looked at each other to make sure there was no stranger among us as we stared at the small window at the top of the stairs to the east side of the yard. That was our great-uncle's room. We chose not to mention it right there and then. That room and its history were always kept confidential.

Aqda'i Mohammad Khan was a highly educated man. He completed his graduate studies in the field of education at the University of Beirut and had written some books on education.[4] He spoke fluent French and Arabic. He returned to Iran and held an important post in the Ministry of Education. He married a stylish young girl, who was a princess from a Qajar family (*Shazdeh*). They had one daughter. Unfortunately, his mental illness, schizophrenia, interfered with his life at a very young age; when he was in his twenties. He was being taken care of in our house.

Having such a brilliant and gentle man in the house brought us a sense of curiosity and importance. Even though he seemed preoccupied with hallucinations, he seemed to be always present. He walked around the backyard and talked to the box trees. He moved his hands as he talked to them as if he were reasoning with them through logic (very much the same body language as his brother Ali during his speeches in the Parliament). Then, he would walk away from the box trees, apparently sensing that logic did not work. He rolled a cigarette in a piece of old newspaper and went up to his room to smoke. His actions were very structured—his steady schedule was much respected in our house; we knew when he was coming out of his room to walk around and when he went back in—we kept the level of noise accordingly. Bibi and Fezeh and at times Nafiseh were ready to run to his room to clean up as soon as he left the house once in a while. We were so curious to see his room. The smoke-filled room was stacked with old books and newspapers. Someone would stand by the front door to let them know if he was approaching, then Bibi and Fezeh would run down the stairs with their broom and bucket most triumphantly. That was a daring move by Bibi, obviously he did not want to let others into his most delicate environment.

Even when Mohammad Khan was hallucinating, he was watchful. He cautioned us in case we seemed to be in any kind of danger, "*Movazeb bash joonom*! (Be careful sweetheart!)" he said. One of the most important experiences from my childhood is when I was allowed to take lunch to Mohammad Khan. Getting that close to him, as I handed him the tray at the top of the stairs, was a magnificent experience. The aura around him was gentle, caring, most sophisticated and powerful; his dignity was in complete charge of his insanity. His voice was like the texture of thick *ardeh* (sesame butter); his clothes were worn out with patches all over, yet very clean—he hand washed them every day and hung them outside on a line to dry. As he took the tray from my hands, he would make eye contact and say, "*Qorboonesh beshom* (I love you)." Then he waited to make sure I got down the stairs safely before he closed his door, going back to his vast world.

The only story we ever heard about an act of aggression by him was when he nonchalantly uprooted a new tree from the backyard and carried it on his shoulders. This was a young willow tree that Aqa ye Bozorg had planted and the late Zan Aqa was caring for. One day as she was watering the plants outside, she saw what Mohammad Khan had done. She cried out in disbelief, "Aqa?" Mohammad Khan turned around and looked at her. She immediately said, "*Shoma zahmat keshidid*?" This was a *ta'arof* meaning that you should not have bothered to do something this difficult; you should have asked someone to do it for you.

We then ran inside the building. Every room had been turned into an office or a storeroom. My cousin Amir pointed to a room as we entered the hallway from the yard and said:

This is the place where I saw a banana for the first time. Khaleh (Bibi) was holding a banana like a magician, then she started peeling it with her fingers! It was unbelievable. The fruit looked like a cucumber and I was sure that a knife or even something sharper was required to peel such a huge strong fruit. Then she took the white fruit out and gave it to me. It was soft and delicious. I never forgot that taste. I also tasted cherries for the first time, right here in this room. My mother and all the family were sitting in this room. I was sitting on her lap as she seeded these round rubies and put them in my mouth. I had the best memories of my life here in this house. Did you know that except for today, I had never walked on my own feet into this house? I was always carried in the arms of so many loving and cheering cousins. When we came to Tehran and turned into this alley, we could feel the rumble caused by joyfulness from inside your house. Somehow, someone would let you know that we were coming. As soon as we got to where the alley narrowed, you all ran out and took me from my mother's arms to carry me into the house and upstairs. Absolute bliss is the only word that can explain how I felt.

To the left of this room was Fezeh's room, always open, facing the stairs and a shelf for the telephone. Next to the stairs was our father's room, also used as the summertime living room. There, we experienced an electric cooler, homemade carbonated lemonade, and vanilla ice cream all for the first time. Our father loved to introduce us to the latest inventions.

Another stairway connected the ground floor to the upper floor and to the roof. Our cousin Aqa Mehdi's room was next to these stairs and had windows to the yard. Aqa Mehdi stayed with us while he was attending Tehran University.

Next to the kitchen was a large pantry filled with woven bags of rice, large metal containers of cooking oil, etc. The pantry, the hallways, every space available was also used to accommodate guests coming from the south to stay, turning the house into a hospice. Some of the rooms were equipped with hospital beds. Many of the visitors came to have an operation and were released from the hospital to continue care in our house. There were cases of broken legs, tuberculosis, cholera, whooping cough, eye infections, etc.

How amazing was it that we were not forbidden to go in and out of these rooms even though the family had lost some of its most precious members to the diseases carried by the random visitors. We played around them, hid under their beds for hide-and-seek. We got in the most serious trouble only when we kept bumping into Day Shokoohi's broken leg suspended from the ceiling of the pantry.

The kitchen was piled up with boxes now, making it difficult to match the present grotesque scene with when we last saw the heart of the house. The concrete oven our father had designed and the windows to the street where Fezeh splashed water at the naughty schoolchildren were still intact.

Then we rushed upstairs. The staircase looked so short. I had once fallen from the top floor down the stairs when I was about two or three years old. I am the only one remembering that because I did not dare make a sound. I could not breathe for what seemed an eternity. I was more afraid of being caught, than actually dying. We were strictly forbidden to slide on the staircases but we all did it; none of us walked down the stairs if there was not an adult in sight; we always slid down.

The rooms upstairs were better preserved. There was no challenge in locating the rooms upstairs—we had lived life to the fullest there.

The children's room, the dining room, the salon, our father's home office, our parents' bedroom, and Abaj's room (later Talieh's room) and most importantly the wooden coatrack with a character of its own. In the event that questions such as, where is my coat? Where are my gloves, where is the hat? Where is . . . were asked, the common answer was, "On the coatrack" and then the case was convincingly closed. There was no blame of carelessness following that. When Bibi's lambskin coat was stolen from the coatrack, it gained importance; not because it was made out of lambskin, it was because it was stolen off the coatrack. There it was, a place in the house with a designated function, a sanctuary for objects.

The struggle that day was to grasp the sizes of the rooms. How could that vast glory have taken place in such small rooms? When last those men and women sat together in the salon upstairs, making decisions for their families and the nation, the ground beneath them rumbled. The rooms seemed gigantic when those people with their giant goals were present. How boldly they talked, how fearless they seemed, how safe the world felt growing up next to such titans.

In addition to the stairs leading to Mohammad Khan's room the other dark and forbidden place for us as children was the stairway to the roof. We were never allowed to go there alone. For the first time I noticed the very beautiful, tall, stained glass window at the side of the stairs. I did remember the strange objects piled up there, such as the many different sizes of sawfish rostrums (some as long as four feet)! We used to think that our father had caught them. The stairs opened to the flat roof where we slept during the summer nights. Still so high above everything else, it gave us a better view of the whole neighborhood.

Most important was the old cypress tree, which was still there, sticking out of a hole in the metal roof they had erected over the yard. The cypress tree had not grown much. It was always this tall, yet younger.

Looking down from the roof, we got a better glimpse at the house and the neighborhood. None of those people live here anymore, not our parents, not our grandparents, not the heroic *mir-ab*, not the Jewish families squeezed into the narrow, dead-end, side streets, not the French midwife running to our house to deliver yet another baby; most are not alive anymore, and the living had taken their lives to other locations.

We had been injected that day with a sense of pride. All that we had experienced growing up in that house was all within us and not in those buildings. The building was now a soulless body to us. We have had our turns; we had showed up for a play and had performed on one of the stages of our lives. It was now the turn of others. So we quietly left that day.

The cyprus tree and the family in Khaneh ye shahr's backyard. Photo: Dashti family album, about 1957.

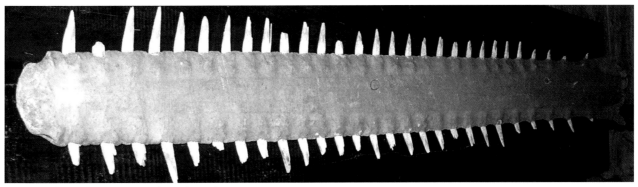

Rostrum of a sawfish. Photo: Sayeh Dashti, Tehran, 2015.

Notes

1   The *koucheh* (alley) was named Borazjan after Aqa ye Bozorg's last name Borazjani. (The alley was previously named Zahir al Eslam.)

2   The neighborhood was named after Majid Mirza Eyn al Dowleh (1845–1927), Qajar prince and prime minister, who was the eldest son of Prince Sultan Ahmad Mirza Azod al Dowleh and grandson of Fath Ali Shah Qajar. http://en.wikipedia.org/wiki/Abdol_Majid_Mirza

3   Nezam Mafi was the architect of *Khaneh ye Shahr.*

4   Mohammad Dashti, *Mabadi e elm e tarbiat* (The principles of education) (Tehran: Kitabkhaneh ye Ma'refat, 1307 [1929]).

Twelve

How Was Reza Shah Forced to Leave?

Bibi told us the details of the events she remembered from the time Reza Shah abdicated and left Iran in 1941. This was following the invasion of Iran by British and Russian forces in August 1941.

When Ahmad Shah proved to be so incompetent, the British chose a man like Reza Khan, a very brave military man from Mazandaran.[1] He became too powerful I suppose!

At the beginning of World War II, when there were only the Italians, French, and England, Reza Khan was neutral. When the Russians and Americans got involved, he helped the Germans.

Germans worked hard for Iran. Most of the important buildings in Tehran were built by German engineers:[2] The Court House, Foreign Affairs Building, the Ministry of Finance, and many more. I was in awe in front of the magnificent buildings. None is like the Ministry of Finance building. 'God bless your soul man,' I said to the face of a *pasdar* (Islamic Republican guard). 'Who are you talking about?' the guard asked. 'Reza Shah, who else?' I said.

The British now wanted to dismiss Reza Shah from his post. One night Reza Shah broke four radios in the parliament—this is when the radio had just come to Iran. The radio was announcing that the Shah has to leave.

Britain was demanding that Iran should expel all Germans from Iran, but Reza Shah hesitated. Eventually he did tell them to leave, but not before he aggravated the British to the point that they ordered him out too.

It was so unfortunate that these countries made decisions for us. We were once the greatest empire in the world, and now they are referring to us as a third-world country! Their employees coming here get extra money (called *haq e tavahosh* (a bonus for dealing with barbarians)), referring to us as savages, whereas we should get that for tolerating them.

Initially, Reza Khan wanted to become president, but Ali Dashti told him that this country is a kingdom and is not ready for it. Aqa ye Bozorg and Dashti from the first day of Reza's reign, and before, were his supporters. Aqda'i was with him when he was *sardar e sepah* (an army general) then a prime minister and then a king.

I remember the night Reza Shah was ordered to leave. The parliament was in session until midnight. Foroughi was the prime minister and Hekmat was the head of the parliament. Ali Dashti was a member of the House of the Representatives before he became a senator. That night they were all there in the Parliament. Aqda'i told us that on that night Reza Shah kicked and smashed four radios as he went from one room to another hearing the same message on the radio. Each time the news was repeated, he broke yet another radio in rage.

The next morning at nine, he came to the Parliament to make a formal announcement on the radio, 'I hereby give the kingdom of Iran to my son Mohammad Reza and all I own, I give to a piece of crystal sugar (*habbeh ye nabaat*),'[3] he said almost in tears.

The rumor that day was that if the lights went off at night it would mean that we were being bombed by Russia. Just a few days before the Russians had dropped a bomb in Saltanat Abad (Pasdaran). Even though Saltanat Abad is in Shemiran, our house shook very hard.

As it was getting dark and we had turned the lights on, we noticed the lights dim gradually. As the lights deemed I felt that life was going out of my body from my head to my toes. I ran to the arch of the basement for safety. My brother-in-law (Zia al Din Ebne Yousef) was there visiting; we were having dinner. He asked why I ran to the arch and I told him the arch was the safest place of the building in case a bomb is dropped on us. He commented, 'If you are so wise, why are you so hysterical!' When your father called from his office to make sure we were safe, I screamed even louder telling him, 'We are not okay, we are going to be bombed and you are not even here with us.' He came home right away!

Then of course we found out that the reason we had a blackout was that Reza Shah was leaving the country!

He was abdicating! The British took him to the island of Mauritius and then to Africa. He died in exile. He was about seventy years old and actually should have left sooner. His son was already twenty-five and was married to Fozieh (sister of Farook of Egypt); he was ready to rule the country. Yes that is how it was (*bale intory bood*). That is how Reza Shah left.

Reza Shah (March 15, 1878 to 26 July 1944).
Photo: Daryoush Tahami.

Notes

1   "Ironside appointed Reza Khan to command the élite Cossack Brigade; Reza Khan would later seize control of the country, and rule as Shah from 1925 to 1941. The precise level of British involvement in Reza Khan's coup détat remains a matter of historical debate, but it is almost certain that Ironside himself at least provided advice to the plotters. On his departure from Persia in 1921, the Shah awarded him the Order of the Lion and the Sun." From: en.wikipedia.org/wiki/ Edmund_Ironside,_1st_Baron_Ironside: Field Marshal William Edmund Ironside, 1st Baron Ironside GCB, CMG, DSO (May 6, 1880–September 22, 1959) was a British military commander, who served as Chief of the Imperial General Staff during the first year of the Second World War. Edmund Ironside, ed. *High Road to Command: The Diaries of Major-General Edmund Ironside, 1920-1922* (London: Leo Cooper, 1972)."There are indications that Reza Khan has worked with the military officials of Britain. There are still controversial views as who introduced him to Ironside, but there is no doubt that he was known to the British before the coup détat 1299." Cyrus Ghani, *Iran and the Rise of Reza Shah: From Qajar Collapse to Pahlavi Rule*. Translated from the author's English manuscript into Persian by Hassan Kamshad. 6th ed. (Tehran: Entesharat e Niloufar, 1391 [2014]): 190.

2   From http://www.iranicaonline.org/articles/architecture-vii: "Shortly after the establishment of the parliamentary system in Iran, a strong desire for preserving and restoring historical monuments was exhibited by educated Iranians and certain influential journals (e.g., Kāva, edited by S. H. āqīzāda in Berlin). Sharing this enthusiasm, Reżā Khan encouraged the founding of the National Monuments Council (Anjoman-e Āār-e Mellī, q.v.). The council, which received support and academic assistance from such scholars as E. Herzfeld, strove to fulfill those aims." From en.wikipedia.org.wiki/ Ernst_Herzfeld: "Herzfeld was born in Celle, Province of Hanover. He studied architecture in Munich and Berlin, while also taking classes in Assyriology, ancient history and art history. 1903–05 he was assistant to Walter Andrae in the acclaimed excavations of Assur, and later traveled widely in Iraq and Iran at the beginning of the twentieth century. He surveyed and documented many historical sites in Turkey, Syria, Persia (later Iran) and most importantly in Iraq (e.g., Baghdad, Ctesiphon). At Samarra he carried out the first excavations of an Islamic period site in 1911–13. After military service during World War I he was appointed full professor for "Landes- und Altertumskunde des Orients" in Berlin in 1920. This was the first professorship for Near/Middle Eastern archaeology in the world. 1923–25 he started explorations in Persia and described many of the countries' most important ruins for the first time. In 1925 he moved to Tehran and stayed there most of the time until 1934. He was instrumental in creating a Persian law of antiquities and excavated in the Achaemenid capitals Pasargadae and Persepolis."

3   This is a symbolic formality when a contract is being dissolved.

Thirteen

Year of Famine (*Sal e Qahti*); Introduction to the Movement in Fars

This time, we were prepared! We had a portable tape recorder, a brand-new blank tape—well equipped to tape Bibi's voice as she told us the story of "The Year of Famine." Most of the time we confused the events—did they belong to the story of "the Year of Ravage," "the Year of Famine," or to another one?

That night (June, 1987) in Nafiseh's house in Leeds, England, we got another chance. Bibi diligently told the story of "The Year of Famine," making sure the facts were spelled out for us. She made certain the tape recorder was working and had us test it a couple of times. She hated hearing her taped voice—she said it sounded childish and loose. She was right, her own voice was much deeper and vibrant than her voice taped on the cheap, amateur, compact cassette player. She immediately ignored the tape recorder and started telling the stories, realizing that it was not about her, it was about something much bigger. She began by saying:

During WWII, Iran had become the bridge of victory for the USA and Russia; they called us "The Persian Corridor."[1] They transported everything their troops needed to Russia and Germany via Iran. The American ships came to Khorramshahr port and then by our railroads they took things to Russia; they also used all our resources to feed their armies. I am telling you, if it were not for Iran, they could not have conquered Germany. They took all Iran's wheat, oil, gasoline, sugar, and bread for the Allied soldiers in Germany. For three years, Iran was packed with the Americans and the Russians. After the war, however, instead of being praised, Iran suffered in famine.

We were in Shiraz for three years after the incident of bombing of Tehran by the Russians. I remember when Sultan, Fezeh's father, went to the market to get bread at six o'clock every morning and finally returned at about nine with only one loaf of dark bread. My niece [Bibi Vajiheh] was only a toddler then. She used to say, "I wish my father was a baker." She must have sensed our disappointment when Sultan showed up almost empty-handed. People were starving. Many families were eating what they used to feed their animals—they would soak the dried-out old bread in water and eat that for dinner.

As a result of famine, typhus became epidemic.[2] So many people lost their lives. All I could do during that time was to put a humongous pot on the stove and simply boil everything—that actually saved us; we all survived, even the babies.

Gradually the Americans left Iran, but the Russians stayed in Tabriz; the Toodeh party [Communist party in Iran] helped them. Some of their members such as Gholam Yahya and Pishehvari were very active in this.[3]

Everything was affected, specially the values of things. For instance a large piece of valuable land in Maragheh (a city in Azerbaijan) that our family had was almost lost. Your father called me one day to see if it was alright to sell it for 20,000 *tuman*s. He wanted me to consult with Zia al Din Ebne Yousef, and Ali Dashti. They both said it was a good idea. I had heard that a customer had run out of the real estate office as soon as he heard that the land was in Maragheh! So actually it was like we lost our valuable property; it had lost its value.

Everything was going wrong. Qavam al Saltaneh became the prime minister and immediately decided to put Aqda'i in prison.[4] Aqda'i was in the Majles and gave a hard-hitting speech against the government of Qavam al Saltaneh who was supporting the Russians' demands from Iran. He had said, "We do not want Qavam al Saltaneh. We do not want Vosooq al Dowleh (these two were brothers); they are traitors!" It was at this time that he wrote the stories that became the book, *Ayyam e mahbas* [Days of imprisonment].[5]

He was in jail for five days, and then he was put under house arrest for a year in his own residence in Shemiran. Your father and I, our two daughters, Talieh and Badieh, and Fezeh stayed with Aqda'i in his house to look after him. I was pregnant with Nafiseh then and my doctor had recommended that I go to a place to get fresh air. Your father went to work every morning and came home at nights. There were two guards in front of each door at Aqda'i's residence making sure he did not leave the house. Aqda'i was on the phone with the Shah consulting him daily. "If you want the Russians to leave," he would advise the Shah, "send a trustee to Bushehr to give all the offices back to the khans [*khavanin*] temporarily, and then after the Russians leave, you can reverse the order. You yourself need to go to Azerbaijan with the army. We are now threatened by the British as well; you must be there," he insisted.

Aqda'i told the Shah that we cannot sit back, we must act strategically. "First we need to control the ports by giving the power back to the tribes [*ashayer*]—they have the power to withstand any attack." Aqda'i was trying to make the Shah understand the delicate politics. Shah accepted it and your father, a man he could completely trust, was chosen for the mission. Your father did a great job.

Shah himself went to war in Azerbaijan. I was seven months pregnant and I saw it in person—we all went to see as the Shah and the army left for the war.

On the 21st of Azar 1325 [11 December 1946], on the day Nafiseh was born, the news came that we had won the war in Tabriz. The Russians had heard that the British were coming! Only then they finally took off.

The next day Nosratollah Amini, the mayor of Tehran, came to tell me, "Last night we had a victory." Then your father called. He was beside himself, crying out with joy on the phone, "We won! Iran won the war." Then he asked me to name the baby Fathieh Azar [the victory of Azerbaijan]. I did not do that of course. "He who was not there when the baby was born does not deserve the right to choose a name for her," I said to myself.

So your father had accepted the mission to go to the South and give the power Aqa ye Bozorg had taken away from the khans, back to them.

Obviously the khans welcomed the opportunity to be in charge again and received your father like a king. I was seven months pregnant with my third daughter when he left and when he returned, she was eleven months old! As he was unpacking he looked around and commented, "It seems like there is another child here? [*na ingar yeki digeh be bacheh ha ezafeh shodeh!?*]"

◆ ◆ ◆

We took a break to put the children to sleep. Bibi was anxious to continue with the stories. She was impatient with the interruptions and as soon as we returned with tea for everyone, she continued:

In June of 1946, your father got the mission from Mohammad Reza Shah to go to Borazjan and give the governing power back to the khans. All government offices such as the customs and the military were to be controlled temporarily by the khans once again.

The chief khans were Nasser Khan Qashqai, Ra'is Ali in Bushehr, and Ardeshir Khan in Shabankareh, Ali Somail and Khaloo Hossain from Dashti. They were so very happy. They believed they are getting their power back for good, but it was only for about eight months.

My own father had the mission to disarm the khans about twenty years prior to that, and now, they were to be armed once again by your father!

We heard that there were duels, man-to-man combats between the khans in Borazjan. Zan Aqa told me, "Hey girl, get up and go! Go see what has happened to this man." Then she sent me to Borazjan to look for your father. I went unannounced with Fezeh and my now three daughters. We first went to Shiraz and then to Borazjan—my sister Abibi accompanied us. Your father had heard the news that we were in Shiraz and came immediately to take us to Borazjan. "Come and see for yourself. It is the same old Borazjan all over again!" he proudly told me.

Sure enough, the entire population of Borazjan had come to welcome us with their gun show. There were so many gunshots celebrating our arrival. I was afraid of guns, yet, as frightened as I was, I was overwhelmed with excitement.

What a scene it was! The crowd was something I had never seen before. They had brought along all the sheep they had to sacrifice in front of our footsteps, as it was the custom of hospitality in those days. The markets were closed so all the people could come to welcome us [*cheh mahshari bood az jamiat va goosfand*]. Then the khan of Shabankareh invited us to his house. His mother was the deputy governor and even more influential than her sons; she had invited us.

I left the baby (Nafiseh) in Borazjan when going to their house—I was embarrassed to show her my three girls, which meant I still did not have a boy! But, as soon as she walked in, she said: "I have heard that you have three girls!"

Ardeshir Khan's wife came in too. She must have expected a woman in my position—having come from the capital—to be so fancy and fashionably dressed. Much to her disappointment, I was too simple and had not worn any jewelry. She herself was dressed up in full *shalvar* (more than forty meters) and had worn gold ornaments from her neck down to her waist. She seemed to be very embarrassed when she saw me so plain. Shortly after she walked in the room, she returned and took off most of her gold. Later, they took us sightseeing to a new dam near Borazjan that your father had helped build and then to Ahram.

The famine was still with us. The flood of people who came to see us daily was so incredible. I remember telling your father, "Why do not you bring some sugar from the Customs?" He looked at me surprised and said, "I am sure you are not being serious." I defended myself by saying "but we will pay for it." Again he refused and said firmly, "These belong to the people and I am their trustee."

A few days later we went to Shiraz. The head of Persepolis invited us for a private visit and to stay in Persepolis. There was a formal ceremony arranged for us. It was most amazing. That night I also found out that your father was not coming back with us to Tehran. I cried all night. When your father came to wake me up at four in the morning, he touched my pillow and noticed that it was soaking wet with tears. "Why are you crying?" he asked. "Why are you so sad? Did you not see all that glory?" he whispered. "You do realize that the two sides are still ready to attack each other. Now they are all armed, and if I am not there, many people will die each day!" he said reassuringly.

Yes! Indeed I had witnessed how he had gone from one side of the road to the other to negotiate with the tribes so that they do not shoot at each other. I was in the car with the children screaming in fear. I was yelling out, "Where are you Reza Shah to save us?"

I told your father, "But what about us? What is our fault here? Why should we suffer?" I just wanted to complain even though I knew he was right; I was sad and disappointed. He tried to calm me down. "We are responsible for our people and our country; people rely on us." "Now what do we do?" I asked. "You have endured all this for our people. Is this not what your own father taught all of us? We cannot ignore the needs of the people; we can never say we do not care," he said that knowing that I understood. "Go ahead and take the children back, I will return in one month," he said before he left. He came back after eleven months! His mission was completed then; he had managed to disarm the khans again and return the power to the central government.

Upon his return to Tehran, he went to report to Mohammad Reza Shah. The Shah was very pleased and said: "*Ajab! Ajab!* [How incredible!] I did not know we still have men like you in this country." Shah then wanted to reward your father: "I have ordered . . ." Your father interrupted him: "I have done this for my home, my people and my country; this was my duty." He refused to receive any gifts from the Shah.

Sheikh Abdollah [she called my father by this name and pronounced it as one word, Sheikhabdollah] worked very hard for our region. He brought schools, electricity, roads, and many other things for the people. Most importantly he worked hard to convince the government to send help for the health services in the south to uproot the deadly diseases.[6] "God bless his soul."

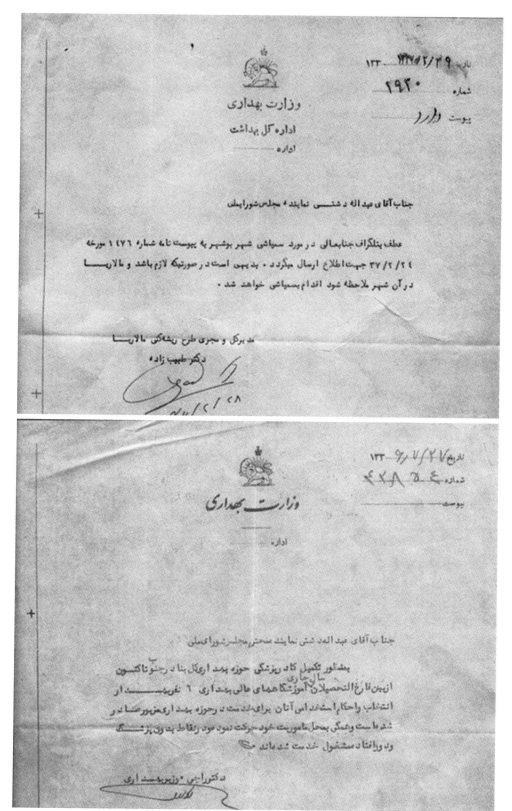

Responses to Abdollah Dashti's letters to the Ministry of Health, ordering the state of Bushehr to prevent malaria.

Notes

[1] "Following Germany's invasion of the USSR in June 1941, Britain and the Soviet Union became formal Allies, providing further impetus for an Allied invasion. With the German Army steadily advancing through the Soviet Union, the "Persian Corridor" formed by the Trans-Iranian Railway was one of the easiest ways for the Allies to get desperately needed Lend-Lease supplies to the Soviets by sea from the United States. British and Soviet planners began to see the vital importance of that railway, and sought to secure it into their hands." John L. Esposito, *Islam and Politics* 4th ed. (Syracuse: Syracuse University Press, 1984): 127.

- "Despite the declaration of neutrality, Iran could not avoid the foreign invasion during World War II. In 1941, when Germany waged war against the Soviets and Japan against the USA, Iran gained a very strategic importance. Especially, Germany's attack on the Soviets put together a communist state and her ideological rivals—the USA and the UK—on the same side. When the war forced these states into an alliance, Iran became a key geography so that the alliance could run. Convening at Placentia Bay, Newfoundland in August 1941, US President Roosevelt and British Prime Minister Churchill decided to provide the USSR with economic and military aid. Yet, there were big difficulties in conveying the aid to the Soviets. The reason for that was the security problem rather than the geographical barriers. The Soviet's Baltic gate was closed due to the German threat and the Far East gate, due to Japan. The Turkish straits and Iran were other alternative ways to establish a connection with the Russian geography. However, the utilization of the Turkish straits was not possible according to the terms that the Treaty of Montreux prescribed. So, there was no other way for the Allies to convey the aid to the Soviets but through Iran." Süleyman Erkan, "The Invasion of Iran by the Allies during World War II," *Codrul Cosminului*, 16 (2010): 112.

[2] Zarafonetis, Chris J. D., "The Typhus Fevers," in *Internal Medicine in World War II* (Washington, DC: Office of the Surgeon General, Department of the Army, 1963): vol. 2, chap. 7. During World War II typhus struck the German Army as it invaded Russia in 1941. In 1942 and 1943 typhus hit French North Africa, Egypt, and Iran particularly hard.

[3] "Ja'far Pishehvari was the head of the Communist party in Iran. On December 14, 1945 he declared Azerbaijan as an independent state. From the book by 'Abd al–Reza Houshang Mahdavi, *Tarikh e ravabet e khareji e Iran: az ebteday e doran e safaviye ta payan e jang e dovvom e jahani* (The history of Iranian foreign affairs: From the beginning of the Safavid era until the end of World War II), 19th ed. (Tehran: Entesharat e Amir Kabir Press, 1392 [2013]): 425.

[4] "Ahmad Qavam (Qavam al Saltaneh) was the younger brother of Vosouq al Dowleh. He was the prime minister of Iran in 1300, 1301, 1321, 1324 and a few days in 1331 Shamsi." From the book by Cyrous Ghani, *Iran and the Rise of Reza Shah: From Qajar Collapse to Pahlavi Rule*. Translated from the author's English manuscript into Farsi by Hassan Kamshad. (Tehran: Entesharat e Niloufar, 1380 [2002]): 81.

[5] Ali Dashti, *Ayyam e mahbas* (Days of imprisonment) (Tehran, 1922).

[6] Abdollah Dashti, *Az Jam/Reez ta Tabriz* (From Jam/Reez to Tabriz). Compiled and edited by Badieh Dashti. (Tehran: Farhang e Hezareh e Sevom, 1385 [2006]).

Fourteen
Doctor Mosaddeq

Man of the year, Dr. Mosaddeq. Photo: Daryoush Tahami.

The history books point us to this incident; Bibi's voice puts us there.

A contract had been signed between Iran and the British during Mozaffar al Din Shah's reign.[1] Under the terms of that contract, England was to exploit the oil in Iran and in return had agreed to build an oil refinery as well as housing and accommodation for the British and Iranian employees of the oil company living in Abadan.[2] In addition, a commitment was made to build a university there in order to train oil engineers, which would have been an exchange program between accredited universities in England and Iran. All the students who were to be enrolled in these universities were to be exempted from paying tuition. The agreement was that when the term of the concession had matured, they were obliged to leave intact all that they had built in our country. During the sixty years of the term of that concession, they were to give fifteen or sixteen percent of the extracted oil money to Iran.

Even though this contract was to be without recompense, the sixteen percent was very low and the deal unfair to Iran. Somehow though, given the situation of the time, and the promises England had made, made it worthwhile to wait. Either way, fair or unfair, the term of the concession was almost over.

Dr. Mosaddeq[3] seemed to be unaware of the fact that there was a conspiracy. The plot was that England foresaw the proximity of the maturation of the term of the contract and was not willing to accept the cost of leaving all that it had built—her share of the bargain—behind.

The British used Mosaddeq through one of the religious leaders, Ayatollah Kashani,[4] to work out a coup through which they could get away from their commitments to Iran. He started provoking Mosaddeq, a devoted nationalist, by saying, 'Why should we just sit here while England is taking all the oil money? Why should they get the oil money when the oil is ours?' Kashani insisted that they should do something; raise the price of oil, get more share, or even ask the International Court of Justice in The Hague to intervene.

Mosaddeq came to Ali Dashti (Aqda'i) one day for a consultation.

Dashti told him, "Doctor, this is not a good thing you do. Do not for a minute assume that you are more of a nationalist than I am. That is not so. I know about the contract they had. They know that the term of the contract is almost due and they need to deliver what the contract dictates. I know that they are using a person like you to do it for them, to start a riot so they can get away with it. I know it. Do not do it. Listen to me. It is a trap. They have expensive commitments. They are making an excuse so we do it ourselves while they are getting away with their commitments to us, and it will look like it is what we wanted, not them."

"No sir!" said Doctor Mosaddeq. "I would rather cover the oil wells with mud than let the hands of England reach our oil," he said. He actually did do that; he covered the wells with mud [*gel gereftand*].

Aqda'i thought there was nothing he could do at that point. Mosaddeq had made up his mind.

The challenges started then. There was no income; we were under sanction. There were not even enough funds to pay the government employees. Mosaddeq had to reach out to people by creating something they called "*qarzeh ye melli*" [national bond, money borrowed from the people].[5] All our children broke their piggy banks to take the money to schools to be collected by the government. People gave all they could afford; a few *rials*, or *tumans*—anything they could give, they did. The situation got really bad, the country was bending down to its knees; it was horrible. Mosaddeq had most people's complete support. One, for instance, was engineer Mehdi Bazargan.[6] He was a major supporter of Mosaddeq and a nationalist himself, a true enemy of the Shah as well. He made a major attempt to dig the oil, but he did not succeed.

Aqda'i had also told Mosaddeq to wait for our engineers to come back so we can do it ourselves. "We are not ready yet. We do not have experts who can do this. Their contract is almost due anyhow. Wait for our engineers to return home from abroad. This is going to take some years," Dashti told him, but Mosaddeq refused.

The Toodeh [Communist] Party welcomed this chaos. They used Doctor Mosaddeq to overthrow the Shah and then they could get rid of Mosaddeq by themselves. Easy! They used to say, "These two are like dog and cat. The Shah being the dog and Mosaddeq, the cat. Let England take away the dog and then we can get rid of the cat ourselves."

Mosaddeq did not take Dashti's advice and took the case to the International Court of Justice in The Hague.[7] Of course England had ordered them to vote for Mosaddeq. Using her influence, he got the vote. This time England was into a bigger scheme with America!

The day he arrived at Tehran International Airport, Mehrabad, people went with so much joy. They celebrated him, giving him a hero's welcome for what he had done; that he had won.

But what had he done? Did he really win? A mindless act! An odd and unjust ruling had taken place much to the disadvantage of the Iranian people. History shows that the British will never stay behind; no matter what! What they did was, they surely did close the Anglo Oil Company they had. Instead they formed another one and called it the National Iranian Oil Company, a consortium. This time the profits all went into their pockets and the sixty percent, which was to belong to us, never actually took place.

Years later OPEC took over. We do not really know what happened that the price of oil went up so high. I assume there was another plot to get rid of Mohammad Reza Shah by raising the price of oil overnight to thirty-five dollars a barrel, extracting about five million barrels a day.[8]

Dr. Mosaddeq became the Prime Minister and the Parliament was in charge of the government. Shah was to be a constitutional rather than an authoritarian figure, much like in England.

The Toodeh Party, however, was not content with this. They wanted Shah to leave. There were riots, daily, all over the country. There were constant demonstrations in front of the Parliament when it was in session.

I remember a woman with an infant in her arms standing in front of the armed soldiers, crying out, "Here, hit me, shoot me," she said. I am telling you, Tehranis are so brave!

One day when Aqda'i was in the Parliament with Jamal Emami [a colleague; member of the Parliament], we heard that there was a riot there. Zan aqa, Abaj's mother, went to the kitchen, took all the knives, scissors, and hammers in the kitchen and along with our friend Mr. Kamaredji, who had a gun and a Jeep, went to the Parliament building to save them!

Luckily they had left from the back door. Aqda'i was so amazed when I told him about Zan aqa. He said, 'Wow! That was so brave [*barekalah Zan aqa*].'

Eventually there were disagreements between Dr. Mosaddeq and Kashani. Of course the Moslems listened to the religious leader, who was Ayatollah Kashani then, like they listen to A . . . Khomeini now.

Dr. Mosaddeq was isolated then and in poor health. Only a handful of people such as Amini, Yazdi,[9] Bazargan, Kazemi[10] were with him. [Most of these families, specially Amini's, were very close friends of Khaleh Abibi and Bibi.] These men were all very young. Amini became the mayor of Tehran. There was Macci[11] and Dr. Hossain Fatemi,[12] who had gone to Borazjan as well. (Fatemi Street is named after him.) These people were all very active.

Mosaddeq wanted Shah to only be the constitutional figure and not a decision-maker. I remember when they went to the Parliament [Majles] and gave a vote of confidence [*etminan*] to Dr. Mosaddeq, which meant that from that moment Shah had handed his power to Mosaddeq.

Bibi is interrupted by Nafiseh asking her about Sha'boon bi Mokh (Sha'ban the brainless), a legendary strongman of Tehran.[13]

Everyone present objects to the interruption, but Bibi says, "No, it is okay. I am glad you brought it up. Sha'boon bi Mokh loved the Shah," she said briefly and continued with her story with new energy.

Mosaddeq did respect the Shah in public, not respecting in the true sense of the word of course. He did things such as closing the offices of all the princes and princesses, sending their employees to the government offices, exiling the Queen Mother and then Ashraf, Shah's sister.[14] It was during this time that the statue of Reza Shah, Shah's father on a horse, was pulled down by the Toodeh Party.[15] The Shah, who was married to Soraya then, began to feel the danger. If they bring down his father's statue, what will happen to him? He secretly ran away to Iraq with his wife Soraya.[16]

Sardar Entesar,[17] who was the ambassador to Iraq at the time, had orders from Mosaddeq not to allow the Shah and the Queen into that country. The Americans helped them and they travelled to America overnight.

After a few days, Aqa E. [a relative] who was an active member of the Toodeh Party, came over; he was overjoyed. Your father was so sad. It was as if his own father had died. Our children were all so sad. The radio was constantly attacking and cursing the Shah. I myself heard on the radio when Dr. Fatemi insulted Shah's father. The Toodeh Party were celebrating. To them, if the Shah left, all their major leaders who were in prison would be released.

103

It was summertime. On the streets of Tehran, they were mostly the Toodeh Party members who were going around doing things, rioting. The rest of the people like us, the *saltanat talab ha* [royalists], were staying home. The military and their families were truly mourning the absence of their king.

The next morning I went to visit our friend Mrs. Haqiqat who had come to Iran from Najaf. I went with my three-year-old son [Dadashi] and Fatemeh, my niece (fourteen), to visit her. In her hotel room on Ferdowsi Square, from the window with a straw blind, we could see the street from above.

We saw a large group of people coming towards Ferdowsi Square and shouting '*zendeh bad Shah*' [Long Live the Shah]. The chanting of "Death to the Shah" had turned into "Long Live the Shah" in one day, by the same people!

We left the hotel right away. I asked a gentleman on the street, "What has happened?" He said "Lady, take your children and take a taxi home right now!" And we did. No, actually there were carriages then not taxis. When we got to our own street, the whole city was under fire. There were increasing gunshots between Mosaddeq's followers and the Toodeh Party. It went on till the next day at two in the afternoon; so many people were killed.

Your father had gone to Shafi Abad in Shahriar (a fruit orchard we owned south of Tehran) with his friends, Malek Mansour Khan and Kamaredji. We were home that night. I saw from the window that a jeep came to our street. The jeep was just like the one he had left with in the morning. They brought out a bloody body of a man. It was a wounded soldier, I later found out. They had brought him to our street to treat him. I almost died thinking it is your father. It was disastrous.

The next day we were in the basement in our room for an afternoon nap. The room was for your father and me. I had never ever seen your father be so happy in my entire life. The radio was in our room. I shall never forget when the lady announcer said breathlessly, "Attention! Attention! We just took over the radio station. Shah is back."

Zereshky, our tenant next door [in the medium-sized building in Khaneh ye Shahr that had a door to my parents' basement room and a door to the main yard] swung open the door to our bedroom, jumping up and down with joy. Your father jumped from the bed so high that he hit the ceiling.

Aqa E., the Toodeh relative of ours, arrived admitting defeat. Jokingly he was touching his nose, "*damagh sookhteh mikharim*," a gesture indicating that they had lost. And the kids on the street were chanting:

"*Sizdeh bedar, chardeh be too* [Outdoors on the thirteenth, indoors on the fourteenth]. *Nakhost vazir, zir e patoo* [The Prime Minister is tucked under the blanket]."[18]

Our home was happier than the Shah's house. You should have heard Fezeh's *helheleh* [trilling or ululation]. Shah arrived with Zahedi who later became his prime minister.

During the three years of Mosaddeq's government, there was always chaos; do not ever think that there was peace.

America had brought the Shah back (he had left for a total of three days). We were incredibly happy for his return. England threw him out and America brought him back.

Shah actually left twice. The first time nobody found out and they quieted Sha'boon bi Mokh. The second time, when Shah was planning to leave, Sha'boon bi Mokh heard about it and went with his red jeep and his followers [*nuchehs*] to the Shah's Palace. He just drove his jeep right through the guards and was blaring, "The King's order, is the order of God. We will raise hell. We would never let our King leave." Shah was very pleased and thanked him—he was happy that one of the heroes of the country was so devoted to him. He promised that he would not leave. When Shah returned, he praised him a lot. He built a club for him and named a street after him and so on. But Tayeb[19] was against the Shah. Shah executed Tayeb as soon as he returned. Yes, that is how it was. It was so good. After three years of riots.

That is how Shah came back.[20]

Sha'ban Ja'fari with large wooden clubs (mil) used in House of Strength (zourkhaneh) exercises. Photo: from Homa Sarshar's book, Khaterat e Sha'ban Ja'fari (Tehran: Nashr e Saless, 1381 [2002])

Notes

[1]   In 1901 William Knox D'Arcy, a millionaire London socialite and investor, negotiated an oil concession with Mozaffar al Din Shah Qajar of Persia. He assumed exclusive rights to prospect for oil for sixty years in a vast tract of territory including most of Iran. In exchange the Shah received £20,000, an equal amount in shares of D'Arcy's company, and a promise of 16% of future profits. This contract was revised in November 26, 1932 with Reza Shah's objections. Changes included the reduction of the area by 75%, better conditions for Iranian employees, and the raise of the Iran's share to £975.000. Stephen Kinzer, *All the Shah's Men: An American Coup and the Roots of Middle East Terror* (Hoboken, NJ: John Wiley and Sons, 2003): 48. Timeline of oil industry in Iran from Mohammad Ali Movahhed, *Khab e ashofteh naft: Dr. Mosaddeq va nehzat e melli Iran* (Tehran: Nashr e Karnameh, 1378 [1999]).

[2]   Abadan, at the Gulf's northern end, had come slowly into existence over thousand of years, built up by silt running from the rivers that meet to form the Shatt-al-Arab waterway. The first well delivered oil in 1911 and before long Abadan was a bustling city with more than 100,000 residents, most of them Iranian laborers. From its private Persian Club, where uniformed waiters served British executives, to the tightly packed Iranian workers' quarters and the water fountains marked "Not for Iranians" it was a classic colonial enclave. From Kinzer, *All the Shah's Men*, 49–50.

[3]   Mohammad Mosaddeq (1882–1967). "From the moment of his birth on May 19, 1882, Mosaddeq had advantages that few of his countrymen enjoyed. His mother was a Qajar princess and his father was from the distinguished Ashtiani family one of whom had served as the finance minister of Nasser al Din Shah for over twenty years. He pursued his education in France and earned his doctoral degree in law from Switzerland (1914)." From Kinzer, *All the Shah's Men*.

[4]   Ayatollah Abol Qasem Mostafavi Kashani (Tehran, 1882 – Tehran, 1962) was a prominent Shia Moslem cleric and former Chairman of the Parliament of Iran. Movahhed, *Khab e ashofteh 'e naft, Az koodeta ye 28 mordad ta soqoot e Zahedi* (Tehran: Nashr e Karnameh, 1383 [2004]).

Also Kinzer, *All the Shah's Men*, 2003. Farsi translation by Shahriar Khajian. 6th ed. (Tehran: Ketab Ameh Publishing, 1391 [2013]): 21, 43, 44, 75, 107, 178.

[5]   Movahhed, *Khab e ashofteh naft,* 1378 [1999] Chapter 9. Vol.2, bk1, ch.9, 355–400.

[6]   Mehdi Bazargan (1907–1995). As one of the highest-ranking students in his class, he was dispatched with a full scholarship to France in 1927 by the Iranian government to continue his education at École Centrale des Arts et Manufactures. Bazargan completed his Ph.D. in thermodynamics in 1934 and returned to Iran. He then completed his compulsory military service and was employed at the Engineering College of the University of Tehran as an assistant professor in mechanical engineering. He later became the dean of the College of Engineering for two consecutive terms and was appointed by Mohammad Mosaddeq as the managing director of the National Iranian Oil Company in 1951 when the Iranian oil industry was nationalized. After the coup against Mosaddeq in 1953, Bazargan returned to the university to teach: Masood Behnood, *275 Days of Bazargan*, 6th ed. (Tehran: Nashr e Elm, 1388). Kinzer, *All the Shah's Men*. Farsi translation by Shahriar Khajian. 6th ed. (Tehran: Nashr e Ketab Ameh, 1388): 145–46, 294–97.

[7]   The International Court of Justice in The Hague, the Netherlands. From the *New York Times*, July 23, 1952.

[8]   The Organization of the Petroleum Exporting Countries (OPEC) is a permanent, intergovernmental organization, created at the Baghdad Conference on September 10–14, 1960, by Iran, Iraq, Kuwait, Saudi Arabia and Venezuela. The five Founding Members were later joined by nine other members: Qatar (1961); Indonesia (1962) – suspended its membership from January 2009; Libya (1962); United Arab Emirates (1967); Algeria (1969); Nigeria (1971); Ecuador (1973) – suspended its membership from December 1992–October 2007; Angola (2007); and Gabon (1975–1994). OPEC had its headquarters in Geneva, Switzerland, in the first five years of its existence. This was moved to Vienna, Austria, on September 1, 1965. www.opec.org.

[9]   Ebrahim Yazdi, born 1931 in Qazvin, is an Iranian politician and diplomat who later served as deputy prime minister and minister of foreign affairs in the interim government of Mehdi Bazargan, until his resignation in November 1979, in protest at the Iran hostage crisis.

[10]   Seyyed Baqer Khan Kazemi (1887–1976), known as Mohazab al Dowleh, held many top positions in the government. A major opponent of Qavam, Dashti supported his positions: Manouchehr Kadivar, *Hameh e mardan e Mosaddeq (All Mosaddeq's men)* (Tehran: Kavir Publishing, 1393 [2014]): 451–65. See Ali Dashti's speech on p. 456.

[11]   Hossain Macci, *Khaterat e siasi Hossain Macci* (Tehran: Entesharat e Elmi, 1368 [1989]). Hossain Macci and Ayatollah Kashani, *Khaterat e Dr. Mehdi Haeri Yazdi* (Tehran: Nashr e Ketab e Nader, 1387 [2008]).

[12]   Hossain Fatemi (February 10, 1917–November 10, 1954), Minister of Foreign Affairs in Mosaddeq's cabinet (October 1952–August 1953): John Foran, *A Century of Revolution: Social Movements in Iran* (Minneapolis: University of Minnesota

Press, 1994): 109. Fatemi was a strong supporter of Mosaddeq: Kadivar, *Hameh e mardan e Mosaddeq (All Mosaddeq's men):* 388-436. Mansoor Moaddel, *A Sociological Analysis of the Iranian Revolution* (Madison: University of Wisconsin-Madison, 1986): "The more militant members of the National Front, such as Hosein Fatemi, were tortured and killed in Prison."

[13] Sha'ban Ja'fari, known as Shaboon bi Mokh (the brainless), (b. Tehran, 1921 – d. Santa Monica, CA, 2006) was a leader of the traditional sport of Iran, *zoorkhaneh* or house of strength. *Mil giri* (exercises using wooden clubs) and traditional chanting of the *Shahnameh* during workouts mark those events. From the book by Homa Sarshar, *Khaterat e Sha'ban Ja'fari* (Tehran: Nashr e Saless, 1381 [2002]).

[14] Movahhed, *Khab e ashofteh ye naft, Doktar Mosaddeq va nahzat e melli e Iran,* Vol. 2, bk 2, 570.

[15] *Kayhan* newspaper, 26 Mordad 1332 (August 17, 1953].

[16] 25 Mordad 1332 (August 17, 1953], the Shah and the Empress escaped to Iraq from Ramsar, in the north of Iran, with their private plane: Movahhed, *Khab e ashofteh ye naft,* Vol. 2, bk 2, 1068.

[17] Mozafar A'lam was known as Sardar Entesar: Abdollah Mostoufi, *Sharh e zendegani e man, ya tarikh e ejtemai va edari e doreh e qajarieh.* 6th ed. (Tehran: Entesharat e Zavar, 1388 [2009]): 3:564.

[18] Shirin Samii, *Dar khalvat e Mosaddeq* (Tehran: Nashr e Saless, 1386), chapter 5 "Bimari e Mosaddeq" (Mosaddeq's illness.] Kinzer, *All the Shah's Men.* Farsi translation by Shahriar Khajian, 91: Mosaddeq suffered from an illness that plagued him throughout his life; however real, no one found out exactly what his illness was.

[19] Tayyeb Haj Reza'i (b. Tehran, 1280 – d. Tehran, 11 Aban 1342). Tayyeb was another strongman from the south of Tehran. He was hanged because of his participation in the events of 15 Khordad 1342 (June 5, 1963] against the Shah. From Sarshar, *Khaterat e Sha'ban Ja'fari,* 289–98.

[20] August 20, 1953.

Fifteen
Winter

Dashtestan gets as hot as 50° Centigrade (= 122° Fahrenheit) and higher in the summer and stays hot most of the year. The moisture in the air, which could be about 80 to 90 percent, retains the heat day and night—in the shade or out in the sun. Before electricity, except for the very deep cavernous basements called *sardab e sen*,[1] there were no other places to escape the heat.

Up to 1931 when Aqa ye Bozorg was exiled to Tehran, our family had lived in the south for generations and were only used to that climate. To them Tehranis were too spoiled when it came to dealing with the heat of summers. "They have no idea what hot means," Bibi always said. Bibi actually complained constantly about the cold weather of Tehran and the drafts, all year round, asking people to close the doors behind them. In the heat of summer afternoons, Bibi leaned back against the wall of the balcony, allowed her spine to touch the hot wall, vertebra by vertebra, and declared, "Now! This is nice and warm."

Unlike the year-round desert climate of the south, Tehran has four distinct seasons. Summer is hot and dry (it gets as hot as 40°C =104°F), winter is cold (as cold as -10°C = 14°F) with powdery snowfalls; autumn and spring are mild and lush. The city's climate changes overnight as the calendar enters each season.

The traditional buildings of Tehran were mostly designed to suit the four seasons. To prepare for the heat of the summer, the majority of the houses had a basement underneath the building and a deep-water reservoir (*ab anbar*) built in the yard to store water, ice, fresh fruit and vegetables; a space to rest in the afternoons. The larger houses had a corner room called *zavieh* (junction), or a *hashti* (octagonal), which had many windows with taller ceilings to allow the airflow. In addition, some buildings had a natural cooler on the roof called *bad-gir* (wind-catcher), which allowed the wind to flow from four sides and carried a cool breeze down inside the buildings; as far down as the basements. Most houses also had a shallow pool in their yards.[2]

When the sun went down, Tehranis came out. They ate breakfast before sunrise and dinner late at night, outdoors. They slept in the yards or up on the roofs. On weekends most went out of town to close-by mountain gardens such as Meigoon. To avoid the afternoon heat, they went indoors into the basements, or to the *ab anbar* in their yards, for their afternoon nap. Any piece of shade, under a tree, in the shadow of a standing donkey or next to a building, created a cool retreat for the people who had to be outdoors.

Knitted straw fans (*bad bezan*), shaped like wings of a butterfly sitting on a thin stick, were handy devices made of bamboo stems, which helped people cool down as well. Sometimes the fans were soaked in water to get an even cooler puff. Straw fans were a necessity at parties and gatherings—a separate fan for each guest was put next to their place settings. Some ladies carried their own hand-decorated fans with tassels hanging; fancier ladies carried Japanese lace fans in their purses.

None of that became a custom in our household; we were Dashtestoonis. Our house did not have the *hashti*, the *zavieh* or the *bad-gir*. The basement in our house was at the ground level and the rooms on the ground floor were used all year round. *Ab anbar* was shallow compared to *sardab e sen* our family's house used in Borazjan. The *ab anbar* was mostly abandoned, used by *mir-ab* who brought water to the neighborhood. In our house, the straw fans were used to blow on the charcoal of the water pipes (qalyan). Our family seemed to be overqualified in dealing with the relatively gentle summers of Tehran.

Winters, however, were a harsh, unknown reality. It was in Tehran (1931) when, for the first time, our parents experienced cold weather and saw the snow.

Our house, like all the other houses in Tehran, had ventilation pipes in the walls conducting the smoke of the kerosene heaters to the chimneys on the roof. The heaters were connected to the vents by long, thin metal pipes with several bends that fitted into the wall. Each heater had a tank of kerosene attached. Adjusting the amount of kerosene for proper combustion was a sophisticated matter. In the event that someone increased the flow to get more heat, the heater got red and got ready to explode. This was when we heard a horrifying noise; an alarming sign. We all ran out of the room with fear and excitement. The brave person in our family, Banafsheh (Fezeh's daughter) was our hero; the wizard of the winters! Her skill was in high demand in winter evenings. She had to be inconvenienced frequently to leave her comfortable and clean space under the blanket of Fezeh's *korsi* (a low wooden table with a heater underneath it), her hand warmed by the gently burning portable heater (Aladdin) in her mother's room, to rush to our rescue. She nonchalantly got a piece of cloth, or the end of her coat sleeves, readjusted the smoking pipes and the flow of the kerosene while her proud mother stood behind her. The windows were opened to let the smoke out and everything was back to normal for another hour or so.

The heaters were greatly appreciated. Not only did they provide heat, but they also were constant lighters for Bibi's and Fezeh's cigarettes, a warm oven to toast the bread, and a useful gadget used to dry and iron the washed clothes, specially our school uniforms. Early in the mornings, the washed uniforms, which were hung outside in a row on the clothesline and pinned by wooden clips, sleeve to sleeve, like a string of frozen paper dolls, were brought in about an hour before school started and two people pulled them from two sides to dry and press. It worked! On our way out of the room, Bibi checked under the arms and the backs of each uniform. She made us take them off in case they were still damp. The socks were laid on the pipes to dry and were checked before and after we put them on.

Socks were a newly introduced part of clothing in my family's culture. We actually never figured out whether it was good to wear socks or not. Whenever Bibi saw us barefoot, she objected and insisted that we wear socks, but when our Baba came home and saw us wearing socks, he told us to take them off. Going to bed with our socks on was a sin. He believed that our feet do not get to breathe properly at nights if we had socks on. The rumor was that we might go blind if we slept with our socks on.

Bibi was ultra-conscious of us catching a cold. God forbid if any of us sneezed, her worried voice came from somewhere in the house, "*Didi badbakht, to ham sarma khordi* (You poor soul! You caught cold, didn't you)?" This message was heard throughout the winter days and nights; it had registered in our minds as a salute response to sneezing.

At the age of seven, on a cold windy day, on my way to school, my hair got caught in an old man's coat buttons. As he struggled to untangle my hair, he sneezed and I automatically said, "You poor soul! You caught cold, didn't you? (*Ey bad bakht to ham sarma khordi*)."

❖ ❖ ❖

The cast-iron heaters were assembled in the classrooms at the beginning of winter. As we entered the classrooms, we gathered around the heaters, trying to defrost our frozen hands and toes; bullying each other to get closer to the heater. We wore black rubber boots all winter until spring school break. The snow on the ground was usually above our boots, filling up the loose boot with frozen snow. The smell of heated rubber filled the classrooms throughout winter. Not a day went by without a glove or a sock burning on the cast-iron heaters. It happened all so quickly that the only thing remaining would usually be a thick black sticky sludge on the heater, creating additional odor and smoke in the classrooms, accompanied with a deep sigh from the owner. The white snow covered the entire playground most of winter. We did not go out to play during recess, but we watched the quiet dance of the snowfall from behind the misty windows and drew faces with our fingers on the glass windows.

There were no cafeterias in our schools, however the school custodian sold sandwiches, *pirashki*s (cream-filled Danish) and Coca Cola from the window of his room. His room was outside the school building, which made it easy to form a line and buy delicious snacks. In the winters though he put a table under the stairway inside the school building. The crowd under the stairs was impossible to break through and the time of recess was short; most of us did not succeed to reach his desk in time.

By the time I was a senior in high school, I got to the custodian's desk quickly and successfully. This was not because I had grown any taller or the lines were any shorter than when I was in elementary school. I had made a friend; her name was Ra'na.

Ra'na was very tall, very distinguished, and bravely accommodating. During recess, she would lift me up and put me on the mantle inside the classroom so we could talk face to face. She also held me by my feet from above the stairs until my hands reached the desk of the custodian. I picked a sandwich for her and a Danish for me, paid the man, and she lifted me back up. I do not recall if anyone noticed that I was upside down the entire time.

❖ ❖ ❖

In addition to the kerosene heater, Tehranis used a *korsi* to keep warm.[3] *Korsi* is a special wooden cage about one and a half by one and a half meters and about eighty centimeters high. A round copper tray is put underneath to hold a metal container (*manqal*) that holds lit balls of charcoal.[4]

Powdered charcoal was used to make tight balls of charcoal about the size of a grapefruit. In our house, Zarafshan was in charge of making the balls for winter. She sat in the front yard by the small storage room for charcoal, washed the ground charcoal in a metal basin, separated out the small pebbles, then formed it into balls and let them dry in the sun; rows and rows of charcoal balls. The larger chunks of charcoal were saved for the water pipes, samovar, and of course they satisfied Zarafshan's cravings during her five pregnancies.

The bottoms of the *manqals* were sealed with plaster and sifted ash. The lit charcoal balls sat on the ashes and were left outside for the smell to go away before they were covered to the top with more ash and brought in under the *korsi*. Every hour or so with a small spatula someone would take a layer of the ash away, to create more heat.

The *korsi* sat in the middle of our living room (children's room). It was covered with a large blanket, about seven by seven square meters specially made for the *korsi*. A white sheet was pinned to the blanket and a bright red cotton cloth with very large yellow flowers, similar to a Chinese painting, was spread on top. The spread was topped with a short tablecloth used and changed for each meal or snack. There were narrow mattresses on all four sides and large cushions to lean on.

Every morning the housekeepers took the blanket, the sheets, the mattresses, and the pillows, put them on top of the *korsi* and swept the entire room. Coming home to a clean *korsi*, tucked-in blanket, and the tray of tea on top was worth all the inconveniences of winter.

A collage of korsi by Helen Zanganeh (Ensha).

Notes

1   Story 3, "German Consul Wassmuss & British Political Agent Cox," in this volume.

2   Ja'far Shahri, *Tehran e Qadim* (Old Tehran) (Tehran: Entesharat e Moin, 1371 [1992]): 4:466–67.

3   In a house in Kordestan something interesting caught my eye that I must write to you about because not only in Kordestan but anywhere we visited in Iran they had it. They do not put the heating fire in a heater. They dig a hole in the floor of a room and call it *tanour* and they put the fire in it. *Tanour* is a rectangular or circular hole about two or three *vajab* (centimeters) deep. In order to get more heat the walls of the *tanour* are covered with baked clay. On top of it they put a wooden table covered with thick cloth that is filled with cotton and it holds the heat. The *tanour* makes the room warm like a heater. They use it when eating, talking, and even sleeping. The persons on the floor sit on narrow mattresses and sit in such a way that their shoulders and backs can lean against the walls where pillows and cushions are arranged for support. The *tanour* is always made in a suitable location with at least two walls of the room next to it. The people who want less heat only put their feet under the blanket and the people who desire more heat put their hands and body inside but never the head. The head should always be out. I must inform you that the heat of this apparatus is so delicious and enjoyable that I have never seen something so useful for conquering the cold of winter and I intend to order some samples of it when I return to Italy." From Pietro della Valle, *Cose e parole nei "Viaggi" di Pietro Della Valle.* Farsi translation by Shojaeddin Shafa, *Safarnameh* (Tehran: Sherkat e entesharat elmi va farhangi, 1348 [1969]): 12–13.

4   Years later an electric heater was invented for the *korsi*.

Sixteen
Bathhouses/Hammam (*Garmabeh*)

"*Salam* Hossain Aqa (Hello Mr. Hossain)"[1]

"*Salam az man khanoom. Hal e shoma*? (My greetings. How are you lady?)"

"Hossain Aqa, how long have you had this teahouse?"

"Oh, way before you were born!"

"But I am sixty-five years old. I used to come to school right here and I do remember your shop."

"Yes, we were here before there were any cars. They used to bring water with horse carriages to put in the water-storage reservoir. Do you remember the water pump we had right here on the sidewalk and people who passed by would take water? The water storage was right underneath this teahouse."

"Yes, of course, I remember. Hossain Aqa, what happened to the public bath here?"

"Do you think these people have fathers or mothers? Do you think they have had one meal on the *sofreh* (spread) of their parents? No! They did not. If they did, they would not do these thoughtless deeds."

"Shah was the only real Shiite Moslem. For him, people came first. He left us each time England threatened the people. He said, "Do not hurt my people, I will leave.""

"Just think when your brother, for instance, comes to visit you after a long trip and wants to take a bath. When he arrives in your home, where should he go? It would not be appropriate for him to take a bath in your house, now would it? He should go to a public bath! Now where would people go? This is only one example. Think of all these workers, where would they take a bath now? These people are claiming to be Moslems! When would a real Moslem do a thing like that, remove the place where people keep clean?" said Hossain Aqa, the owner of the teahouse near Elahieh House.[2]

113

Water delivered to a neighborhood in Tehran. Photo by Daryoush Tahami.

Every couple of weeks, we were handed a personal *boqcheh* (bundle) to go to the public bath with an adult companion. The public bath near our house in downtown Tehran (*Khaneh ye Shahr*) was called Hammam e Zan Oosta.

For most families going to the public bath was a mini-celebration and a feast; for us, it was an ordeal we wanted to avoid. Tehrani women brought trays of refreshments: cucumbers, cheese, bread, herbs, pomegranates, and all kinds of sherbets (sweetened flower extracts such as rose water), stayed there for the whole day, and socialized. Sometimes, when they brought a bride or a woman who had just delivered a baby, they took a box of cookies around for everyone. Then they turned the trays into drums and sang and danced for hours. Some took care of their medical procedures such as cupping their backs for pain, or putting leeches on their legs, and they did the threading of their facial hair, putting henna on their hair, nails, and feet right there in the *hammams*.[3] We, on the other hand, went to the bath, were washed one by one and were sent out to the dressing room to an aunt or a cousin to be sent home right away.

Some of the hammams had two separate entrances to two parallel bathhouses—one for men and one for women. Some places had one hammam but they separated men and women either by the days of the week, weeks of the month, or hours of a day. Hammam e Zan Oosta was for women only. The hammam for men in our neighborhood was a few blocks away in Sar Cheshmeh and was called Mirza Khan e Vazir.

From the women's entrance in Pamenar, it took many steps to go down to a large wooden door to enter the hammam. The hammam keeper sat next to this door on a bench to take money, sell bathing items, and assign a *dallak* (bath attendant) to the patrons. That hallway led to another hallway called ("*sar e bineh*") where there were benches all around and hooks on the walls to hang the clothes. We took our clothes off, opened our *boghcheh*s, hung our fresh clothes on the hooks, wrapped a thin cotton wrap around our chest and with much bashfulness walked from the "*sar e bineh*" to running water in the channels on the ground to rinse our feet before we entered the main *garmkhaneh* (the hot house). We said hello as we entered each section and were greeted with a compliment that embarrassed us even further, "*Mashallah, dokhtarha ye Bibi hastand. Mashallah, cheh zagh o boorand*" (God bless them. They are Bibi's daughters, look how white they are).

The floor of the *garmkhaneh* was so hot it was almost impossible to walk on. The *garmkhaneh* was a large circular room with a high ceiling and a couple of tinted glass domes at the top. Once in a while, from an open vent, we could see the red wraps (*longue*) pinned to a clothesline, flying in the wind, and we could see puffs of clouds going by. There were shower cubicles all around the *garmkhaneh* with no doors. Those were usually reserved for women who did ablution or applied depilatory cream (*vajebi*) on private parts of their bodies. They sat with their backs to everyone but sometimes forgot to hide the paper wrap of the cream!

The *garmkhaneh* had stone platforms on two levels where people sat and were washed. A hexagonal tiled tub was in the center with fresh warm water and copper basins and ewers around it to fetch clean water for rinsing.

We sat on the back of a tray we brought from home on the first level of the platform of the *garmkhaneh* waiting for the masseuse (dallak) to attend to us. Each hammam had several dallaks, each with a different reputation, status, and rate. They were important people with a sensitive job. After all, in their profession they had the opportunity to handle people from all walks of life, right under their hands; capable of bringing out the people's most vulnerable part: dirt!

Sediqeh was the best and Bibi's favorite dallak—she was very pale with straight hair and had very strong hands. Bibi believed that her hands performed miracles! She first poured a pitcher of hot water on our dry skin and asked us to hand her our bath mitten (*kiseh*) and got started. She began to rub our bodies with the rough coarse kiseh that she wore like a mitten.[4] If our adult companion was not looking, Sediqeh got a soaked tablet of *sefid ab* she herself carried, and put it on the kiseh and started rubbing the entire skin to make sure all the dead skin came off. Bibi did not allow *sefid ab* on our skin for health reasons. Besides she wanted to see the actual extra skin come off like candlewicks.[5]

Another pitcher of hot water washed the candlewicks of gray dead skin and some white good skin off our bodies and another pitcher washed them down the drain. This was the peak of the dallak's performance.

Sediqeh then asked, "Have you brought your comb? *Sedr* (jujube powder)?"

"Yes," we said while handing her the comb and the green powder as our heads were bent down.

Before there was any shampoo, we used jujube powder (*sedr*) that is a natural substance from an evergreen tree (*Zizyphus Spina Christi* or Christ's Thorn) to wash our hair with. *Sedr* is extremely coarse and it gets caught in the hair, especially long hair. Sediqeh put the jujube in my hair and put my head in her bosom and started clutching so hard. She would not stop before my neck was twisted and stiff and my legs and arms ran in the air, trying to get away. Then

Mrs. Bersabeh Hosepian and the first kindergarten in Tehran, established 1310 (1931). Photo: Daryoush Tahami.

she poured a pitcher of hot water to wash the jujube stuck in my tangled long hair and on to the second wash. After the two *sedr* washes, relief came with the application of "*gel e sar shoor* (fuller's earth)" which is like a conditioner and smells like flowers. The gentle chunks of fuller's earth made it so easy to comb our hair. While she did the final rinse of the hair, we polished the soles of our feet ourselves with a pumice stone (*sang e pa*). Another bucket of hot water and then it was time for the final step of soap smothering all over our bodies and right into the eyes with a hand knitted soft *lief* (glove).

A couple of years later shampoo was invented and was introduced into Iran from Germany—Glemo by the Schwarzkopf Company. It came in small cubes of plastic capsules, enough for two generous shampooing. The dallaks were greedy and used a lot of it and rubbed their shampooy hands on their own hair. Most people did not hand over the capsules and applied the exact amount of shampoo to the hand of the dallak themselves.

Finally it was time to have a quick rinse and leave. Some people went from the *garmkhaneh* to a hot tub (*khazaneh garm*) and then a cold tub of water (*khazaneh sard*); we never did. We were rinsed with our pitcher filled half with hot water from the hot tub and half with cold water from the cold tub and a quick rinse from the shower.

A towel was brought to the door for us to wrap up in. Then a pitcher of water rinsed our feet before we put our feet, one by one, on the *boqcheh*—not to touch the ground anymore. We quickly put on layer after layer of clothing. The sleeves of some of the layers were rolled on top and made it really uncomfortable to wear another layer and a jacket, irrespective of the weather outside. We were rushed home. Bibi was waiting with a fistful of Vaseline and an anxious face. "Hurry! You are going to catch a cold, I know it," she would say. We were tucked under a blanket or the *korsi* and were taken good care of, at least for the first day and night; again, no sour things to eat for at least a few days.

By the time we moved to Shemiran, the public bathhouses had private bathrooms called *nomreh* (number), where each family went to a private bathroom and the dallaks visited them there. The hammam near our Khazar house was called Garmabeh Naz, which had 12 private cabins next to "Sangaki bread shop" and Hossain Aqa's teahouse. The other one was called Garmabeh Karoon, which was close to our school.[7]

Most of the houses had begun to have their own baths and a system of heating water inside the bathrooms. Butane Gas brought gas cylinders around the neighborhoods to use with the water heaters.[8]

Many times, in the middle of shampooing, with soap in the eyes, the water turned freezing cold and/ or it ran out; the bathroom door was banged on with worried Bibi and/or Fezeh to bring the boiling pot of water inside and get us out. Either way when a person took a shower or a bath, someone had to be on call, to sit behind the door making sure the gas is not killing us, the water is not cold and when it was time for the kiseh, the person entered to rub your back. This had to be done or you were not considered clean.

Our neighbor, a friend of Aqda'i and Bibi, had a son who had married an American girl. The family had a hard time accepting her as a clean person: "Imagine, she has never been washed with a kiseh in her life!" the mother-in-law told Bibi.

Every woman had her personal items for her bath in a bundle. When girls got married, the first thing the family prepared for her to take to her husband's home was a complete bundle for her bath. The bundle usually consisted of:

A handmade thin carpet for under her in "*sar e bineh*;"

A handmade tapestry (*termeh soozani*) with satin lining to put on the carpet for her to put her clean feet on;

A white cotton spread to put over the tapestry to prevent moisture penetrating it;

Two wraps (longue), one of good quality and hand crocheted for coming out of the bath and a thin cotton one to wear when going inside the *garmkhaneh*;

A scarf in the shape of a triangle to dry the hair;

A deep tray to turn over and sit on top of;

A smaller tray to put the bathing items in to carry inside; items such as: kiseh, *leif*, soap, *sefid ab*, *gel e sar shoor*, and a pumice stone (*sang e pa*). Some of the stones had a silver top;

A copper pitcher and a basin.

These items were taken to the bathhouses by a *boqcheh kesh* (a servant carrying the bundle) a few hours before the women started walking toward the bathhouse. The bath keeper put their things in their special places and notified the dallak to get ready for them.

❖ ❖ ❖

For centuries, hammams were an integral part of community life in Iran. Every neighborhood had its own hammam. These bathhouses were built below ground level for the security of the building against climate change, winds, storms, and so on. The ceilings of the bathhouses were about the same level as the streets, a little higher. At the top of their roofs there were glass domes to let in light and get energy from the sun. The traditional public bath in Iran was a very calculated structure designed to secure the health of the people who were exposed to heat, moisture, and relaxation for many hours. The bathhouses and the water were heated by a furnace underneath the hot tubs. In the old times those furnaces were heated by coal. The labyrinthine architecture, long stairways down to the ground, several turns to hallways before and after entering and exiting the bath, and the doors covered with hanging carpets securing the air in each section, guaranteed that. We still salute people who come out of the bath as having had their bodies made vulnerable (*afiat basheh*).

The hammam in Borazjan was called Hammam e Salem Khani. Even though the air outside of the hammam was more hot and humid, the hammam had the same structure of being built underground. "On Fridays they restricted public access (*qoroq kardan*) for our family to go to the public bath," my cousin added.

Also on Fridays the barber came to our house to shave all the men's heads and trim the beards of the grown men before we went to the *hammam*. All the boys in our family had to have a "number four" haircut, which was really short. We cried and wanted our hair to be as long as the governor's sons, yet we were refused every time. The other boys could have white German or number one or two haircuts; ours was always number four." My cousin was still mad.

Another day of the week the baths were cordoned off and closed to the public for the women of our family.

My cousin was not sure how it was for the women so he dismissed my question about hammam for women in Borazjan.

The experience of the public bath was entirely different for women. Men and boys were washed and soaked and got a manly massage called *mosht o mal*. They were given a couple of dark red cotton loincloths called *longue* or *khoshk*. The men were loud and once in a while there was a very loud yelp heard from the men's bath; I wonder what the masseurs did to them! Then they slapped themselves to shed the water from their bodies and called out, "*khoshk.*" One of the bath employees ran in with a stack of dry wraps. They put one wrap around their waist, down to their ankles, one on their shoulders and the more important men got another *longue* for the top of their heads, my cousin said.

Aqa Reza (our housekeeper in Meigoon since 2002) from Sanandaj, Kordestan has similar experiences of hammam. According to him the structure and the services they received were identical to hammams in Tehran and Borazjan.

One day Aqa Reza's wife, Homaira, told me with the naughtiest smile on her face: 'In Sanandaj, the *hammam* was one week for women and one week for men. Aqa Reza and his brothers accidentally went to

the *hammam* on a day that the *hammam* was closed to men and was reserved for women. Do you believe that?' she kept laughing bashfully.

Once a week the *jar chi* went to the top of the hill and announced, "*nobat e marde, ohoy, nobat e mardast* [it is the men's turn this week]" or he announced, "*nobat e zane, ohoy, nobat e zanast* [it is the women's turn this week]. But these boys had not heard him and walked with their bundles right into the *sar e bineh*!!!"

The villages and towns of Iran are still being modernized. The streets of Iran are still being torn up to install gas pipelines. Tehran has had gas pipelines for many years now and Meigoon is beginning to get gas.

Taking a full bath with hot water continues to feel like a luxury. I considered it a special treat to allow my children and now my grandchildren to soak in hot water in the bathtub at home with perfect temperature, while playing with their action figures for hours.

A private bathhouse near our school. Photo: Sayeh Dashti, 2014.

119

Notes

1   This conversation took place in August 2014.
2   See Story 40, "A Precious Gift," in this volume.
3   Some men phlebotomized in the *hammam*s.
4   The *kiseh* is made of woven rough fibers of sackcloth and is used for exfoliation of superficial skin layers.
5   *Sefid ab* is made from fat, sheep's spinal cord, and the fine powder of a kind of stone called 'marl' (which mainly contains zinc or tin minerals).
6   Both *garmabeh/hammam*s were still there in 2014. However, Naz Garmabeh and the buildings around it were about to be demolished for a new shopping mall.
7   Butane Gas Company, established in 1954, still delivers gas cylinders to the rural areas of Iran and to neighboring countries.

Seventeen
Or Else!

In some ways, Bibi was like the Godfather. For one thing, she had many agents at her disposal, making sure things were done her way! She mostly stayed in her home, a headquarters if you will, and had her devoted agents carry out her orders!

Going to most public places such as schools, offices, markets, etc., did not appeal to her. On rare occasions, like the New Year's clothes shopping, she accompanied us to the Grand Bazaar. The places she herself went to, willingly and regularly, were to visit her friends, when of course she preferred not to take small children along. This is what we usually heard from her: "I am going to an old lady's house; it is too boring for you."

We were taken to doctors, dentists, public baths, schools, or any other place necessary, by a nanny or a relative; one of her devoted agents!

My nanny, Nanneh ye Hassan, had the mission to take me to Bersabeh Nursery School every day. She carried me on her shoulders—despite my constant crying. I beat on her head and kicked her all the way to the nursery school. I hated to leave the comfort of our house, especially the solitude under the dining room table. Nevertheless, Nanneh had to carry out Bibi's orders. She had her chador wrapped around her waist; her scarf pinned under her chin, my lunch box in one hand as she held onto my legs with her arms.

Our father was the one who did our yearly shopping for school items and the delicate job of shopping for the New Year's treats. Stacks of notebooks, pencils, erasers, and sharpeners for so many students in our household, for a whole year, filled up his office in the house up to the ceiling. The sweet homemade candies and cookies and pistachios were ordered from "Yas," the well-known bakery in Tehran. Those were stored and locked up in the guest room ready for NoRouz. When our father was in the city, he usually came home with a pickup truck filled with watermelons, cantaloupes, and other fruits.

One of the male servants (Mammehdi, Rajab, Vali, or Ahmad) bought fresh food items such as meat, vegetables, and bread daily from the neighborhood stores; many other goods and services were sold by vendors who came around to all neighborhoods and to our door.

Fezeh, a lady herself, would not go out to public places alone either. If no one else were available, she would take one of us girls along and in case we accidentally got some distance from her, she would call us by one of our brother's names (it was improper to call out a lady's name on the street; she called all of us Abbas.)

On those occasions where communication with our schools was a necessity, Bibi sent out our two aunts—her younger sister, Abaj, who was tall, and her own aunt, Khaleh Zakieh (Ali Dashti's half sister), who was short—in order to implement her decisions.

The tall aunt and the short aunt were very fashionable and extremely confident in carrying out Bibi's orders. They usually wore their unique black *aba* and high heels to walk to the offices of the principals with a message/order from Bibi.

There were times when Bibi and the aunts took a long shot for the sake of amusement. For instance, together they had decided that I was ready for first grade when I was only five years old (the cut off age for first grade was seven). Not only was I underage, I was also very petite and usually decorated with fluffy dresses and ribbons in my hair by my older sisters.

That day the principal laughed in their faces telling them, "This is not a dollhouse and she could not possibly accept their order." They talked and laughed about that adventure for years.

◈ ◈ ◈

Established in 1931, Sa'di School was the most innovative school of its time. The state-of-the-art building was constructed on two levels. On one level high school graduates were being trained to become teachers. The other level was designed for the first through six graders. They were being educated while participating in the most advanced educational programs offered in the country.

One of the unique programs they had implemented was to introduce school plays in the form of poetry. As part of the curriculum, the first-grade teacher had chosen a poem by Mrs. Parvin E'tesami,[1] a contemporary female poet of Iran. Her poems have a dialectic characteristic, a great opportunity for the students to participate in a playlike debate via poetry.

My sister Talieh, a first-grade student, ran home that day to tell Bibi that she had been chosen for the leading role in the school play; a true honor. Everyone took a seat in the living room waiting for her to perform. Tea was ready and the living room was filled with relatives and guests in the house. Unaware of the possible consequences, my sister started reciting the poem with such compassion:

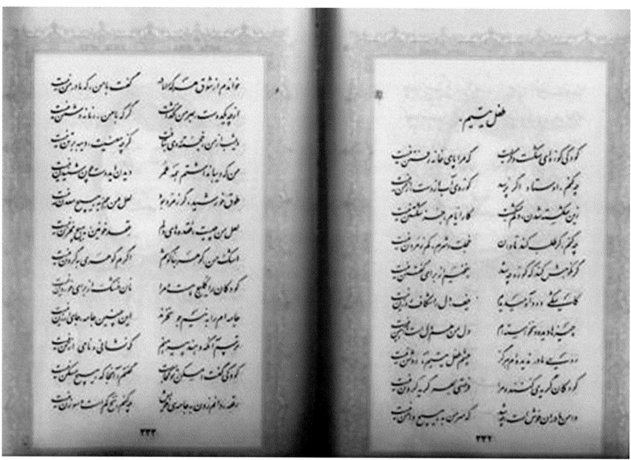

The poem "Tefl e yatim" (The Orphan Child) by Parvin E'tesami. Photo: Sayeh Dashti, 2012.

The Orphan Child (*Tefl e Yatim*)

A child broke an earthen jar and cried,
"I cannot drag my feet home, now!
What do I do if the master finds out?
The jar of water was his, not mine.
My heart is shattered into pieces with this calamity.
That is what life is all about: failures and calamities.
What would I do if the master asks for its cost?
Shame and embarrassment is no less than dying many times.
What if he scolds me,
demands to have the earthen jar?
There is not a word I can come up with. I am helpless.
I wish there was a vent in my heart, to release the pain of my cramped sigh,
Much I have endured; none had I ever asked for.
Oh why?
Tell me.
Is my heart made of steel? Believe me, it is not.

Eyes of the orphans like me are dim.
Never seeing the faces of our mothers has not given them light.
Other children have the right to have tears in their eyes,
I do not even have the luxury to cry."

This was the exact moment! Bibi got up! She did not even wait to hear the rest of the poem before she ran to Talieh to stop her and said, "What? Tahereh, Khaleh Zakieh, you are sitting here and my daughter is going to play an orphan child? Not only that, her earthen jar has to break too?"

In spite of Talieh's crying all night, Bibi gave the aunts the mission to go and inform the principal that there was no chance her daughter would play that part.

"The role of a happy child, maybe!" She was being considerate. However, playing a miserable child? She wouldn't hear of it!

"First of all, she should not play an orphan because she has her family. Secondly, her jar should not break! We have so many jars. That is unacceptable!" Bibi told the aunts to make sure the principal gets the message. "Close the school if you have to!" she had ordered.

Abaj and Khaleh Zakieh got ready the next morning. With their high heels and abas on their heads, they got ready to deliver Bibi's orders.

The principal of the school, Mrs. Kiani, was a highly educated and well-respected woman. She was shocked by our family's behavior. She later told Talieh that she expected women from our family to be very appreciative of such advanced programs in their school. "Frankly, I thought they had come to thank us for choosing you as part of such an innovative program. I was sure they had come to maybe even donate a jar or something!" she had told Talieh in disbelief.

The aunts' mission was clear. Bibi would have it no other way. The message was firm, leaving no other option for the principal.

Notes

[1] Parvin E'tesami was born in 1907. Her family moved to Tehran from Tabriz when she was a small child. She attended the Iran Bethel School and American Girls College in Tehran. She is best known for her work as a classical poet. From the book *Divan e khanoom e Parvin E'tesami*, 2nd ed. (Tehran: Entesharat e Elmi, 1382 [2003]): 232–33. Calligraphy by Davood Ravasani.

Eighteen
Elections

Persian Gulf ports and the islands had two elected representatives in the House of Parliament. The parliamentary elections were held every two years, and the men of all provinces voted for their candidates. For four consecutive terms, terms sixteen through nineteen (1949/50 to 1958), our father was one of the two elected representatives from Bushehr, Dashti, and Dashtestan in the Majlis.[1] There were three different prime ministers during the time that our father was in the Majlis: Mansour, Mosaddeq, and during his last term in the House, Manouchehr Eqbal. The head of the Majlis was Sardar Fakher (Reza Hekmat). He was a distinguished man with a distinguished nose like Charles de Gaulle and a distinguished car, a black Cadillac. Friday mornings some members of the Majlis came to our house (*Khaneh ye Shahr*) to have their meetings. When Sardar Fakher came to one of the meetings, Bibi bought strawberries. Bibi served the strawberries with powdered sugar, and that was the first time we had seen that fruit. The incredible scent of strawberries filled the entire salon. A driver stood next to his car to guard the car against the curious kids in the neighborhood. Mohammad, Aqda'i's butler, took the driver trays of tea, strawberries, and cookies as the street children followed him to peek at the tray and to get closer to the Cadillac. Our Baba avoided such attention in the neighborhood. Actually he did not have a car and took the bus to the Majlis—he was the only one at his social level who did not own a car. *Tofiq* magazine, the most popular political satirical publication in Iran, published a cartoon of our Baba getting on the bus with the tails of his tuxedo tucked into his pockets. On the days when a special ceremony was taking place in the Majlis or when the dignitaries went to visit the Shah in his palace—this was called *Salam* ceremony—they all wore tuxedos. Our Baba did in fact fold the tail of his tuxedo and carried it under his elbow in the bus and also when he came down the alley to enter our home.

◆ ◆ ◆

All our cousins call Bibi *khaleh* (aunt) and call our father *amoo* (uncle). The rest of the aunts and uncles are referred to by their names preceded by *aunt* and *uncle*, i.e., "Khaleh Robabeh" or "Amoo Ebne Yousef." Clearly Bibi was their special aunt and Baba was their special uncle; they had a unique bond unlike any other. All the nephews who were old enough to be out and about had campaigned for their uncle during the elections.

Our cousin Sadri was in his teens when he campaigned for our Baba. He recalls going to some of the prominent people like the mother of Sohrab Khan, Shah Mansour Khan, and Ardeshir Khan, khan of Shabankareh, informing them that his uncle was about to run for a seat in the Majlis.

Our cousin Sadri recalls:

The mother of the khans was a powerful woman. She was the sister of Ghazanfar al Saltaneh who had married Ebrahim Khan, a khan from Borazjan. All we had to do was to let her know that our uncle was running for election. She then instructed all the related families and tribes and they all voted for my uncle.

On July 1949, the term of the 15ᵗʰ Majlis came to its natural end. Abdolhossain Hazhir, the Shah's interior minister, initiated preparations to hold the elections of the 16ᵗʰ Majlis. The election term for the House of Parliament was two years at the time and now is four years. Uncle, bless his soul, was a great man. The people of Borazjan never forget all the sacrifices he has made for their region. Even though he had the mission to arm and then disarm the khans in the south, he had shown his loyalty to the khans and their families. For instance, when Ra'is Ali Borazjani, one of the khans of Borazjan, was sentenced to death by the government and was assassinated at the airport in Shiraz, your father got an amnesty from the government for the khan's family to come to Tehran. They stayed in your home and everyday Khaleh (Bibi) went to Ali Dashti to help release them and your father went to Shah to get pardon for them. His two daughters, Iran and Khorshid, stayed with Khaleh (Bibi).

Those times, the campaigns were not in the form of the advertisements you see today. There were no banners or flyers; it was the word of mouth and what the wise men said was good for our region. The candidates also made speeches and told the people what they were planning to do for them.

Uncle did so much for our people: he brought water pipes, the first electric plant, the first ice factory, and also a lemonade factory. He made bridges, roads, and loved to bring the latest developments to our region. He paid out of his own pocket; whatever he had—he even put up *Khaneh ye Shahr* as collateral to get a loan from the bank to build the power plant. He worked hard to convince the Ministry of Health to vaccinate the people of the south and provide pesticides against the deadly infectious diseases that had killed so many. He is the one who finally uprooted those diseases from the south. When the good of the people was at stake, he put his life on the line. People knew all this and voted for him.

His opponents were rich, powerful people like the heads of national newspapers and big businessmen, but they had no chance next to my uncle.

He was elected four times in a row: the sixteenth, seventeenth, eighteenth and nineteenth terms of the Majlis for Bushehr, Borazjan, Ganaveh, Sa'd Abad, Dashti, Khormooj, Dayyer, Bandar Abbas, Qeshm, etc.

He and Baqer Boushehri were the two elected representatives during those terms. However Uncle was the one with incredible background: He was the man people trusted the most. He had high respect for our people and our traditions. Aqa ye Bozorg, Aqda'i, and the Shah always went to him first when there was something sensitive and efficient at stake for the country. In 1949 he became the editor-in-chief of *Shafaq-e sorkh* [Red dawn] newspaper.[2] He was the man in charge of Aqa ye Bozorg's family and also his son-in-law [Bibi's husband] and the Shah chose him to take care of issues in the south and also Tabriz (1320).[3] He was one of the few members of Iran's parliament who was sent to London for the forty-sixth international Conference of the Inter-Parliamentary Union [*confarance e etehad e bein al majales*].[4] We all went to Mehrabad Airport when uncle was returning home. He had a suitcase with him that we called a 'magic suitcase': he had things for everyone as souvenirs and kept pulling more things out of that suitcase for months! He did all that and he never ever wanted or expected anything in return.

The heads of all the khanates of Khosravi, Papari, Najjari, Solat al Dowleh, Hayat Davoodi, everyone, everyone was devoted to him. Ra'is Ali Borazjani, Gholamhossain Tangestani, the heads of Ahram khanates, Sheik Davood were all his supporters.

The ballot boxes were put in the government building. On election day, all men aged twenty-five and older went to vote. Women did not vote until after 1963 but some of the women like Day Abdoo, one of our maids, would not hear of it—they let her make a homemade ballot, a piece of paper with uncle's name on it—and put it in the ballot box. The ballot boxes were protected but not like these days. So one time, some people from the side of our opponents came to tamper with the boxes, but Asheikh Davood, your father's devoted friend, set the box on fire, cancelled the votes and demanded that people should vote again!

When we got the votes and Amoo was elected, we first sent a telegram to Khaleh and then we all came to Tehran to celebrate.

◆ ◆ ◆

Once upon a time there was a king who had a son, the heir to the throne. The king and the queen were looking for a perfect girl for their perfect son—someone suitable to be the future queen. He was offered many beautiful young ladies from all over the country. The prince refused them all, waiting to fall in love first before he chose a bride.

One sunny day on a hunting trip with his father, he had an encounter with a gypsy girl who was fetching some water from a stream around the hunting grounds. The prince fell in love with the girl instantly and wanted to marry her.

The king and the queen mother were very sad and disappointed, but could not tolerate to see their son suffer any longer. He was not eating or sleeping and was getting pale and depressed. Eventually they decided to go and ask the gypsy family for their daughter's hand in royal marriage.

When they were preparing to go, they designated the most decorated men of their court, along with the most valuable gifts, to ride to the gypsy camp, announce the prince's choice, and bring the girl back with them.

As soon as their caravan became visible, the primitive gypsies started to attack their caravan with shouts and by throwing rocks at the king's representatives. The caravan returned and tried again the next day and the next day, each time taking more presents and more of the dignitaries, yet to no avail.

The prince who was hopelessly in love was getting very ill and his royal family by his bedside were completely helpless.

The court had a prime minister who was known for his wisdom. He decided to intervene by telling the king how they should approach the girl's tribe. He said to the king, "Your Majesty, each time you have gone with such dignity, you have been attacked. Have you ever thought that you are not speaking the language of those people? They are a primitive and wild tribe who have never been treated in such a way; they are not at all familiar with your language; you need to communicate with them with a language they understand."

So the next day a group of men rode to the hunting ground and settled at a distance from the gypsy camp. One of the messengers started hollering from the distance, "Hoy!!!!!" Again, "Hoy!!!!!" And then all together they hollered, "Ahoy!" After a while a voice came from the campground, "Ahoy!!! Who is calling?"

"It is us, we want your girl. Bring her to us right away? Or else!"

The wooden gate opened and the girl appeared with her bag outside of the gate waiting for them to take her!

This story was told by Bibi to our father's opponent, Rasool Parvizi,[5] who had won the election to the House of Representatives. The man had come in shame to personally apologize for what had taken place. He was admitting that the election of that term (twentieth) was manipulated by powerful politicians such as Asadollah Alam, the closest adviser and confidant of the Shah.[6]

Our father was in bed with a broken leg when he received his opponent. He was firmly instructing Bibi not to insult the man while he was visiting our home. So she waited, served the guest properly, and then met him once he was outside the house and on the street. She was accompanied by Fezeh. He stood next to her, nodding at her every word, guarding her as she took the last puff on her cigarette and got ready to confront the man (I was one of the kids who stood in line worrying about a fight):

"I do not have much to tell you," she said powerfully yet calmly. "But I want to tell you a story so that you understand that we do not speak the language of the bribe. Our way was too sincere, a luxury for this government. You go ahead and take the girl (the nomination), you and the prime minister speak the same language," Bibi said.

Main gate of the Iranian Parliament. Photo: Daryoush Tahami.

Notes

[1] These terms mark some of the most important terms of the Iranian parliament: "Both Mosaddeq and Ayatollah Kashani were members of Parliament in the 16th term of Majlis. This was the time when the negotiations for the nationalization of oil and the movements for democracy and Iran's independence from foreign influence was at its peak." Quoted from Homayoun Katouzian, *Iranian: doran e bastan ta doreh e mo'aser* (The Persians: Ancient, Mediaeval, and Modern Iran), 4th ed. (Tehran: Nashr e Markaz, 1392 [2013]): 267.

www.iranchamber.com/history/constitutional_revolution/constitutional_revolution.php: History of Iran: Constitutional Revolution, "Sixteenth Term (February 9th, 1950 – February 18th, 1952). A tumultuous period, deeming Gass-Golshaiyan contract amendments against government interest, Majlis expressed its opposition. The Select Petroleum Committee submitted its proposed amendments for Nationalization of Iranian Oil Industry. The British Government lodged a complaint with the International Tribunal in Hague. The Tribunal issued a restraining order preventing the Iranian government from measures it had already taken for transfer of oil industry to Iranians. Quoting inattributibility of the Tribunal in the case, the Iranian government deemed the order as being invalid. The British closed their consular offices in Iran.

Some of the noteworthy bills passed by this session of Majlis were:

Revoking of all press laws, except for 1908 law.

Resolution for nationalization of the Iranian Oil Industry.

Bill for establishment of piped water and sewage system utilities for Tehran.

Seventeenth Term (April 25th, 1952 – December 19th, 1953)

This session, like the one before it, was plagued with political turmoil and unrest. Election was carried out with some difficulties, with some seats remaining vacant throughout Majlis abnormally short life. Only 80 representatives were present out of 135. The issue of oil predominated most of the discussions.

The British government did recourse to International Tribunal in Hague, this time the Iranian Prime Minister attended the hearings. In a vote, the International Tribunal ruled that it is incompetent to deal with British claim regarding nationalization of oil industries. It is noteworthy that the British arbitrator did cast its vote in favor of the motion, which was passed nine to five. This led to complete break of political ties with the British government. The Majlis terminated the Iran-Soviet 1927 Caspian Sea Fisheries agreement and nationalized its facilities.

Shah was put to exile, only to be restored to power in a CIA-sponsored coup d'etat. Upon return, he promptly dissolved both Majlis and the House of Senate.

Of the bills passed during this period one could mention the following:

Special Powers Act in favor of Prime Minister Dr. Mohammad Mosaddeq.

Nationalization of the Iranian Telecommunication.

Bill of Establishment of Public Shuttle Services.

Charter of Iranian Telephone Company."

[2] Sayeh Dashti, "Ali Dashti: His Life and Work." *The Realm of Sa'di* (Costa Mesa, CA: Mazda Publishers, 2013): xiv: "Dashti . . . started his own newspaper, *Shafaq-e sorkh* (Red dawn), a candid publication through which readers became acquainted with his nationalistic ideas and quest for lawfulness. Published three times a week at first, it later became a daily paper. His style of writing, courage, and frank criticisms not only provided guidelines for lawful governing, but also opened a new chapter in Iranian literature."

[3] Abdollah Dashti, *Az Jam/Reez ta Tabriz* (From Jam/Reez to Tabriz). Compiled and edited by Badieh Dashti. (Tehran: Farhang e Hezareh e Sevom, 1385 [2006]).

[4] The 46th Conference of the Inter-Parliamentary Union was held in London in August of 1957.

[5] Seyyed Ja'far Hamidi, *Farhang'nameh e Bushehr* (An encyclopedic dictionary of Bushehr) (Tehran: Vezarat e Farhang va Ershad e Islami, 1380 [2001]): 189: Rasool Parvizi (1919–1976) was born into a family from Ahram. He was a writer and a politician. His most popular works are: *Shalvarha ye vasleh dar* and *Looli e sarmast.*

[6] Amir Asadollah Alam (April 1, 1919–April 14, 1978) was an Iranian politician who was Prime Minister from 1962 to 1964. He was also minister of the Royal Court, president of Pahlavi University, and governor of Sistan and Baluchestan Provinces. Katouzian, *Iranian*, p. 280.

Nineteen
Technology

The little boy from Dashtestan was running around our backyard hollering: *"Oonasho. Oonasho!* (There it is! There it is!)" Breathlessly he kept pointing his finger to the sky. Everyone was running out of the building in panic, worried about this little boy who was about to pass out with excitement and confusion. His eyes seemed to be popping out as he kept pointing to the cloudy sky. Finally we all saw it. It was an airplane fading in and out of the clouds. It was his very first time to see an airplane. We of course could not help but feel superior; we had seen airplanes before.

His eyes in awe were very similar to our own eyes when we saw a television set for the first time. My father had brought home a magic box that worked with electricity. When plugged in, it showed a lighted page with millions of gray dots that made the most unfamiliar noise. Sometimes there were lines that went horizontal, and at times the lines danced obliquely. Such an astonishing object it was. We sat around it for hours to see the designs it made, wondering what they would look like on fabric. Then of course we bragged about it among our friends and the neighborhood children. As a result our living room soon turned into a community showroom. Children and adults, some complete strangers, rushed to our house to see the magic box, a real dilemma.

Bibi was furious with what our father had brought home. The house was totally out of control. It was especially difficult for the housekeepers who believed they had to wash everything after the neighbors' kids whom they believed were not sanitary.

The crowd was getting out of hand when someone finally came up with the idea of putting the box on the windowsill on the second floor, facing the street. All we had to do then was to plug it in and let the neighborhood watch it. This went on for weeks before a temporary television station was set up in Tehran.

A newspaper seller went around the neighborhoods announcing the names of the newspapers and the headlines with a rhythm. His rhythm changed with the names of the newspapers and/or the headlines. That day he sang, "Hey, it is today's paper! Hey, it is very important! Hey it is *Etela'at*, it is *Kayhan*, it is *Tofiq*, it is in *Keyhan Mosavar*. Hey it is very important."

Whenever he showed up in our neighborhood, the children and adults on the street followed him around to ridicule him like they would a fool. "It is a lie! It is a lie!" His nickname had become *doroogheh* (a liar). The poor man usually brought the headlines to the people around the time that people had lost faith in the government and the news. Not long ago he had announced that "The Shah is leaving; read all about it." The next day he had said, "The Shah is arriving, read all about it!"

As soon as the kids heard him, they ran around the alley shouting, "It is a lie, you are a liar . . . " They were circling him and making fun of him. He stopped, pulled himself together, and shouted, "A television station has opened up in Tehran; read all about it." He said that and started to run.

When he announced such news that sounded absurd, Bibi opened the window and told him off: "It is a lie." She quickly closed the window not to hear him curse back. He had looked up in disappointment as he did not expect the very open-minded lady who usually protected him against the naughty kids in the alley and was always very curious about the news to repeat the same insult. Ironically this time he was telling the truth.

The television station had its grand opening, and the box started to show one or two programs, usually classical concerts from Europe; Florian ZaBach had become a household name.

Before television, we were attached to the radio and its one radio station. The radio was punctual, and we told the time by the start of the programs, time to walk to school. The ticktock of the noon hour and the holy sound of *azan* made Fezeh run with her rice to the yard, and at nights, we looked forward to snuggling in our beds to hear the bedtime story, *One Night of One Thousand Nights*. If we were dosing off under Fezeh's *korsi*, the two o'clock declaiming of poetry *Golha ye rangarang* (the colorful flowers) warned that we were late for the afternoon session of school; we ran all the way to school, while every adult went to sleep to the soothing voice of Roshanak.

One early morning at dawn, my sister woke up and started hopping to the radio across the room. She was about five years old, but she still wore a diaper at night. The cloth diaper wrapped her body from under her armpit down to her feet and was secured with a long cloth strap like a miniature mummy. Many guests who had arrived from Borazjan the night before were sleeping on the floor in the living room. She had reached the radio and turned it on to the sound of a man coming from nowhere. Two of the women ran out screaming, "*Jinn! Jinn!*"

It was not only our father who was passionate about new advances in technology, our government was also in a hurry to modernize our country. Electrical elevators were installed in all the tall buildings and the hospitals. The first escalators were installed in 1958 in the first modern American-style department store called Forooshgah e Ferdowsi. Every one of these was a main attraction for the people to come and experience. People of Tehran and people around the country travelled to Tehran to see for themselves the latest technological developments.

Day Abdoo was an amazing woman. She was the daughter of one of the workers in Aqa ye Bozorg's household in Borazjan and the mother of Abdolhossain, her oldest son—that is why we called her Day Abdoo, meaning the mother of Abdolhossain. She came to Tehran to stay in our home most summers. She had problems with her eyes and was always very curious to know about the latest advancements in the field of medicine. Whenever a doctor friend visited us, she was in the front of the line asking about her eyes, knees, her son's indigestion, etc., no matter what the doctor's specialty was. She listened hard and asked questions, not to mention that after all she heard, she went ahead and followed her own traditional way of treatment—she burnt the manure of a cow, put a towel on her head, and got a full facial and eye treatment. Her curiosity encouraged her to follow anyone who was going to see a doctor or a patient in a hospital.

On one of her visits, she came along with us to see a friend of Bibi's in Pars Hospital, which was equipped with elevators. We stood in front of the elevator. Bibi was hesitant to go in, believing that no wise person would willingly lift his foot off the ground. Yet she had to be more modern in front of us children and Day Abdoo from Borazjan. Day Abdoo had no idea what was about to happen. The door to the elevator opened, she took her shoes off and said an eloquent hello before entering the empty room. Her lips formed as though she wanted to whistle a couple of times but couldn't. She kept looking at Bibi with her good eye and wanted to know what was going on. She looked at us, too, but she was not getting any responses from anyone. When the elevator started moving up with a big jerk, she let go of her *maynaar*, stretched her arms to the sides of the elevator's door and asked for God's forgiveness! We arrived on the fourth floor safe, and Day Abdoo walked backward not to have her back to the elevator door as a sign of respect. Bibi walked out solemnly and thanked the elevator for taking her to the fourth floor without having to walk up four flights of stairs.

Bibi appreciated the conveniences of modern life—the washing machine, the juicer, and the portable radio had her approval; the answering machine was the hardest to get used to. She had called her doctor, who happened to be the son of her close friend, one day. The voice of a lady said, "This is the office of Dr. Kazemi . . ." Bibi immediately responded, "This is Dashti, I would like to speak to the doctor." Then she heard a beep and then silence. "Alo! Alo!" She hung up and dialed again. The same voice came on, "This is the office of Dr. Kazemi." "Yes, I would like to talk to the doctor. This is Mrs. Dashti," she said, making sure she was heard. Again a beep and silence. She looked around the telephone, checked the plug and the receiver, and dialed again. The same voice said, "This is the . . ."

"God damn it! I know where that is, I need to talk to Davood right now!" Again she heard the beep in the middle of her talking. She hung up the phone, got ready, and went to see her friend, the doctor's mother, to teach her a lesson on raising polite children.

I wish the little boy from the south were there when I was witnessing my daughter's engagement ceremony over the Internet. I wish he could see how I was able to use the webcam; how the page was divided into four compartments as the family in Tehran, Esfahan, New York, and San Francisco connected. I would not be surprised actually, if he himself has turned into a hacker!

If the young man in the village of Meigoon is constructing a squash court claiming that his daughter is googling the measurements and if my housekeeper's wife, who cannot read or write, gives me back the DVD I gave for her children to watch and tells me, "Here, I had it burnt on the hard drive," if you need to sacrifice a sheep and you get to call the shepherd on the hills on his mobile and you hear him say, "Text your address," then everything is possible. Then I should not blame my mother for not allowing my brother to put his laptop in her closet believing that it was a live creature and should not be hidden in her closet. I can completely understand why she warned me not to point the remote garage door opener toward her. She saw the possibility of it all: "If this thing can open this heavy door, then surely it can split me open!"

Ferdowsi Department Store: The first department store in Tehran equipped with escalators in early 1960s. Photo: Daryoush Tahami.

Twenty
Dragging Homa (Homa *Keshoon*)

In spite of our very large family, our house seemed empty without a crowd of relatives and friends of the family. We had our extended families, Bibi's sisters and their children, people from Dashtestan who came to ask for a job or just to escape the scorching heat of the southern summers, people who needed surgeries or other medical care available in Tehran, families with youngsters who came for their vacation, college students who got their room and board there, etc. They came and they stayed with us for months or even years at a time. Their lives and their stories became ours; every room, every corner of the house was occupied by our visitors.

I remember an older man, an attorney, with a cast all the way to his hip, his leg supported by many pillows, staying in our house in one of the guest rooms for more than a year. I took his lunch tray to him many times.

Day Shokoohi, a woman maid from Borazjan, was literally hung by her leg in the basement. She also was in a cast and her leg was not to be moved. There were many times when we ran around the house and into her room as well, hitting the chain which supported her leg. Her leg swung, and we got in trouble!

Most of these people refused to go to a hospital or to a hotel. As long as our father and Bibi were there, nobody dared even contemplate the idea. Those places were for people who had nobody.

Fezeh of course had her own relatives who came to visit and stayed with us. Her in-laws also paid a visit once in a while. Bibi's order then was for us to behave and call Fezeh *banoo* (lady).

Bibi was a very sociable person herself. Her personal guests were the wives and the mothers of the politicians of the time. Our father had his friends and colleagues who had their meetings in our house. During election times, our house was swarming with campaign managers. Both the supporters of my father and his opponents stayed in our house.

The house was never ever empty. It might have happened just a few hours in my life at home that any of us were home alone. Actually, it never did happen to me!

As children we too were most welcoming. When Bibi's friends came to visit, we either sat with them and listened eagerly or went to our own rooms with such feeling of security; the world was safe out there.

We shouted with joy when the doorbell rang and a dear friend showed up. And when they were leaving, we would hide their shoes so they could not leave.

As we came of age, we each had our own friends visiting us at the house. There were times when about ten kids from the neighborhood would be jumping on our parents' bed before Fezeh or Zarafshan got there to kick everyone out. The older we got, the more welcome our friends were, and in return, our friends loved to visit our home.

My sister Talieh had her friends whom everyone respected; our parents and everyone else received them with joy. One special friend of Talieh's was a classmate of hers, Homa. Homa lived a few blocks away with her mother and her teenage brother Ahmad. Her two sisters were already married.

Ahmad was a genius. He had invented the first manual intercom system for their house. Their house was built in two separate parts, north wing and south wing. The entrance from the street (Pamenar) opened into the south wing. There were a few rooms on the street level and a stairway down to more rooms. I have no idea what they were for, or who lived there, all I know is that Homa's family lived in the north wing. There was a well-kept yard and then again another stairway to the north wing.

Homa's house. Photo: Ahmad Qazinoor, 2011.

A petite older housekeeper was always sweeping the ground of the immaculate yard. I am not sure if she had a hunched back or it was the way she bent for hours at a time, with a small broom in one hand and the other hand on her waist. During the long hours, I was there I never saw her stretching up straight. At times she would just bend some more to pull a weed from around the jasmine tree.

Homa's mother was the most dignified woman. She was tall and very focused. Their home was very much different from ours; it was quiet.

When someone rang the bell from the street, one of the ladies in the house, or Ahmad himself, like a church bell ringer (campanologist) proudly pulled on a white sport shoe (*katooni*) which was hung from the ceiling of the porch in front of the north wing.

The shoe was attached to a long wire, the wire travelled from the porch to the yard, making a line in the sky. It continued to the back stairway, ran into some small hooks on the wall of the long vacant hallway, every fifty centimeters or so, and finally came down to the door knob and to the latch in the lock. When the shoe was pulled down, the latch was pulled to the left, and the door swung open.

I know all this because I watched it happen many, many times.

Everyone in our home loved and respected Homa. Her cool sense of humor and her selflessness drew everyone close to her. Her being there made our sister very happy, and that was important.

My sister called Homa most evenings, asking her to come to our house. She always said no, first. Then my sister would insist, "Homa, c'mon. Please come over, please. For the sake of God, please," she begged. Some days she said yes, but most of the time she refused to come. It was then when my sister sent her special agent (me) for Homa *keshoon*.

I must have been about three to six years old. Talieh was like my mother. She dressed me up and did my hair every day. She took me with her to her friends' houses and to school sometimes. My hair was long and heavy; having it in an imperfect braid or tied back loosely could bring me such frustration, feeling like a knot in my stomach (I called it *qomboli goshneh*). She was the only one who knew how to pull my hair up very tight into a ponytail.

On school days, I would go to her room first thing in the morning and knock softly on her door with my comb. She combed my hair and pulled it till my eyes were stretched to the point where I could hardly close them. Then she asked me, "*Qomboli goshne at raft?*" (Is the knot in your stomach gone?) I would smile with relief and run out of her room to go to school. By the time I got to school, my face was red from the loving pinches on my cheeks from Talieh's high school classmates: "How cute, she is Dashti's sister (*khahar e Dashti ye*)," they said.

When Talieh gave me a mission, of course I was committed to do it to the point of completion. To begin the mission, someone took me to Homa's house for Homa keshoon. The doorbell was rung, and the door swung open. The person who took me (I think it was mostly Banafsheh, Fezeh's daughter), would put me inside the building and leave.

I sat on the stairs of the south wing of their house and just stayed there. I sat and sat for hours not talking to anyone and not eating or drinking any of the food they offered me. People would come and go, pat my head, and make their way past me to the door or to the house.

Until it would happen. Right before dusk, I would hear her mother say, "Homa, take this innocent child to her home (*Homa, madar, in bacheh bi gonah ra bebar khoonash*)." Homa finally showed up. She took my hand and cursed Talieh all the way to our house, and she called me "*kaneh*" (tick). When we turned into our street, we could hear the cheers from our house. "Homa keshoon!"

I then let go of her hand and ran home into my sister's arms in triumph.

Homa came in joyfully after all.

Twenty-One
Order / The Games We Played

The world is not to be put in order: the world is order incarnate. It is for us to harmonize with this order.
—Henry Miller

My younger sister Sepideh and I held hands as our short wobbly legs led us from home at the end of a cul-de-sac to a glorious adventure around the corner. We had saved a *qeran* (about a penny) and had gained the courage to go buy pieces of sour candies the size of our fingernails. The rush of adrenalin shook our bodies, made it hard to walk. We kept telling each other not to look toward the other side of the street. The other side of the street, a maximum of twenty meters away, was another world, unknown, "full of strangers," as we had been warned against. Even when we grew older, we were conditioned to go to the main street, turn left and left again at the light to go to school. The other side of the street was a "black hole." The owner of the small corner store, Nabi, stubbornly gave us only three candies instead of four, which would have made it so much easier for us to be fair to each other when we shared. So we spent a long time trying to cut the third candy into exactly two portions. We measured the pieces against each other's, and if there was any discrepancy, we cut the extra piece with our teeth and then cut that in half as well. When done, we performed a ritual—we sang our special song before we put the pieces in our mouths. This was to make sure that we ate at exactly the same time:

Bekhoram ya nakhoram
Mikhaii bekhor, mikhaii nakhor
Mikhoram, baleh
Aam!

[Should I, or should I not eat it?
Do you want to eat, don't you want?
I will eat it, yes
Yum!]

Only then was justice served, the mission accomplished, and we returned home with our heads up, legs strong.

This was a mission for Thursdays. In addition, on our agenda every Monday at 6:00 a.m. during summer we obliged ourselves to make lemonade for the two of us, a daring action beyond our means at the ages of five and seven.

Every Monday morning in the summer, Sepideh and I woke up around five in the morning. One sat up in the dark and found the shadow of the other sitting up right on time. We then crawled out of the wooden beds in the yard where we slept with at least twenty other adults and children next to us.

Our mission was to make lemonade and drink it at six o'clock in the morning. The challenge was to get the lemon juice out of the room of our cousin, Amehdi, who was a college student boarding in our house. We went into his room from the large window in the backyard that had been left open for air. One of us waited outside as the other crawled in the total darkness, got the freshly squeezed lime juice stored on the lower shelf of his bookshelf, and handed it to the partner anxiously waiting outside, guarding. Then it was time to get the sugar. We had to pass Fezeh for that. We believed that Fezeh never slept. Like two little puffs of cloud, the two of us managed to go past her room into the pantry next to the kitchen. Sometimes, just our luck, the round leather spread with red cloth lining was left outside of the pantry. This was used to break the large sugar cones into sugar cubes. If we were lucky, there was still some powdered sugar left in it. If not, we had to climb on top of each other to get the metal box of sugar cubes, which we did. Then the cups and spoons then they were made; we never failed!

The lemonade tasted like triumph. We had claimed our territory from our older cousin and had challenged a supreme power such as Fezeh. However, the order of choosing Mondays leaves me with no clues.

Usually the first thing all of us children did when we woke up was to set things straight: who was first, second, third, and so on, in getting to do things. Whoever was first to wake up had the advantage of waking the others up and quickly declaring: "First toilette, first plate of breakfast, first to choose a game, and on and on for at least ten things. The list was getting longer and harder to follow when we made it short and said, "First everything." Shotgun!

In all our make-believes, a great deal of our time was spent on establishing order and, by declaring detailed rules, making the images as vivid and clean-cut as we possibly could.

Sepideh and I wanted to build a school. In our make-believe games, we had to first figure out how we were going to get the money. The easiest way was to win the lottery, we thought. Then we went into great detail as to how we were to announce it to avoid the stigma of buying lottery tickets? Handling so much money and of course the threat of greedy or needy people was a nuisance. After giving so much of it to others, how do we split the money to be fair? What do we buy? And so on. It was all so exhausting that we, at times, decided with relief that it is better not to win it! However, the incredible force of fantasizing or bringing our own desired images close to reality was much stronger than the limitations we feared. We never bought the tickets!

Eventually we would settle with some of the fortune left for us with the valued goal of making a school. Then again the structure of the school, the children's uniforms, the location, the teachers, the curriculum, etc., went beyond our tolerance, creating much anxiety, but we had to do it. The effort was worthwhile;

the make-believe went on for hours as we went around our perfect school, feeling satisfied with what we had created in the virtual world. The careful arrangements and the orders we set and followed did help us. It made it easier for us to engage in play when the rules were protecting our rights. It was like our mother was watching.

Games We Played Beyond the Borders of Our House

Once we stepped out of the house into the neighborhood alleys and to the schools, the games became more serious and intense. The games we played were not just a pastime or fun time or simply acting out our fantasies, where we ourselves were in control of our imaginations; they became a test of power and our social standing among our peers. There were no adult interventions nor their considerations; the games were our territory; in it, there was no mercy!

The games were structured with unbendable regulations—a leader and the followers who had agreed upon the rules of the games. The leader was more like a hypnotist or a movie director who had a vision. He or she would tell us how it was supposed to be, and we agreed to follow. There was no bargaining once the rules were set. If we had agreed that our fingers were guns, we had to die in case we were shot with those fingers!

Hide-and-seek (*qayem mushak*): Hide-and-seek was one of the games we played in the old neighborhood in downtown Tehran. It was an intense and potentially dangerous game. Most of the time, we played it when it was dark, and we were out on the streets. The curfew for us and also for others in the neighborhood was when our father, Mr. Dashti, came home. The participants were children of all ages and the game was played at several levels. The older teenagers were advanced, and the small children were led to believe that they were actually part of the game, but it was made easier on them (a little consideration here). Even though all children were allowed to play, the more serious players called them "*nokhody*" (a bean in the soup), they did not count.

We took the liberty to hide anywhere—sometimes we just walked into a house without even knowing the residents. It was simply enough to declare that we were playing hide-and-seek, and somehow it was acceptable to them or maybe even exciting for them to be a part of this far-reaching game; happy to offer us refuge.

The seeker (the wolf) would knock at every door and would look behind every bend to find his prey. There were always nosey neighbors, spies here and there, leading them. One or two of the players were the best and hardest to find. Nafiseh was the hardest to catch. She was a champion who was welcomed in every house and knew every nook and cranny while the rest of us were afraid to go far. She hid in the kitchen or the closet of some stranger if she had to.

What I did though was to run! I ran and ran and ran deciding where to hide and finally returned, breathless, declaring, "Here I am." The game was usually over by the time I got back, causing my sisters trouble for having left me alone.

***Gol Koumal*:** When our older cousins came from Borazjan or Shiraz, the games got tougher. One Dashtestani game we played was *Gol Koumal*.

We sat around in a circle with a cover on our laps. One of the players put a crumpled piece of paper called *gol* and took it behind his back, hiding it in one of his closed fists. Then he brought both hands in front for us to find out which hand held the *gol*. The skillful player had a poker face while the others, one at a time, tried to guess where it was hidden. The guesses were calculated—we measured the distance between the two fists by our wide open fingers stretched out. Then we brought our two hands together—if one of our small fingers stood higher than the other one, it was an indication that the *gol* was in that fist. We watched carefully how the player held his wrist—whether it was loose or tight—we also listened to the pulse of that fist; we stared into his eyes as we touched each fist, examining carefully if his eyes dilated when we were close to guessing correctly; we looked for any sign of stress. We weighed the fist and so on. Finally we chose one. If we were correct, our team won; if not, we were harshly punished.

One of the penalties was called the "burning mustache" (*sebil atashin*). With two thumbs, a member of the winning team pressed on the loser's upper lip as if he is drawing a mustache; it did burn for hours. When smaller children were playing the punishment was called "cotton mustache" (*sebil panbeii*), a very soft drawn mustache. Another common sentence was a "donkey ride"; the loser would give a ride to the winner on his back and around the yard or the room. Basically, the winner could ask for anything he or she wanted. However, some rules were there to limit the winner's demands.

Taking Turns: The privilege of beginning the game—who got to start first—was just as important as winning or losing. All games had their own rituals to give the right to a person or a team to start the game. A song made of nonsense words, for example, was one common way to start a sitting game:

Almman navaran, doo doo escatchi, ana mana kalachi, soozan va qeichi, atchin o vachin, yek pa to var chin (fold one leg).

The person with the last leg outstretched got to start the game.

We quickly sang the song *palam, pooloom, peeleem* as we moved our hands on top of each other's. This was the quickest way; we did that when we had no time to waste. The person with the palm of the hand on top of everyone else's got the first turn.

For standing group games such as jump rope and hopscotch, two members stood at a distance walking. As the tip of one foot was touching the heel of the other, they approached each other, while many eyes watched for exact measurements. Whoever had his foot on top of the other person's foot would start.

Yek qol do qol: The best place to find the pebbles for *yek qol do qol*, a sit-down game, was at the bakery. The bakery made a whole-wheat flat bread called *sangak* (*sang* means stone). The flat bread is made in the stone oven and laid on pebbles to toast; when the bread comes out, pebbles are stuck to it. Around the bakery and under the table where customers brush the pebbles off the bread is the best place to find the evenly sized stones for the game. This had to be done behind the baker's back.

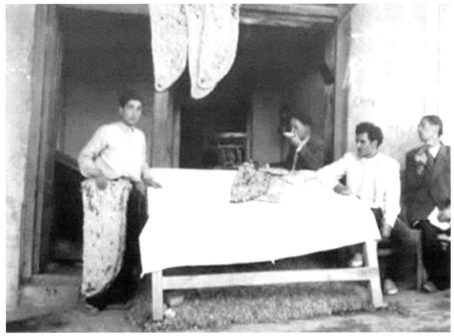

A sangak bakery. Photo: Daryoush Tahami.

Inside the oven of a sangak bakery. Photo: Mohsen Jazayeri, 2016.

Kids who went out in nature to the gardens around Tehran usually had the most amazing stones. The pros carried their own personal stones in their pockets.

Glass marbles were also available for this game. They were incredible to look at, but we still preferred the stones and kept going back to them.

About five of us sat around in a circle with our knees touching. One by one we spread five pebbles in the middle of the circle, then by holding one stone in the palm of our hand we started:

First round: We picked up the other four stones one by one by throwing the one in our hand up in the air, as high or as low as we wanted to—it depended on our style. Each style demanded its own skill. Older girls who had manicured nails usually preferred high style; it simply gave them more time to show off the nails as they swapped the stone on the floor and waved the hand like a ballerina in the air.

Second round: We threw the stones in the middle, and this time we picked a stone from the floor in a way that it had to hit the stone in the palm of our hand making a sound (*beshkan*).

Third round: We threw the stones in the middle and this time picked up each stone one by one. This time around the stones had to be picked up without hitting the stone in the palm of our hand (*nashkan*).

Fourth round: Like a hen, we laid an egg by picking up two stones, we laid our fist down to lay a stone. We exchanged it with the stones on the ground, one by one (*tokhm kon*).

Fifth round: This time we had to pick up all four stones on the ground as we threw one stone up in the air and caught it. Once we caught the stone, we gently threw all five stones on the back of our hand, threw them all up, and caught them all at once and called this spraying perfume (*golab pash*).

These five rounds were the basic rounds. For the more advanced girls, we went to another round of a more challenging game:

Putting the stones in the gate we made with our other hand, and collecting the stones on either side of the gate. Making an open hole and putting the stones in the middle. Making a closed hole and pushing the stones in the hole.

Scattering the stones one by one to a fair distance and collecting them two by two. The more skilled we were, the farther we scattered the stones. We carried our five stones in our pockets at all time. When we fell asleep, they fell out of our pockets. They were the first things we looked for when we woke up.

By the time I was in twelfth grade, I had become the champion of our high school. We played rough and with precision; there was never any bending of any rules. We had our own special corner on the tiles at the top of the stairs at school, while rows of students stood around silently to watch us play.

***Laylay* (hopscotch):** Every neighborhood had its own hopscotch drawn on the ground. Thanks to the dry weather of Tehran, the lines were in place for weeks or even months at a time. The street cleaners swept gently over the lines drawn by means of scratches on the pavements, chalk, or charcoal on the ground in the alleys and smaller streets. The lines were renewed and drawn over when there was a new player or a tournament, or in case it had rained.

Our neighborhood played the form of hopscotch that consisted of six or more side-by-side squares, numbered from one through six or eight or more (always an even number). At the left-hand side of the bottom, there was a semicircle that we called *jahanami* (hell). The player slid a flat stone to land on one of the squares. We had to make sure it did not go into the jahanami. If it did, we lost the game. (We lost our turn if the stone landed on a line, on the side or in the middle of the board, and in case our foot landed on the lines.) Then we hopped with one foot and kicked the stone into the next square and returned. We started from the first square and went all the way to the last one. On the way out, we made sure it did not go on the jahanami semicircle.

As we moved to different neighborhoods, we got to know different styles of hopscotch. I personally got to do three different kinds (simple rectangular, circular, and Hungarian type). As pros, we had our personalized hopscotch rocks.

Tanab bazy **(long rope):** Sepideh and I were the champions of skip rope through elementary and high school. We jumped over a long and thick rope swung so that one or two or more players could jump over and allow the rope to go under our feet and over our heads. When the rope touched any player, she would go out. Eventually two players were left for the semifinal and they jumped till one was out. We had one-time jump (*yek dar row*) where we would run in the middle of the swinging rope, jump once and go out, one by one. Then we had two-times jump (*do dar row*) where we came in, jumped twice, and then left one by one. The lines were sometimes very long and with ten or more initial participants. At the end there was only one player left who would do the two-feet jumping very fast until it was over.

Other Games

When someone brought a ball to school we played dodgeball tirelessly, coming back home with bruised legs. We played Ping-Pong and volleyball too.

We blackened the pages of our notebooks with games such as "*esm va miveh*" (name the names and the fruits), hangman, dot to dot, etc. and when we got older, we challenged each other in math by playing with numbers in games such as "chicken lay eggs," "hop at number seven and its multiples." *Twenty Questions* was played on the radio, and we followed it by creating our own game and so much more.

In all the games we played, we longed for the moments of perfection—moments where we performed our best; when the opponent was a perfect match; not too easy, not too hard. When the ball hit the perfect location on the racket, when the opponent hit it back to where you could hardly reach it, yet you did, when the hands were in a perfect position to hit a ball, when the stones sounded shallow on the ground, when there was a silent moment of order!

Toys. Photo: Daryoush Tahami.

Twenty-Two
The Music in You

Most summers we moved to the countryside, to the northern part of Tehran, Shemiran, to be close to our great-uncle. In the summer of 1959, we moved and ended up staying. The difference between downtown Tehran and the northern part of the city, Shemiran, Elahieh, Tighestan,[1] was as great as the difference between two countries. Most of the neighbors were dignitaries, ministers, artists, or ambassadors, and most embassies had their summer villas there with vast grounds in Elahieh.

Fortunately, being a large family made the outside world nonthreatening for us. We had everything we wanted right there in our house. Nothing had to change in our household due to our move. Something about us, however, was the urge to create a community no matter where we went!

The decision was made among us children and we started to plan an event to invite all the children in our neighborhood to a play.

The terrace in front of our living room was turned into a stage. We brought bricks and mud from the large vacant backyard to raise the stage and brought about twenty chairs from everywhere in the house for the audience. I have always wondered how our parents allowed us to do such things, but the will of a large team of siblings, all eight of us ranging from two to nineteen, made it difficult to say no, and usually when Banafsheh joined us, Fezeh made it happen.

We made tickets and took them door-to-door to the neighbors. My sister Badieh was the most imaginative—she plugged in the electric teapot to prepare rice and saffron to serve as refreshments. Everything was set.

The neighborhood children started coming in with their nannies to fill up the chairs; they were dressed up and well behaved. The refreshment was served and the show started:

The main performance was a choreographed ballet by Badieh. It was called "The Butterfly." Our youngest sister, Sepideh, sat in the middle of a circle with her head hidden between her knees. Three of us circled around her on our toes like ballerinas, for a long, long time, singing softly: Butterfly lalalalalala . . . Dream . . . Butterfly lalalalalala . . . Dream . . . Butterfly lalalalalalal . . . Dream . . . (*parvaneh lalalalalalala afsaneh* . . .). The brothers accompanied us by banging on pots or chairs to keep the beat—the adults were watching with pride and excitement from inside the living room.

The second act was an opera:

Standing by our small pool which, in our imaginary world, was as large as a sea, next to the terrace, Nafiseh and I performed, in pretend Italian, a grand opera! None of us knew Italian or any other language for that matter, not even the languages of our neighbors. For us every nonsensical word related to a certain meaning. We were in awe of ourselves and what we were presenting.

The opera was the story of a married couple in love. The man had gone on a long journey to serve his country and the beautiful young wife had suffered; counting the moments until his return. As the ship appeared in the distance on the sea, and as the figures came vividly to the imaginations of the child-performers, the soundless music got louder in their souls. The audience was dumfounded. The artists were at the peak of their performance. How intense it was to do such a scene. The soprano choked, and the tenor led her backstage. Again the audience started clapping and cheering.

No one knew what it was all about, and it did not actually matter. Perhaps we had figured out that it was the rhythm that was able to break through differences and to introduce new ideas. We had begun to realize that once our own thoughts were harmonized, our listeners maintained focus to our message; they heard us: "We want to be friends."

What that musical show did for us was more than we had ever planned. We had become the stars of the neighborhood. All the children wanted to come to our house everyday to play with us.

After that victory, we learned to use the same art, breaking through the uproar of our own family's life in full demand. We begun to realize that the beat, the high and low, the strong and weak beats, repeated in harmony could get us what we wanted and we started using it:

We made an ensemble of all children and performed a repertoire conveying our messages: First we wanted a Ping-Pong table and we performed this repertoire every night for weeks, peacefully and seriously.

Meez Ping-Pong [strong beat] [a Ping-Pong table]
[weak beat of silence]
Meez Ping-Pong (strong beat)
weak beat of silence
Mikhaheem (strong beat) [We want]
Meez Ping-Pong (strong beat)
weak beat of silence
Meez Ping-Pong (strong beat)
weak beat of silence
Mikhaheem (strong beat).
[Fast pulse:]
Meez   e   Ping-Pong,   meez   e   Ping-Pong mikhahiiiiiiiiiiiiiiiiiiiiiiiiiim.

Musical note for our song "Ping-Pong Table" written by an unknown artist, 2016.

Meez e Ping-Pong, meez e Ping-Pong mikhahiiiiiiiiiiiiiiiiiiiiiiiim.

We repeated this for a very, very long time, moving around in a circle in a trancelike mode! It was effective and we got the Ping-Pong table.

Bibi was getting into this as well. She, like most Iranians, used poetry to express herself; now she was adding a beat to it. To reflect the limit of her tolerance for the long exhausting summer holiday, she created a song for the night before school started, and we accompanied her with clapping and stomping our feet:

Soloist (Bibi): Kay farda sobh meesheh? [When, oh when, will it be tomorrow?]
All the children: Enshallah mobarekesh baad [May God bless this day].
We, the younger sisters, had made a song when we found our brothers stronger and taller than us:
Eefeloo bi ensaaf shodeh
Saaf shodeh, eye saaf shodeh

[The Eiffel Tower is being unfair
Unfair, so unfair]

This part was accompanied by clapping and stomping our feet on the ground as well. It worked like magic; they stopped being so physical with us.

The following song was made with complete nonsensical words; it became our family song; even our aunts and uncles sang it:

Sham al abali
Sal kalamo nabaatio
Oh oh. Oh oh; oh oh misaghieh.
Shamal abali sal kalamo nabaaghio
Oh oh. Oh oh; oh oh misaghieh.
Shamal abali
Sal kalamo kapashmaneh
Oh oh. Oh oh; oh oh kapashmaneh.
Our brothers had made a song of their own, claiming their identity:
Aqa ye Abdollah e Dashti, baba ye ast bandeh.
Khanoom e Abdollah e Dashti, madar e ast bandeh.

[Mr. Abdollah Dashti my father, he is. Yours truly.
Mrs. Abdollah e Dashti my mother, she is. Yours truly.]
We made many such songs and dances depending on the occasion. Songs were made either for the sheer art of music; a group emblem; a way to express ourselves; a peaceful approach to be heard. We were dancing with our childhood.

At one of our performances: Abbas, Sepideh, Sayeh, Dadashi, Badieh, and Nafiseh on top. Photo: Dashti family album, 1956.

Notes

1   Tighestan is now called Dashti Street.

Twenty-Three
NGO

A taxi pulled up to our gate one early morning. The taxi driver got out of the car to take the lady's suitcases out of the trunk and left waving good-bye. It was still dark as her tired body pushed the suitcases a little closer to the gate to ring the bell. Before she reached for the doorbell, however, she noticed something unusual that caused her to panic. She had come to the wrong address! This was not her niece's house! The large sign installed on the front gate read: "**The Institute of Bee Supporters (bongah e hemayat az zanbooran).**"

Exhausted from her bus trip from Esfahan, she picked up her luggage and began heading away with so much disappointment. Fortunately, however, our father, the host, who was taking his morning stroll while sipping on his thumb-sized teacup, ran into her and said, "Welcome! Where are you going?"

"What is going on here," she protested in confusion. "Where do you live? Have you moved?" Khaleh Zakieh inquired.

"No! We have not moved!" he was confused too. He took her suitcases and led the way. She followed him confidently knowing that soon he is going to be proven wrong when he sees the sign on the gate.

❖ ❖ ❖

At the ages of seven, eight, and nine, my sister Sepideh, my brother Dadashi (Mohammad Hassan) and I had established an organization of our own whereby we protected bees. Our father had brought home a couple of mud cylinder beehives to get honey. He had put the beehives at the farthest distance from the house in the yard so Bibi would not object to them. He loved his bees and would do anything to protect them. Everyone else hated them. The house would be filled with bees by the end of summer and whoever could catch one would kill it. Years later when we moved by the creek (*rood khooneh*), our Baba got more beehives; this time made out of wood.

There was a flood one time and the raging water was carrying away the beehives. Our father was devastated. He called the fire department and went in the water himself to save the bees. I do not know how he survived the floodwater and all the bee stings all over his body. The firemen were dancing outside with bees all over their faces and bodies. It was not until Bibi's screaming got out of hand and not until he saved the beehives that our father finally came inside. We pulled his T-shirt off gently and saw that the white T-shirt was almost black with bee stings.

Enough was enough! We had decided to protect our father and his bees. The three of us announced that no one is allowed to kill a bee. If we found a dead bee anywhere, we cross-examined everyone. Of course no one ever admitted the murder, but we were suspicious of everyone.

Our whistling was heard throughout the day like a siren; we were pretend ambulances running around the house. In addition, we had made a couple of miniature stretchers out of used matchboxes for the injured or dead bees. We took care of the injured bee by putting it in a flowerbed and watched over it. They usually passed away in a few minutes. Then we solemnly mourned their deaths.

We had designated an area in our backyard as a graveyard for the bees. We carried the dead bee in the matchbox, took it out of the box for more proper burial (we also needed to save the hard-to-find matchbox), and buried it. We put a tombstone (a flat pebble) on their graves and performed the whole ceremony of eulogies and tears.

Our headquarters was in the backyard on a ladder. My brother, who was the head of the organization, sat on the top step, I was next, and my younger sister sat below me. Our older sister, Nafiseh, who seemed only to want to make sure we were having a good time, just served us. She swept the ground under the ladder and brought us things to eat. Still a child herself, she seemed to be above it all. We sat there for hours and hours every day spelling out rules and regulations of our NGO. We all wanted to be called Aqa ye Nambordeh (Mr. So and So [John Doe]). We picked up that name from overhearing our father's meetings at home with other politicians. They used the name *Nambordeh* in order to avoid using specific names, we later found out. We had assumed that Mr. Nambordeh was a really important man that everyone talked about.

The decision was made. We cut out a big piece of board (about one meter by one meter), painted it yellow, and our brother, who was skilled in the art of calligraphy, wrote on it in black ink:

"The Institute of Bee Supporters" (Bongah e Hemayat az Zanbooran)

The sign was ready, and we agreed to hang it out on the front gate and go public!

The NGO had become very active. We were adding new members, and adults were becoming more cautious about killing bees until one day it happened! An unfaithful bee stung our brother, the head of the organization! We immediately renounced bees. The new sign read: **"The Institute for Combatting Bees"** (***Bongah e Mobarezeh ba Zanbooran***).

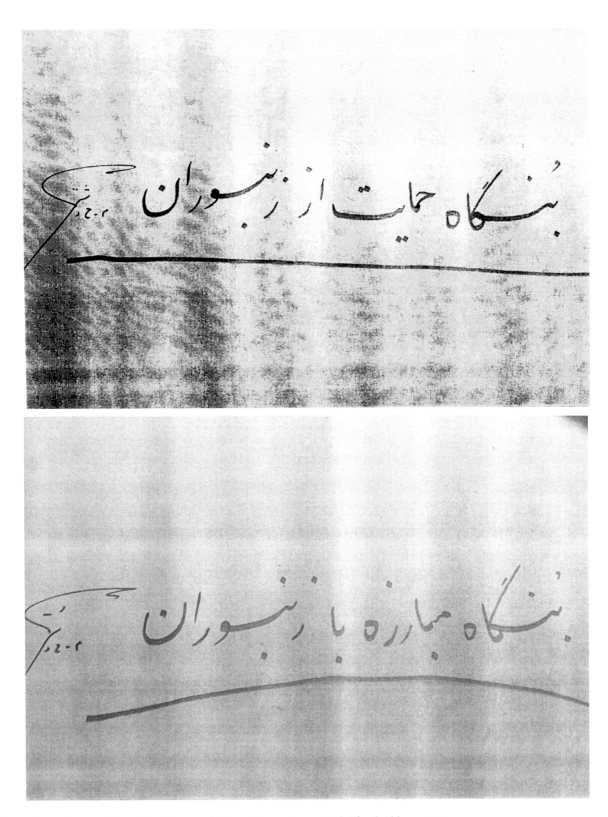

بُنگاه حمایت از زنبوران

بُنگاه مبارزه با زنبوران

The two signs written and signed by Mohammad Hassan Dashti. Photo: Dashti family al-bum, 2015.

Twenty-Four
School

Yek o do o seh
Zang e madraseh
Madam bia peesh
Nokhodchi kishmish

[One and two and three
The school bell rings
Come forward, Madam
Chickpeas and raisins]

Once upon a Friday we were invited to our school to see Khalil Oqab perform.[1] That Friday of Fall 1955, our elementary school, Sa'di, was honored to lend its grounds to the performance of the Iron Man of Iran. For the first time, we saw the large gate to our school wide open—usually the small door in the side of the gate was open for us to come and go—that day the large metal gate was opened to allow many trucks loaded with men and animals, plus some equipment, to enter the school grounds.

We were seated on the benches assembled specially for that day, around the schoolyard, in two and three rows. We sat there, in the freezing weather, with our families and waited for the program to start. Finally Khalil Oqab was driven inside the schoolyard in a small truck that had his picture on top, like Zampano.[2]

The strongman Khalil Oqab did things that if I had not seen them with my own eyes, I would never have believed. For one thing he lifted up a donkey with his teeth and started to swing the donkey. Then he laid on the ground and a truck filled with men went over him! I saw it with my own eyes. Then two large trucks went around the schoolyard from two sides and approached him with speed. We stopped breathing for a moment, in fear. Were they going to smash him? Much to our relief, the trucks stopped next to him before touching him. He grabbed two chains from under the trucks and held them in his arms. Both trucks put their gears in reverse trying to back up, but he would not let them. The tires were spinning so fast, but the trucks could not move back; only the front of the trucks were raised in the air. He stood in the middle with his bent knees and stopped them with his arms; he was punishing those trucks! He wrapped the thick chain around his chest, picked the heaviest weights up off the ground, and walked around as if he had done nothing.

Photo: Khalil Oqab, Photo: Khalil Oqab's personal collection.

Khalil Oqab at ninety-two. Photo: Sayeh Dashti, 2016.

Each school day started at eight o'clock in the morning with the sound of a hammer on a rectangular piece of metal. The students who were late stood by the gate waiting for the national anthem to end and the three-colored (green-white-red) flag with the inscribed lion, sword, and sun, to be raised to the top of the flagpole, before the custodian allowed them in to their class assembly. We stood at arm's length of each other, quiet and courteous. The principal and the teachers stood in front facing us as we all saluted the flag of our country and prayed for the well-being of our king. Then it was time to introduce the best students and the worst students. The good students stepped up to the principal to get their awards, usually a set of pens, and the bad students stepped out of the lines and stood there to be shamed.

When the second bell rang, each grade, row by row, starting from the first graders, walked into the building to go to their classrooms.

The classrooms at Sa'di Elementary School were spacious and full of light. Each class consisted of three rows of wooden benches that were attached to a desk with three compartments. We were each assigned a seat and walked to them as we entered the classrooms. A few weeks after the beginning of school, the more courteous and the smarter students were moved to the front rows and the back of the classrooms was reserved for the naughty, the gossipy, yet the cool kids.

The class representative (*mobser*) kept a notebook with everyone's name in it and kept putting "+" and "-" in front of our names in order to report to the vice principal. The cool kids got a hold of her notebook and started erasing the "-" or made it into a "+." Some of us just kept begging her to reconsider.

The classes started with an inspection by the vice principal. We put our drinking cups (folding plastic cups), our handkerchiefs, and both our hands on our desks for the vice principal's careful examination. If anyone's nails were long and dirty, if she did not have a cup or a handkerchief, she was sent to the principal's office. "Come back with your parents!" the principal ordered. Calling the parents was the worst thing that could happen to us, the same as the end of the world. The parents were completely on the side of the schools; being respectful and obedient toward the school staff was nonnegotiable and was considered a holy order.

The vice principal then left the classroom, and the teacher walked in. Each time they came in or when they left, the class representative would call out, "*Bar pa*" (On your feet), and as they left, she called, "*Bar ja*" (On your seat). We had to raise our right hand with our index finger outstretched to ask permission to ask questions, answer questions, and when we wanted to go to the bathroom, "*Ejazeh? ma berim dast be ab?*" (Permission, may we [I] go to the washroom?)

We called each other by our surnames—it was not unusual not to know the first names of our best friends. We also addressed our own person as the plural "we," and never "I." "I" or "me" was rude and selfish. "*Khanoom ejazeh, inna ma ro mizanand!*" (Teacher, they are [she is] hitting us [me]!) "*Aqa ejazeh, inna darand khoraki mikhorand*" (Permission, sir, they are [he/she is] eating, sir), one of the students in the classroom would report. My husband recalls:

The teacher came to the accused boy and told him to open his mouth. He had his mouth full of rock-hard, dried apricots. The teacher got his ruler out to hit the boy for eating in the classroom. "*Aqa ejazeh. Aqa be khoda dashtam khiseshan mikardim baraye zang e tafrih, Aqa ejazeh*" (Sir, we [I] were [was] soaking them for the recess, sir).

The bell rang after two hours for a half-hour recess. We all went out and walked around in the yard; two by two or at times five or six of us holding on to each other's elbows circling the yard. Some girls were very popular, and many other girls would want to walk around in their group. The fans were called *barooni*. The word means "raincoat," but I have no idea why it was used as a term for devoted fans who literally worshiped their idol and were willing to do anything for her. Some girls were barooni for the teachers. They waited for the teacher to come to school and followed her from the street to the teachers' office and walked her home after school, one or two steps behind.

Most girls kept a diary and had their favorite people write in it. The most common things to write were poetry from our many poets. For some closer friends we bought beautiful postcards of a rose, a kitten, or a cute baby, and glued it in their memory book. For the most special friends, a flattened, dried-up flower, was added.

Morning sessions ended at twelve noon when we all went home for lunch and then again walked back to school for the afternoon session at two o'clock, rain or shine.

We wore gray uniforms on top of our clothes called *ropoosh e ormak*. They were made of cotton broadcloth, and we wore a separate white collar. Our uniforms had two pockets. Backpacks had not been introduced to us yet, so we carried our few books in our hands and never left any of our school materials inside our drawers; we carried the smaller items such as pencils, erasers, snacks, stones for our games, and so on in our pockets.

Our snacks consisted of dried fruits, especially figs, salted roasted chickpeas, and raisins. The school custodian sold some snacks, and we bought *lavashak* (fruit roll) on our way home.

For physical education we wore puffed-up green shorts and white shirts. During the hours of physical education we performed synchronized movements. Some of our best performers prepared to perform in the parade on October 26, Mohammad Reza Shah's birthday.

Each elementary grade had one main teacher (home teacher) who covered all the subjects. In upper grades, third grade and up, other teachers for calligraphy, Koran, sewing, and so on were added. English as a second language started in seventh grade. However, private schools taught English from first grade. All the textbooks were given to us by the Ministry of Education and were the same across the country. We were required to keep our books clean and return them to the school at the end of the year (no one ever did!). Therefore we spent the first night of the school year making covers for our textbooks with clean construction paper, and we glued a label on the front with the name of the book. It was improper to write on or draw in our books; the cleaner we kept our books, the better. Some of us had to read the books so many times that by the end of the year the book looked swelled up! I usually buried my books after the finals; they were dead!

The Koran was specially guarded. We were not actually allowed to put our fingers on the holy words so we made an arrow (*choob* or *chooq alef*) out of paper to use to point to the verses.

In first grade we started learning the alphabet and the numbers, and in a short time we were required to memorize poetry. Graduating from the first grade was a big achievement. The first sentence of the second grade book read: "Thank God we have come to the second grade." Homework in elementary school mostly consisted of writing from the Farsi book in our notebooks and memorizing prose and poems by Sa'di. If we made a mistake in writing any of the words, we were assigned to write that word numerous times—the parents made sure we do not write them in a column (*raj zadan*); somehow it was faster to write letter by letter, a hundred times in a row!

In reality, almost all students, no matter how slow, were allowed to pass the first couple of grades. Seldom did a so-called lazy student have to repeat the first grade. Even then with someone's recommendation the school allowed him or her to graduate to at least third grade to be called literate. He or she sat in the class as a visitor *"mostame azad"* (auditor) and was not responsible for homework and was never called upon to go to the blackboard.

In third grade the subjects of history, geography, religion and Koran, essay writing, social studies, drawing and calligraphy were added to the curriculum, which made the third grade one of the most challenging. I hated my third-grade teacher and had dreams of seeing her being dragged on the floor of the school hallway, night after night. She was thin and tall, with a haircut above her ears and absolutely no sense of humor. She wore a dark gray suit and the same suit all year round. Our first-grade teacher was so much more stylish; the second-grade teacher was round, kind, and homey.

The grading system was from zero to twenty. Report cards were made of thick papers in different colors of blue, yellow, or pale orange. The grades were written using fountain pens—the zero was highlighted with a line on each side to secure it (-0-) and the grade twenty was written nice and clean followed by the word "*afarin* (bravo)."

Our Baba had bought a bag of tangerines on his way home. Bibi went to him and said, 'How could you not get a present for Sayeh? She got such a clean report card with all twenties and a hundred *afarin*?' Our Baba was quick to say, 'I got her a bag of tangerines!

I am proud to say that I got a bag of tangerines for my second grade 20 GPA! The best present I have ever received; I ate all of them.

The day we got our report cards was exciting for some and dreadful for others. Those of us with good report cards waved it all the way home as we ran and those of us with bad report cards hid it and said that it was not ready yet.

"*Tamam e noomeh daroon, noomeh darand* (All who have achieved have their papers to show with pride).

Man e bi noomeh sar dar peesh daram (Not me, my head is down in shame; nothing worth showing.)," Bibi recited this poem with a sigh.

Due to the heterogeneous nature of the students' learning abilities, success in a grade had become a team effort. It had become an unwritten obligation to help each other pass the exams or do our homework; we did not consider this cheating. In fact when a student bent over her examination sheet so no one could see, putting a book or a barrier between herself and the student next to her, everyone resented her, calling her stingy; she was not to be trusted as a friend. The rest of us went out of our way to yell out the answer or leave our examination sheets wide open and at our friends' disposal.

Any incident out of the ordinary routine was a sudden lift of the pressure and made us laugh from the bottom of our hearts. When the normal pattern of the classroom was interrupted for any reason, we found a chance to interact from the front of the classroom all the way to the last rows. Even the least curious of us would leave her seat and start to run around wanting to participate in change, making it a struggle for the class representative or the teacher to restore order in the classroom. Those interruptions could be anything from tripping over on the way to the blackboard to when the teacher dropped the chalk or even a sneeze; all of those were welcomed. When a student from an upper class was dragged to a lower class for punishment, not only was she not humiliated, she was celebrated for having brought some novelty; she became a hero in our eyes. Those students usually stood in the corner of the class and made us laugh.

Some of us in our family went to public school throughout elementary, middle school, and high school, and some were sent to private schools. The private elementary school was more modern, European style. They went from morning till four in the afternoon and had lunch in their cafeteria. They had ballet and music lessons. The principal of a private school was a foreign-educated man who also hosted a children's program on the radio. The program started with a musical theme: "*Chish Chish, ghow ghow*" and then Mr. Bani Adam's voice announced, "Let's Make a Better World." He was a friend of our Baba and had talked him into sending one or two of his children to his school, Jahan e Tarbiat, and of course Nafiseh and Banafsheh were always up to the challenge.

Most of us went to Sa'di public school. Sa'di was one of the first teacher training schools for girls and the elementary program was part of their training.

◆ ◆ ◆

Our generation had just come out of the traditional schoolhouses of our parents' time. The traditional schoolhouses were called *maktabkhaneh*, which were meant to teach the Koran to boys and girls. The girl's *maktabkhaneh* had added domestic skills such as teaching sewing and embroidery to young girls. Bibi and her sisters had home schooling in Borazjan—the woman from the *maktabkhaneh* came to their house to teach them the Koran, Sa'di, and basic math. The men of the family went to *maktabkhaneh* for elementary education and were mostly sent to Najaf or Karbela for higher education in religion. Most men of our family, including our father and great uncle, Ali Dashti, and his brothers who were among the best-dressed European-style gentlemen, wore the Islamic turban at one point.

Starting in the 1920s, many young people of the upper class families were sent to the boarding schools of Europe, especially Switzerland, France and England. At the same time, many European schools opened branches in Tehran: French, German, and Italian schools. Some of our friends (Shohreh, Afsaneh, Ashofteh) went to a Catholic school near our Khazar House (Sohail School). They told us amazing stories about their adventures as they disobeyed the nuns, much different from our uneventful school days.

Talieh and Badieh were sent to the Baghchehban school for the deaf and mute before they went to regular schools. This was not because they had any problems with hearing or speaking, it was only because Mr. Asgharzadeh (Baghchehban) was a friend of the family and the school was conveniently located right next to our house (*Khaneh ye Shahr*). Both my sisters had learned some sign language. When Baghchehban school moved from our neighborhood, a very large co-ed Jewish elementary school was established in its place.

Mr. Aziz Hayyem, the principal of the Jewish school, was kind enough to let us sit in the classes and to participate in their ceremonies and celebrations simply because we were their neighbors. They had Hebrew, French, and music as part of their curriculum. We had learned some of each and practiced the songs and the dances at home. Our plays were then spoken with a French accent, not knowing the meanings of the words:

Contra poolo van do jan, lap rem yer e mash de van,
lance konci laprom ye
latra zema shodeh yeh.
The rest of the lyrics were replaced by:
La la la la la la la . . .

The public schools we went to were mostly within walking distance of our residence. Sa'di and Dori elementary schools and Parvin E`tesami High School were about a half-hour walk from our house, *Khaneh ye Shahr*. When we moved to Shemiran, we walked from Qolhak (Fereshteh Elementary School) to Elahieh and our brothers went to elementary school next to our house Elahieh Elementary School). The junior and high schools (Jannat and Shahnaz girls' high schools, Jam and Shahriar for boys and Nakhshab private school for Nafiseh and Banafsheh), were also within a half-hour walking distance from our houses in Shemiran. When my brother Mohammad Hassan (Dadashi) finished elementary school, he was sent to

Alborz College. Doctor Mohammad Ali Mojtahedi, whom my parents deeply believed in, was the head of Alborz.[3] Almost every day, Bibi walked to the bus station by the British Embassy to receive him. If he were a minute late the whole neighborhood found out about it! Abbas, my younger brother who had a passion and an extraordinary talent for mechanics, was entrusted to the capable hands of Nafisy Technical School.[4]

From Sa'di, we walked home challenging each other by walking on the edges of small canals (*jooy*), down small alleys, and hopped on the hopscotch drawings on the ground for a quick match. As we got braver with age, we challenged the boys who walked home on the other sides of the streets as they sang:

Pesar ha shirand, mesl e shamshirand
Dokhtara mooshand, mesl e khargooshand

[Boys are lions, as sharp as swords
Girls are mice, they are like rabbits]

We sang back reversing the order:
Dokhtara shirand, mesl e shamshirand
Pesara mooshand, mesl e khargooshand
or
Adasi, farda morkhasi [Lentil says, "Tomorrow is the day off."]
to which the response was:
Loobia, farda zood bia [Chili bean says, "Come early tomorrow."]

On our way to and from high school, we walked home faster and were more careful not to be distracted by cars passing by honking, mothers blocking our way looking for a nice girl for their sons, asking for our addresses, gypsies following us to tell our fortune, or young boys studying on our street. Elahieh streets were crowded with young men preparing for the university entrance exam (*konkoor*). They walked under the mulberry trees, by the open canals, or by the creek. Some of them camped out and studied all day, way into the night, using the streetlights and the serenity of Tighestan; another obstacle in our way.

Rote learning was used in the mastery of all the subjects, complex or basic. We memorized everything, phonics in reading, multiplication tables in mathematics, history, geography, and all the other subjects; walking around and studying out loud with a rhythm seemed to help. We were so used to moving around that when we were called in front of the class to read, we swung back and forth, back and forth. When our memory was blocked, we begged for a clue: "Would you say the first word? Please, would you?" After much begging, someone whispered the first word and away we went, all the way to the end; we memorized the books, word by word not leaving out a single vowel (*vav ja nemigzashtim*).

Bibi was certainly intrigued by the whole process and made us practice at home. She asked us the multiplication table: 7x8=? 9x6=? and so on and she quizzed us all day, wherever she found us. She also asked us to recite the poetry we were supposed to memorize; she knew them all herself. She corrected our history lessons, geography, and most every subject.

❖ ❖ ❖

I wonder who Bibi would have become if she had had *A Room of (Her) Own?*[5] Would she have been a writer, a politician, a judge maybe? She certainly had the gift, the genius in her. She was adventurous, had imagination, and cared about the world as much as our father, our great-uncle, and her father. She was well read and she spoke her mind, but all that did not leave the house. Instead, she insisted that all her children have the highest education possible, both her daughters and her sons. Talieh was one of the first women who went to the University of Tehran and finished her master's degree, so did Badieh. Badieh was sent to England to pursue her education and career; they both became career women. Our brothers too were sent abroad for higher education.

She expected us to have a major role in society. She could not hide her disappointment if any of us did not accomplish that.

I had worked hard to make a beautiful home and an extensive social life while I was raising my children. When Bibi came to visit us in Los Angeles, I carefully asked, "Mamman, do you see all this?" "Yes, but what do *you* do?" she said sarcastically.

Students performing at Jahan e Tarbiat School. Photos: Dashti family album.

Students parade at the Shah's birthday. Photo: Dashti family album.

Notes

1   From historicaliran.blogspot.com/2013/01/khalil-oghab.html: "Khalil Oqab was born in Shiraz in 1924. During his younger years he was active in *Varzesh'e Bastani* (an ancient sport) and subsequently became involved in strongman shows. He was the founder of the first strongman show in Iran that charged an admission and included other acts such as music, acrobatics, and animal tricks. He was also the first man to bring back lions and bears from India for trained animal acts."

2   Anthony Quinn in the 1954 movie, *La Strada*.

3   Y. Armajani, "Alborz College," Encyclopædia Iranica, I/8, pp. 821-823; an updated version is available online at http://www.iranicaonline.org. Doctor Mohammad Ali Mojtahedi (1908–1997) who was one of the one hundred students sent to Europe on a government fund (1931) had returned to Iran to serve his country (1938). He was chosen as the head of Alborz School (1944). Besides many other academic and governmental positions, in 1965 he was assigned to establish the Aryamehr Technical University (Sharif University). "For thirty-seven years Mojtahedi was the head of a school which produced 50,000 graduates— the best of the best." From the book by Habib Ladjevardi, *Tarikh e moaser e Iran be ravayat e tarikh sazan: Khaterat e Mohammad Ali Mojtahedi*. Iranian Oral History Project Harvard University. (Tehran: Safheh ye Sefid, 1st ed., 2006; 3rd ed., 2012).

4   Habib Ladjevardi (compiler), *Nafisy, Habib*, Harvard Iranian Oral History Project, Harvard University, interview conducted in 1984. After finishing his practical training in Germany, Habib Nafisy returned to Iran in 1938. In 1943 he became the Director of Labor Affairs in the Ministry of Commerce and Industries. In this position he was instrumental in drafting the first comprehensive labor laws in Iran in 1946. After the establishment of the Ministry of Labor in the same year, he became Undersecretary of Labor, a position he held until 1950. During the Mosaddeq period, Habib Nafisy was instrumental in establishing the Ministry of Industries and Mines, with himself serving as Undersecretary, a post he continued to hold under the Zahedi cabinet in the mid-1950s. In this position he was credited with establishing one of the first industrial estates (industrial zones) for light industries at Karaj west of Tehran. In the late 1950s, Nafisy was named Undersecretary for Technical and Vocational Education in the Ministry of Education with the mission to reinvigorate and expand that type of education, which had been initiated during the reign of Reza Shah Pahlavi. In that position he established some one hundred technical and vocational schools throughout Iran. He established the Tehran Polytechnic University (now Amir Kabir University) as well, which emphasized practical engineering education. He also established the Technical Teachers College (now Elm o Sana't University), and the Higher Commercial College (Madresseh Aali e Bazargani), both in Tehran. In 1963, Habib Nafisy was appointed Cultural Councilor, with the rank of Chargé d'Affaires, and Supervisor of Iranian Students in the United States and Canada at the Iranian Embassy in Washington, D.C., a position he held until 1966. He established the Nafisy Technikum, a private, combined technical college and secondary technical school, which placed emphasis on practical work. He spent most of his effort in the 1970s on developing that institution. At the same time in the 1970s he was asked to serve as Undersecretary for Human Resources Development at the Ministry of Transportation, on a part-time basis. He held these two positions until the 1979 revolution.

5   *A Room of One's Own* is an extended essay by Virginia Woolf. First published on October 24, 1929, the essay was based on a series of lectures she delivered at Newnham College and Girton College, two women's colleges at Cambridge University in October 1928.

Twenty-Five

NoRouz: It Happened Once a Year

NoRouz 1338 (1959). Left to right: Sayeh, Badieh, Talieh, Mohammad Hossain (with back to camera), Sepideh (above), Aqda'i, Bibi, Mohammad Hassan (Dadashi), Nafiseh, and Abbas. Photo taken at *Khaneh ye Shahr*, Tehran.

The bazaars were filled with shoppers, rushing, bargaining for a better price, buying a few items of new clothing for NoRouz. Most shops offered candies and cookies creating a festive experience.

We were told repeatedly not to get too excited in front of the shop owners who would raise the price based on the sparkles in our eyes, an instinct most difficult to hide. It was equally challenging to hide our embarrassment when the suggested price was suddenly cut to one-tenth or even lower by the adults (usually our aunts) accompanying us. The vendor and the shopper would get into the most outrageous back and forth bargaining, all part of the ritual of shopping for NoRouz. He would come up with a random price, she persisted that what he had was worth nothing and that her children hated it anyhow. We would have tears in our eyes; she would drag us out of the shop reassuring us that the man is going to come after us and he usually did. She would warn us not to look back. We could hardly breathe with apprehension. He almost always called out after we had gone about twenty meters passed his booth, or he sent his workman to bring us back. If that happened, we had won. The bargaining would start again; however, this time, it was geared toward a compromise. If by any chance he did not call us back in, we went back to him defeated. All that was resolved once the roll of fabric was thrown in the air to allow the fabric to flow down the vendor's stall. He took a hold of the large roll from both ends, pushed it to his chest several times to allow the stream of material to get longer and longer to the exact measurement. To make up for his guilty feelings of overcharging, he would give a few centimeters extra as a present in the spirit of NoRouz. He then took the large scissors, blew on it for blessing and said, "I hope it blesses you (*mobarak basheh*)," a win/win situation.

The men vendors sometimes had an old Koran to swear by; promising that the price was right and that they are not making any profit out of the deal. They went as far as threatening to tear up the Koran or to step on it, just to convince us that they were telling the truth. Most vendors standing behind their stalls on top of many rolls of fabric had a Koran in their hands, shaking it while calling out loud for customers to visit their stalls. No sin is bigger in the minds of a Moslem. We knew that they were not Moslems—the textile industry in Tehran was run by Jewish people—in our minds no one, of any religion, should ever disrespect the Holy Book. Therefore, in spite of that information, it did have an effect on the Moslem shoppers. Bibi never had the patience to bargain, and before things led to blasphemy, she gave up each time and we got the goods; it was definitely more exciting to go with our aunts.

A feverish joy mixed with excitement and doubt usually followed. Our older sisters including Banafsheh and Bibi had a tailor, Asad. "Could he do it on time?" we worried. All the tailors were booked before the New Year's, and Asad happened to be the best in Tehran. How could he possibly cut and sew, do the first fitting and the second fitting in just a few days? No one seemed to have planned ahead!

Our little brothers were dressed in formal suits and ties from a store called General Mode in the shopping district of Lalehzar, Tehran. General Mode was the first American-style showroom of a factory that produced ready-made suits for boys (late 1950s). The store carried all sizes of suits for boys. For some reason the suits were chosen one, two, or three sizes larger, just in case. Nafiseh, Sepideh, and I were dressed with the most special clothes from a store called Pechela on Lalehzar, Berlin Koucheh. The shop imported European clothes from Italy and France. We got new shoes, new socks, new everything from top to bottom. Somehow, luckily, with the help of many aunts, friends of the family, and the sewing machine running all day and night, everyone in the house was ready on time, even if it was a few minutes before NoRouz.

It all happened once a year; it was an obligation for all families to go shopping for their children a few days before NoRouz. Even the very poor found ways to dress their children with new things for the occasion. Piles of new clothes and shoes were collected at every school, at businesses, and in most neighborhoods for the children who could not afford new outfits.

NoRouz marks the first day of spring or the vernal equinox. It is celebrated on the day of the spring equinox, which usually occurs around March twenty-first or the previous/following day depending on where it is observed. The moment that the sun crosses the celestial equator is calculated precisely every year and it marks the beginning of the year in the Persian calendar, the beginning of spring. Regardless of the hour, families stay awake and alert to celebrate the event with certain rituals.

A cloth spread (*sofreh*) filled with designated items called *haft seen* (seven S's) was arranged in our house in the salon, the best room of the house. The essential elements on our *sofreh* were a mirror—symbolizing the sky; a book of Hafez's poetry and the Koran—telling us what to look for in the coming year; candles—symbolizing fire, one for each child and two for the parents; live goldfish—symbolizing animals; and seven items starting with the letter "S" each symbolizing an aspect of prosperity: earth (*seeb* [apple]), love (*senjed* [oleaster or wild olive]), rebirth (*sabzeh* [wheat sprouts]), color of sunrise (*sumaq* [sumac]), old age (*serkeh* [vinegar]), affluence (*samanu* [wheat germ]), and for health we put (*seer* [garlic]).[1]

We painted the eggs by putting them in solutions of dyes and watched them turn blue, green, and pink. The *sabzeh* was prepared about ten days before the New Year. We grew wheat in a couple of large plates—they began sprouting from the seed in silver roots and then green stems appeared like a miracle. By the time it was the thirteenth day of NoRouz, we had to throw them away. It was a good thing that we did, because they started to have a bad smell by then and were growing so tall that they hung from the sides of the dish, looking old.

Tehranis have always been very big on ceremonies. They grow all kinds of beans for NoRouz such as: wheat, lentils, vetch, or chickpeas. They grow them artistically in dishes and even on and around an earthenware jug. They put ribbons around them and trim them to be all perfectly even. They look after their *sabzeh* compulsively, while having many superstitions about the way their *sabzeh* behaves—interpreting its growth with the character of the person starting it, or how the year was going to turn out. Our family had none of that. *Sabzeh* was lucky to be there! Our *sabzeh* was completely natural and untrimmed with no decorations. It looked uneven, but it was beautiful, having made it against all odds. The event or circumstances never dictated how things were supposed to be or who we were. The only thing we did not like was when one of the candles went out before its time. They should have burned for hours until finally extinguished. The candles stood erect, planted in soil in an oval-shaped serving dish. By the next day, the wax had spread and integrated into a beautiful abstract design, like the icing on a chocolate cake.

It also mattered that we were all in new clothes and seated by the *sofreh* at the exact moment the sun crossed the spring zone no matter what time of the day or night. If NoRouz happened to be in the middle of the night—two or three in the morning for example, we were all woken up, showered, and dressed in new clothes and sat by the *sofreh e haft seen*. Without an exception for some reason, however, someone would run to get something while everyone else worried, "What if the person does not make it in time?"

It was so essential that we wore a smile, did not fight, and felt genuine happiness, believing that the emotion we felt at the *sofreh* we were going to feel it throughout the coming year.

Our father read a poem by Hafez as we made a wish and then we marched around the table counting down from ten to zero bringing the house down with joy as soon as the New Year was announced by the radio, or television, accompanied by the sound of cannons going off from one of the main squares in downtown Tehran (*Toop-khaneh*). We then stood in a row according to our ages to kiss our parents' hands as they kissed our foreheads; an exchange of eternal love demonstrated once a year; so complete there was no need for reconfirmation during the year.

The beautiful city of Tehran with its four perfect seasons participates fully by suddenly turning from dry colorless winter into fresh green and multicolored spring. The streets are washed and cleaned; there are no traces of the muddy piles of snow. The small streams of water running alongside the streets (*jooybar*) are sparkling with fresh water. People look renewed and the houses are immaculate.

For spring cleaning of our house, every single item in the house was usually taken outdoors to be washed, repaired, or replaced before it was allowed back inside—carpets, drapes, every piece of china, utensils, clothes, . . . none were exempt. The *korsi*s were put away and some of the furniture would be rearranged. The storerooms, the basements, and the stairways to the roof were emptied and cleaned. Even the yards were cultivated, fertilized, and new plants, flowers, and grass were planted. The special flowers for the New Year are pansies (*banafsheh*), hyacinths (*sonbol*), and daisies in a variety of colors. The aroma of freshness and cleanliness, the excitement of getting everything ready for New Year's Day is shared by every one of all ages.

Aside from the immaculate habitats, the hearts too are obliged to be cleansed of resentments, hatred, and anger. Friendships are to be renewed and differences worked out by that day. The tradition is for the younger people to pay a visit to the older people first, and then the visits are returned. Our judgment whether anyone is liked or disliked, good or bad, is irrelevant; if they are related, they must be respected and visited. At any hour of the day for twelve days everyone is ready and dressed up to receive guests or to go visit family and friends.

Clearly a special part of the New Year for children was getting gifts (*eidi*) from the family. Everyone had new bills to give to the young, depending on the amount they could afford. Everyone was extremely generous and gave away money no matter how poor they were.[2]

When NoRouz, the purest, most joyous, and wondrous event arrived with such rich history, we felt that we were part of its glory. The house was most festive—the kitchen was busy with a hired cook and so many fancy meals were prepared to welcome our guests of honor; our great-uncle, Ali Dashti, and his guests usually gave us the honor first. Men wore suits and the ladies were fashionable and beautiful. We would run around in the hallways waiting for things to happen. Our new shoes sounded new on the tiles. In the next few days when the squeaking wore off, we sprinkled sugar on the tiles to get the same glorious effect. On those days we were allowed to go in and out of the guest room to join the adults. The smells of perfume, freshly peeled oranges, and foreign cigarettes were intoxicating.

Every time we got our *eidi*, we would run out to the hallway to count and compare our riches with each other. We got the most *eidi* from our great-uncle; he was thoughtful enough to remember which one of us had come to the age of getting a present instead of money. So we knew when we had been confirmed as young ladies or young men, according to his gifts to us—a perfume or an expensive pen.

A group of guests would eventually get up to say good-bye. Unfortunately for us they would continue the farewell talk for an everlasting time in the hallway as we, the kids, waited impatiently to sneak into the guest room to eat cookies.

Our family was the first to be visited. After the first few days of NoRouz, it was our turn to visit them back. The priority was with the families who had lost a loved one during the past year. After that we visited the elderly and the friends who had visited us. Our extended families did not live in Tehran. Nevertheless,

Bibi and our Baba had a large circle of friends who had to be visited. They did not take all of us along; not to every visit; we were chosen randomly. Bibi must have calculated the expenses of the hosts. We also never stayed for a meal during NoRouz. The visits were limited to a tea and a cookie. We knew we should not accept the offer of fruits. "It is too costly for them," Bibi always said. Some people were allowed to give us *eidi*. Mr. Kayvan, a friend of the family, gave us fountain pens every year and Mrs. Ayatollah Zadeh, Bibi's friend, gave us small change from the middle of a Koran. It was supposed to be blessed but we hated it. Nafiseh of course never let her get away with this and insisted on getting more. She stood there like Oliver Twist and kept asking, "May I have another one?" That is how brave she was!

The holidays brought many special events. Many vendors would come to the neighborhood selling special treats from their wagons or loaded on their donkeys. They were eloquent and had usually made a song announcing their spring goods, "*Ay gol pooneh na'na pooneh, Nobar e bahar e gol pooneh*" advertising the fresh spring herbs. And the ice-cream man came with his bucket of ice cream on his head, "*Ay bastani, ay bastani, nobar e bahar e bastani, qand o gol ab e bastani* (ice cream, ice cream, it's the first of the season, sugar and rose water, ice cream)."

It was our family's tradition to go see a play once a year during the NoRouz holiday. The plays were mostly comedies. Great comedians such as Tafakori or Arham e Sadr made us cry with laughter. Suddenly movie theaters replaced the playhouses in Tehran; however, our tradition prevailed; we went to see a movie instead. Some of the films were made in Iran, and some were romantic musicals from either Egypt or India. It was not until years later, in the 1950s, when Western movies, dubbed in Farsi, found their way into the Iranian movie theaters.

On the thirteenth day (*sizdeh be dar*), our family rented a big bus to go out of the city and into nature. It was a blessing that the picnic was nonnegotiable. It was mandatory for all families to get out of the house and out of the city to spend a day outdoors in nature. No one could be visited on the thirteenth day of NoRouz. Bus after bus, rows of cars, motorcycles, carriages, etc. took people of the city to the parks, gardens, or alongside the roads in the countryside.

By the thirteenth, the families, already exhausted by constant visits, were ready to leave their homes. The roots of the *sabzeh*s were dense by that day and could easily be lifted from the plates, destined to be thrown into the running water. The vehicles carrying the families also carried their *sabzeh*s; they were put on the roof of the cars, on the antennas, or held by a lady sitting on the back of a motorcycle with the rest of her family as the husband let the handles go once in a while to dance to the music of the cars passing by.

The Argani family (Zohi's family), who were our family's closest friends, joined us on *sizdeh be dar*. Bibi always sat behind the bus driver, making sure he did not fall asleep or was not distracted by his helper sitting next to him in the front passenger seat. Bibi made sure the guy also stayed alert; she sat there by herself. Behind her were the other adults of the two families (I do not recall my father or Mr. Argani accompanying us on any *sizdeh be dar*). The rest of the bus was occupied by all the children, about fourteen of us. All the way to and from the picnic, we sang and we laughed—we were as loud as our throats permitted; no inhibitions. The Arganis were able to break our pattern. The back of the bus was filled with a humongous pile of heads of Romaine lettuce cut in half, wrapped in a sheet, bottles of oxymel (vinegar and honey), samovar and teapots, plates and silverware, pots of cooked rice mixed with lima beans, dill and lamb, plus all the leftover cookies, nuts, and fruit from the houses of both families. We drove out of the city for about two or three hours and eventually parked in a green and vast area to spend the day.[3] We performed all the rituals: playing dodgeball with a soccer ball, "*joftak char kosh*,"[4] "*alak do lack*,"[5] throwing thirteen rocks into the water (symbolizing parting from thirteen evil deeds), secretly tying the grass or weeds (symbolizing falling in love or getting married). We ate and drank and dipped our lettuce heads into the oxymel.

Finally, exhausted from all the excitement, it was time to return home and get ready for school the next day. It was a moment of harsh reality for all who had not worked first to play later! As we tried to finish or, in some cases just start, the inhumane, cruel load of homework, the parents could not help but seem relieved!

Sizdeh be dar with the Arganis (1956). Photo: Dashti family album.

Notes

1   Recent additions to the *sofreh* of most families are photos of family members around the world. As soon as the New Year is announced, everyone is walking around the *sofreh* with cell phones trying to reach their families abroad.

2   A beggar lady gave me a large bill this New Year (2014)!

3   Khazar Street, our address now, was once a large vacant lot where we went for *sizdeh be dar* in the early 1950s.

4   A game from Dashtestan: Four people bend over as the last person jumps over the three and if he succeeds, he bends over and the first person gets up and jumps over the other three. The big challenge is to jump without the use of your hands.

5   A game with two teams: each team tries to toss a short stick, using a longer stick, towards the opposite team.

Twenty-Six
And the Colors Testify There Is a God

A gift from my cousin Amir Mahallati, 1992.

Our father knew how special the thin shiny metal foils were to us. He usually saved the chocolates he was offered at parties; he put them in his pocket to bring us the magical chocolate. He brought them home and watched our eyes light up when we saw the colorful wrappers.

With the backs of our thumbnails, we flattened and smoothed the thin foils, yellow, green, red, and blue. Besides the basic colors, occasionally there were incredible surprises. Our Baba, like a loving magician, took a chocolate from his pocket; his fist still closed, he opened it gently in front of our wondering eyes. He was holding the sun, a gold wrapper!

A drawing was prepared ahead of time by an adult. A pencil drawing of a house—a sun shining in the sky, a person nearby, and some clouds scattered around—was the usual theme. We held our breaths as the adult confidently, rather heartlessly, cut into the drawing, around the lines and made a hollow house, a hollow sun; the human drawn by the house turned into a frightening ghost when its face was cut out. Quickly the thin layers of the wrappers that were kept flat in the middle of a schoolbook were handed to the artist one by one. The drawing was turned over and the foils were put into place. A thin layer of *serishom* (fish glue) attached the edges of the foils in their proper places. The world seemed inside out for a while, during which time nothing made sense, a void. Then the artwork was turned over; a colorful and playful masterpiece was created.

As the hues processed in our brains, the drawing gained meaning: the sun started to shine bright, shedding light over the roof of the house that turned it into a glowing mansion. The sky, well represented with a drop of vivid blue (we did not have enough blue to cover the whole sky), became touchable, and the human figure turned into a person, every pigment brought life!

An artwork made with chocolate wrappers. Photo: Dashti family album.

Tehran is in a basin surrounded with gigantic mountains interlaced with bare hills, a towering display of grey and earth tones. Before the 1970s, there were very few visible green spots in the city—and the colorful private gardens were usually hidden from the eyes by tall brick or mud-brick walls. Most everything our eyes met was either in black, white, or very subtle colors. Color prints were not introduced in our country before the 1950s. Our schoolbooks were in black and white with dark tan covers.

The television, the movies, the photos were all in black, white, and shades of gray. Buildings were mostly made of earth tone bricks; there were no colorful billboards on the streets. The traffic lights caught the eyes, as they turned to bright red and then green. The proper color of clothing for men, women, and children was a subtle color and the very bright patterned fabrics were considered rustic, lacking the sophistication of the elite lifestyle. Gray school uniforms, black-and-white schoolbooks, black ink, black pencils, etc. were what our eyes knew the most.

Bibi had a red satin dressing gown that we only saw in her closet and adored. The ruby of a pomegranate seed, the bloody wild tulip in the middle of a plain, the turquoise color of the eyes of our Queen Soraya, a postcard of a princess holding an umbrella in full color with glitter, which my sister Badieh owned, brought us true rapture.

The dominant cliché that "black is for funerals" made the color black forbidden clothing in our family. The color black is now a new black! Even though the Tehrani girls wear mostly black at parties, we were the few who wore colors.

For years, none of us owned a black dress—an overcoat in black was acceptable, but nothing black was allowed to be attached to our bodies. When there was an actual funeral, we were presented with a dilemma—we could not find a solid black outfit in our wardrobes hence we had to mismatch it by borrowing from each other. When we did finally wear black to a funeral, we had to take it off before we entered the house, certainly before Bibi saw us. For her own funeral, we had to shop for black clothing and most of us did not wear black for more than the first forty days (*chelleh*) after her death.

◆ ◆ ◆

Once or twice a year, usually around NoRouz, there were street entertainers who brought the kingdom of colors to our alleys. A man carrying a golden metal device (a Mutoscope) on his back, walked around our neighborhoods and showed us colorful slides, ten *shahi* (about a penny) for a minute; a true bargain. He put his magical golden box (*shahr e farang*) on the ground and called out: "*Shahr e farangeh, az hameh rangeh, bia va tamasha kon* (Come! It's a fantasy land, it is in every color, come and watch for yourself)." Every child and adult ran out to the street and paid him to put their eyes on the peepholes to watch the colorful slides, as the man turned the slides and told stories about the pictures. The device had couple of viewer windows, where three to four people could watch at the same time. The slides were random pictures of some places in Europe, a skier, a horse carriage, some pictures of the queen of some foreign land, etc. None of the subjects actually mattered to us. We were not after identifying the characters or the locations, we were not after increasing our knowledge; we were thirsty for colors and the device took us directly to the kingdom.

Shahr e Farang. Photo: Daryoush Tahami.

"Why was it that even though our homes, all the rooms, and sometimes the hallways were carpeted with Persian rugs with the most amazing colors, we were still thirsty for colors? Why was it that the abundance of colors on the Persian carpet did not surprise our eyes?" I asked my brother who is an astrologer.

My brother Mohammad Hassan (Dadashi) had the answer:

The colorful design of the Persian carpet is beautiful and so gentle to the eyes; it tells the story of creation in the most artistic way. The colors and symbols are representations of the cosmos as it is known in our ancient culture. The design and the colors of the carpets embody a galactic, solar and philosophical coding system. They also match the four elements of the universe: Water, Fire, Earth and Wind, 'The Four Sacred Elements of Nature' originated by the Persian prophet, Zartosht [Zarathustra].

The sun = orange
The moon = green

176

Mars   = red
Mercury = turquoise
Jupiter = yellow
Venus   = light blue
Saturn = purple
Jupiter = yellow (color of saffron)

Most rugs also include the two colors of infrared and ultraviolet, symbolizing the two hypothetical stars where the energies of the earth and the moon meet.

The knots are so delicately woven (as fine as more than hundreds of knots per square inch)[1] they feel like the density of our own body; a sacred part of nature we had learned to be respectful of without being mindful of it.

Reaching the edge of a Persian carpet, we take our shoes off: cosmos under our feet!

Persian carpet. Photo: Sayeh Dashti, at the Persian rug exhibition in Tehran, 2014.

Notes

[1] In Iran the carpet density is measured by *raj*, the number of knots in the length of a regular cigarette on the back of the rug.

Twenty-Seven
Have I Been to the Zoo?

As part of its modernization, Tehran, like any other major city, acquired a zoo. And, as any civilized family would, our family felt obliged to visit it. We had all been looking forward to visiting the zoo for a very long time; we had almost made a song and a parade for our request! Finally one day, we got to go. Permission, however, was not granted to all. My older sisters were allowed to take some of us—a couple of children were left behind to avoid the possible dangers of an unknown place.

We all promised that our lips would be sealed and we would not mention, in any way, that we had been to the zoo. If the siblings whom we had left behind ever found out, there would have been a catastrophe no one could have handled. Anyhow, the order was sealed and we all pledged to it, including our five-year-old brother Abbas. "**No mention of the zoo!**" he was instructed. The pressure of keeping such a big secret was intense. Most of us handled it though, but some were not old enough to understand the consequences of things or what keeping a secret meant.

Tehran's zoo was a peculiar place by any standards. The garden of a charitable rich man in North Tehran had been converted into a zoo. I remember, as its main attraction, a wrinkled elephant was fastened to the ground by the entrance with a short, heavy chain. The lions did not look as powerful as we expected. They appeared so tired that looking at them instilled no fear in us as children. I was certain, even if their cages were open, we could outrun them! We first asked which was the way to the snakes' exhibition hall. This was to make sure that we did not go that way! We had all agreed on that.

The giraffes were fascinating to us though. No matter how much we had heard about giraffes, what we saw was beyond our visualizations. The adjective "tall" went as tall as the pine tree in our backyard or maybe our two-story house. The giraffes provided a new definition of height for a living creature. Their big eyes seemed like windows to unknown souls, decorated with very long lashes; making it peculiar to look inside. They moved and reached for our small hands to take the leaves we were holding with fascination.

The flamingoes and the other birds were more like decorative statues. Again the color combination of the birds and the fish played with our imaginations.

We did not stop by any cage for more than a second. Our restless group was just running around the zoo in one single line; mostly quiet and even wearied. We wanted it to end soon. I suppose the experience was similar to going to a museum of science fiction, fascinating, yet too far from reality.

When we finally finished our visit and sat there outside for ice cream, the real fun started.

Usually when we went out together, an adventure took place. My oldest sister Talieh was our driver; she was one of the first few young girls who drove a car in Tehran. Our first family car was a black 1959 Opel.

Our father's chauffeur was a man called Aseyyed Ali who was an experienced driver. He taught our sister to drive like a professional. When we went out to places like the zoo or just for a ride, all of us sat in that car on top of each other. One time on a *sizdeh be dar* trip, sixteen people sat in that Opel, young and old, family and friends of the family, and our workers. Some of us sat in the open trunk of the car, singing all the way.

Bodies were hanging out of the car windows, wind blowing in our faces as we screamed with excitement. We were not merely passengers in the car; we had work to do. In case the horn was not working, for instance, around each bend, we were ordered by our sister to honk. From the deepest point of our guts, we screeched BOOOOQ. And then laughed like crazy. The following order was to be quiet. "Quiet!" Until the next bend on the street, "Okay, ready? Honk!"

As a routine when we finally got in the car to go out, we made sure to first stop by a certain house in the neighborhood to ring its bell. This is a house on a street parallel to Khazar (Vaseq e Nouri). It is a beautiful garden with a green gate and stone walls. Next to its gate, there is a hemispherical metal window grill with a camel bell inside it. The handle is sticking out of the metal grill, attached to a bell. We took turns and one of us would jump out of the car, grab the handle, and pull it madly to hear the camel bell. Then he or she would run to the car, which was on the move and we drove away. Many times the person running would have to get in the car from the open window headfirst; the car was too full to risk opening its door. Once the kids in the back seat looked back and reported that the gardener had come out and was swearing, our mission was accomplished.

That day on our trip to the zoo, we had many of these adventures. We returned home saturated with pure fun and charged up with excitement.

What now? How was it possible to hide all that?

To help us distract attention from the big secret, we sat around and started playing *Twenty Questions*. This was a serious game. The way we played this game was as rigorous as it was on the radio show *Twenty Questions*, if not more so. We engaged in this game to test each other's sharpness. The panel of judges was merciless and intolerant of any mistakes made by any of the contestants. One would keep count of the questions. No one was allowed to talk or make any comments that might have led to a clue. Even the way we asked the questions, how we categorized our questions, mattered. It was in some ways a test to qualify as a member of some exclusive club (the older siblings).

Abbas was desperate to be part of the game. Bibi begged us to let him play just for one time. So the game began and our five-year-old brother was chosen to be the first contestant.

Abbas's first question: "Have I been to the zoo (*man baagh e vahsh raftam*)?"

A riot erupted!

The same house, the gate, and the doorbell are still here (2014). Photo by Sayeh Dashti.

Twenty-Eight
The Opera Singer / The Pianist

There was no room for the old wooden cabinet when our family moved to a new rental house in North Tehran. It ultimately landed in a small room shared by me and my sisters, virtually taking up the whole room. In some ways it was flattering to have that piece and the special china in it in our room; we were trusted with items of value.

This piece came to be used as a chest of drawers for our clothes, our school stuff, and most importantly, it became my piano! Our guests were led to the small room to watch me perform. I had drawn a keyboard on top of it and spent hours playing that piano. I wonder whether a real performance in front of an audience would have caused me the same stress as when I played the cabinet.

I had created my own soundless music by moving my fingers on that keyboard; obviously irrelevant to how a real piano and notes of any specific music are played. Compulsively, I followed my own notes written as numbers 1, 2, 3; black or white and so on, on papers, in the pages of my school notebooks. If by chance I missed a note, I became utterly embarrassed. I had no knowledge of music nor did I know how to read notes; I simply was a world-renowned pianist in my fantasy world!

Months later, the desire to be that artist gave me the courage to ask my sister, Nafiseh, if she would ask our mother to ask our father to get me a piano, an impossible request! The idea was dismissed immediately. "My daughter? A showgirl? How could anyone of us contemplate such an idea?" was my father's direct response.

We expected that response from our father, yet my sister and I decided not to give up. She was thirteen and I was eleven years old at that time. She wanted to be an opera singer and I wanted to be a pianist. One day we got the courage to visit our next-door neighbor, Monir Vakili,[1] who happened to be one of the most famous opera singers in Iran. Her daughter, Zaza,[2] was our playmate and a regular audience to my piano performances and my sister's operas. We had made an opera just for her—we performed it as a duet over the wall between our houses, calling her to come play with us: "Zaza . . . *zoodi bia* . . . (Zaza, hurry up and come to us . . .)."

Zaza insisted that we should meet with her mother. She was confident that her mother could lead us to our dreams.

Monir Vakili was born into a family of music lovers. Her father had encouraged her love of opera and supported her decision to study abroad in the field of music. Monir Vakili was the creator and founder of the Academy of Voice in Tehran and the founder of the first opera company in Iran. She was one of the pioneers of the Tehran National Conservatory of Music. She was Madama Butterfly as well as all the main characters of the major operas performed in Iran. Her performances were televised, and we watched them with admiration. For her performance as Madama Butterfly, she got a gold medal. We all watched the ceremony on television. Zarafshan could not quite digest the concept regarding our neighbor. She commented, "Oh well, she comes on television, she screeches some, and she gets a gold pen for it? I could do that too!"

One sleepless night, my sister and I decided that we would take the challenge. Indeed it was a challenge to leave the house without anyone finding out where we were going. What do we do? What excuse could we come up with? Without the adults' supervision we could not even find a proper thing to wear.

We must have looked ridiculous wearing our formal New Year's clothing with the rubber boots we wore to school. Somehow we managed, but I do not remember what excuse we came up with, if any; maybe we just disappeared. We ran next door.

Everything about her house was a confirmation of an artist's residence. The black royal grand piano in the middle of the living room, the giant crystal chandeliers, the antique statues, and a butler who led us into the small guest room. He brought us tea and cookies in china on a silver tray. My sister and I were squeezing each other's knees with excitement; we were on our way to fame.

And then the most beautiful woman, much more beautiful than we had seen her on television, came in to the room; so elegant. With her kind smile she welcomed us. She boasted that she knew our parents well. After hearing the story about our love for music and the fact that our parents would not allow it, she seemed puzzled. "But your parents always praise me for my art. How could that be?" My sister and I exchanged glances knowing my parents had complimented her to be polite. This gave us more courage to continue asking her for guidance.

She took us to the grand piano and sat me beside her. Her fingers rested on the keyboard with such ease. My fingers were touching a real keyboard for the very first time. My fingers were so ready, but I was paralyzed. Those keys were alive! I pressed them and the keys actually made a sound! Nafiseh told her, "She is shy, otherwise she can really play."

Ms. Vakili said, "I can see that; her posture is perfect. Zaza has told me about her playing." She told me gently to follow her fingers, but I could not move.

Then it was my sister's turn. She patiently gave her a chance to rehearse with her, asking her to sing along and follow the notes. She seemed impressed by our enthusiasm.

The magic took place; we were stepping up to our dreams, we thought. She picked up the phone and called the Tehran Conservatory of Music, introducing us. She told the manager that her two young friends, mentioning our father's name, would be coming to attend the solfège and basic piano lessons.

We did not know how to react. We just ran out with excitement. Did we properly thank her for her hospitality? I do not remember if we did. We were simply exuberant with joy.

The complications of the real world were gently introducing themselves to our dream world. All right? Now what? How do we get there? Where do we get the money to do it? How do we tell our parents? Is this really what we want to do? None of those questions had been a concern when we played on the wooden cabinet or when we freely mimicked a pianist or an opera singer, not until after we woke up to the reality.

Once more, we got ready and left the house. We had never gone more than a few blocks from our home anywhere; we had never gone that far unless attended by an adult.

We must have walked on the clouds as we left the house with an excuse and took the bus to the conservatory. We entered as two celebrities would, went to the classes with impatience, and took the bus back home.

The bus was overcrowded. Our young feverish bodies were squeezed against the tall glass front windshield of the brand new bus. We were facing the streets and the pavements that ran underneath us, while we imagined ourselves in an airplane flying to Vienna; we felt so ready. Our dream was complete. Unfortunately the complications of reality were real and we quickly decided not to go anymore. Somehow we felt satisfied with that much; we were more comfortable dreaming.

Nafiseh never became an opera singer. She told me she practiced opera when she yelled at her kids. At the age of nineteen, I did get the opportunity to pursue my dream—when I found myself away from the family and in the land of the free. Little did I know that being the greatest pianist meant starting from the basic do-re-mi and that it required practicing hours and hours, day after day after day; a realization! I thought of it as an insult to the perfect image of the pianist, to settle with being just a beginner. Consequently, I abandoned the whole dream! It was beneath me, I thought, to press a key and then concentrate for more than a few minutes to find where my fingers should go next. No! Not in a hundred years.

Being a pianist in the world of fantasy was so effortless. I never became a pianist and I have no one to blame now but my misunderstanding of the reality; the real world required real effort. Monir Vakili was a real artist who had devoted her life to music; I was just a dreamer in love with an image.

Monir Vakili, winner of the Charles Cros Grand Prix award for Album of the Year 1958. Photo: Zaza Saleh collections.

Monir Vakili performing the role of Madama Butterfly in Puccini's opera. Photo: Zaza Saleh collections.

Monir Vakili's house on our street in Elahieh. Photo: Sayeh Dashti, 2014.

Notes

[1]   www.monirvakili.com

Twenty-Nine
Language of Love

Did you know that female turkeys are the most loving mothers among the animals? They love their babies so much, and they express their love with a particular sound they make. When the poults hear that sound, no matter where they are, they run and snuggle up their mothers, and the mother turkeys passionately envelop them. Psychologists have done research and found out that even when they put the recorded mother turkey's sound inside the body of a stuffed bobcat (the turkey's greatest enemy), the turkey poults run to it blindly to hug the bobcat.

Human beings, so well equipped with many means at their disposal to express their love and affection for each other, have such difficulty communicating the same message. People raised in the same culture or even in the same household, people who have lived together for years, have difficulty receiving or expressing the message of love. In fact their language of love usually varies and is foreign to each other. Some people's receptors receive the message of love by hearing the words, some need to be touched and held, some need to receive costly gifts, some need to show control, and some need it all plus something vague unknown to them and to the people who love them.

The language of love for my father was to let my mother sleep in the morning!

To see the expression of the most delicate passion from my father was to wake up very early in the morning, as early as five or six, and watch him prepare breakfast for the eight of us.

The most common breakfast in my country consists of bread—bought daily from the neighborhood bakery, butter or feta cheese, and tea freshly brewed on a samovar. In our family we ate bread (*sangak*), butter sprinkled with sugar, and lots and lots of tea.

The stick of butter, about 226.8 grams, was cut in ten equal pieces of 22.68 millimeters, not a millimeter thicker or thinner. When the water in the samovar began to boil, my father put a butter knife in a glass cup filled with hot water. As the knife was getting hot he got the tea ready and then like a capable craftsman, sliced the butter in front of our curious eyes making sure each child's piece was precisely the same as others, and it always was. When it was my turn though, he moved his hand just a few millimeters. An exchange of a secret glance between him and my appreciative eyes, sometimes objected to by my siblings, was a gift of love. The next step was to make a pile, what we called a "mountain," made out of cut fresh, thin, whole wheat bread (*sangak*) in equal sizes, a piece of butter, sprinkled with sugar, and then we were served.

As we eagerly ate our breakfast, he stirred his small, thumb-sized glass teacup forever with the little spoon as he walked around the living room waiting for us to get ready for school, inviting us to silence, making sure we did not wake our mother. As a result, we all started our day with warm hearts.

His love for his children was spoken softly; expressed with a language we understood perfectly. His language of love of life was his full participation, an absolute devotion to any role he had in life, while putting no weight on the shoulders of others. He was neat and had healthy habits. He never required service from others in order to serve his own needs. He slept early, prepared his own light dinner and washed his plate. He quietly went down to his office in the house and slept and woke up very early. He read for hours and he kept a journal of his missions for his country.[1] He never smoked or drank alcohol. Bibi never smoked in front of him, both out of respect for him and his disapproval of Bibi endangering her health. Alas, in spite of his perfectly balanced nature, our Baba died of lung cancer. Everyone present during his sick days said that he did not even complain while he was suffering with the pain of cancer. He was only sixty-one years old when he passed away.

◆ ◆ ◆

The language of romance between two human lovers though is a different matter and seems to be universal. Our father was a man from the south, a nomad by nature. He had lived most of his young years in battles to arm or disarm the khans of the southern region. His essence was made of palm trees, dates, heat, adventure, and nationalism. A completely selfless man but hopelessly primitive when it came to romance.

In many traditional homes, showing romance publicly used to be sinful. You could not even sit next to your husband in public or in the presence of any other. Time and again my siblings and I, then all married, were scolded for that matter and reminded that if you need to sit together, go to your bedrooms!

Our father was usually gone for many months in a year, as long as eight months or so at a time, in battles or campaigning for his election to the parliament. For the birth of many of his children he was not in town. A telegram was sent to him to announce the births and the health of our mother. A return telegram though had only expressed his gratitude for my mother's health. Seldom did he send letters home to my mother, and when he did, it was usually to let her know that he is alive or maybe reminding her of some chores in the house that needed to be taken care of. With so much disappointment, my mother would hand the letter to the maid and sarcastically tell her, "Here, the master has written a letter for you!"

One of Bibi's many failed efforts to teach him romantic language was to show a letter from Aqda'i sent to her, "Look at this and see how delicate and loving this letter is. Can't you write the same way?" Bibi had told him. A very hard act to follow my father must have thought. Ali Dashti was a writer, known for his delicate nature. How was it possible for our father to match up to that? So he hopelessly copied it to send Bibi a letter:

My beloved niece; the light of my eyes . . . !

Our father's personal teacup (estekan e kamar barik) and bowl. Photo: Sayeh Dashti, 2012.

Abdollah Dashti.

Abdollah Dashti, 1965.

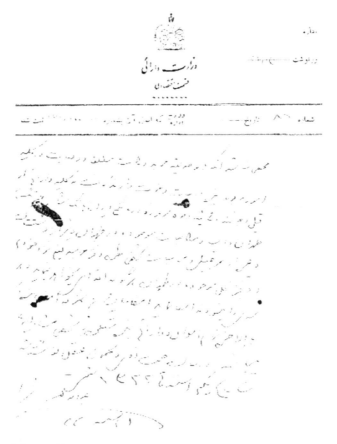

The legal document signed by our father, 1944.

Translation of a legal document signed by my father:

Ministry of Finance
Department of Economy
February 21, 1944

Let it be apparent that Lady Sediqeh Mojahed has absolute power of attorney in the entire affairs related to all my assets such as cash, goods, money in the bank, the deeds of all properties in Tehran, Shiraz, and Dashtestan. She has full authority to act upon all my personal and legal documents.

Her signature equals my signature. All I own now is equally owned by her.

The above is written in my perfect and complete physical and mental stability on this day of Esfand 1, 1322 [February 21, 1944].

Abdollah Dashti

Notes

1   Abdollah Dashti, *Az Jam/Reez ta Tabriz* (From Jam/Reez to Tabriz). Compiled and edited by Badieh Dashti. (Tehran: Farhang e Hezareh e Sevom, 1385 [2006]).

Thirty

A Kal Kokab Story: "The Farting Goat"

The blue of her eyes took us to the depths of clarity. Still standing tall, taller than other women around us, she managed to walk with a hidden limp. She was homeless, yet most welcome in any house she visited for as long as her pride allowed her to stay. Every once in a while, she came to stay with us.

As soon as she turned into our street, the news travelled and many excited children with ear-piercing screams of joy ran out to get her small sack of clothes and literally dragged her into the house.

All her belongings fit in a piece of cloth tied into a neat ball, the size of a small purse. She was very clean, ate very little, and still managed to be low maintenance at the age of ninety-something. Above and beyond, she carried with her a wealth of fairy-tale stories; fascinating, charming stories that filled our summer nights with humor and words of wisdom.

She was permitted to say words we would never dare say or hear otherwise. She freely talked about male and female body parts in her humorous stories of people, animals, fairies, monsters and so on. Coming from her purest mouth, with the purest intentions of bringing innocent joy to our naïve ears, made it all so decent. Everyone laughed; even the adults could not resist.

She began to tell the stories as we sat around her. No one moved; no interruptions were permitted. We never put her on hold or pause. The only pitfall was that the stories ended too soon. The endings started a riot. Again! Again! Again! Sometimes she was made to repeat a story more than ten times, before a caring adult showed up and released her from our forceful demands. When she told a story, she told it exactly the same way every time; not a word out of place.

Hardly a day goes by without a blessing on her soul, along with a childish smile in one of our faces, as we encounter an application of a situation matching one of her stories. All we need to say or think then is "God bless Kal Kokab's soul."

Kal Kokab, about 1952. Khaneh ye Shahr, Tehran. Photo: Dashti family album.

Here is one of Kal Kokab's stories:

The Farting Goat

Yeki bood yeki nabood [once upon a time . . .] there was a young bride who lived with her husband, her mother- and father-in-law, and a goat. They lived in a small one-room house.

Every morning after the husband and the in-laws left the house, she swept the room. One day as her broom reached the goat, the goat stubbornly refused to move. Instead of pushing the goat out of the way, she lifted it and then . . . Bam! She let out a fart!!!!!!

She got really scared and worried that the goat might tell the in-laws and then they would tell their son about the accident. She begged the goat: "Dear goat, please do not tell my mother-in-law that I farted." The goat says, "Maaaaaaaa, *ya'ni migom* [I will tell]." so she assumes that is what the goat is saying. Helplessly she brings her best clothes and hangs them on the horns of the goat and continues begging it not to say anything. The goat keeps saying, "Maaaaaaaa, *ya'ni migom* [I will tell]."

She hopelessly sits in the corner and cries. Meanwhile her mother-in-law walks in and sees the clothing on the goat's horns. Frantically she asks the young girl to tell her what has happened and why she was crying. The girl tells her, "I was sweeping the floor and wanted to clean under the goat. The goat was too heavy. I could not help it. I let out a fart!" she cries. The mother-in-law bangs on her own head, realizing the disaster.

"Dear goat," she cries, "please do not tell my husband or my son what has happened. She is very young and if her husband finds out, there will be a disaster." The goat goes "Maaaaaaaa, *ya'ni migom* [I will tell]," so they interpreted.

The mother goes and gets her jewelry box and good clothes and puts them on the head of the goat trying to bribe it. "Here, are you happy now? Will you keep this a secret?" But the goat says: "Maaaaaaaa, *ya'ni migom* [I will tell]."

Then the father-in-law walks in and witnesses the scene. He questions the strange scene and his wife tells him: "Our bride was trying to sweep the floor and when she tries to clean under the goat, she lets out a fart. Now the goat is saying that it will tell on her."

The father in-law too, goes to his closet and brings out his best clothes and puts them on the goat asking him solemnly, "Mr. Goat, my son is a very serious man and if he finds out that his wife has farted, he will leave her and leave this house. Will you keep this a secret?" The goat says: "Maaaaaaaa! *ya'ni migom* [I will tell]."

Eventually the young man walks home and finds his family all shaken up, scared and embarrassed; the goat loaded with clothes and gold and a turban on top of its head.

"What in the world is happening here?" he asks. The father tells his son the whole story with so much shame.

The young man, fed up with his family's idiocy, announces that he is leaving them not because she farted, but because they are so brainless.

So he leaves the house, his family and the town.

He walks and walks and walks from one village to another.

On his journey, he first gets to a village and notices that people of that village are mourning. "Why is everyone mourning?" he asks. They tell him that the daughter of the chief of the village had tried to get some shelled walnuts out of a jar, and now her hand is stuck in the jar. They had decided to chop her hand off and of course now everyone is really sad about that. He tells them hurriedly: "No hold on! I know the secret."

195

They quickly take him to the house of the chief and then lead him to the little girl whose hand was stuck in the shelled walnut jar. He puts his mouth to her ears and tells her quietly, "Let go of the walnuts in your hand!" [Here Kal Kokab acts out the scene by holding the wrist of one of us sitting close by, and slaps it softly. Each one of us wanted to volunteer for the slap!]

The girl successfully pulls her hand out. The village celebrates with relief and gives him a bag of gold pieces [*ashrafi*] as a reward and a good meal to eat.

The next day he starts on his journey. Later in the day he arrives at another small village and finds its people mourning and depressed. "Why?" he asks. "Why is everyone so sad and depressed?" he wants to know.

He is told, "Our chief's son is getting married tonight. He is too tall to get into the bridal chamber. Now they are preparing to chop his legs short."

Horridly he says, "No! Wait! I have the secret. Take me to the chief's house."

They take him to the house of the chief and to the entrance of the bridal chamber where a crowd is mourning and the groom standing tall with his waist to the top of the small door.

He is led to the groom. He puts his mouth to the ear of the groom and tells him softly, tapping his waist, "Here, bend your back from your waist and walk in there." He does it successfully and the crowd cheers. [Again, here one of us volunteers or is rather chosen to go and be tapped by Kal Kokab. The chosen one had to hurry back; it was as if someone stood in front of the television set in the middle of the most exciting movie or the World Cup.]

The chief takes him to his house and rewards him with pieces of gold [*ashrafi*]. He is then served as the guest of honor.

The next day he starts on his journey. He walks and walks until he gets to a stream of water. He sits there to rest— all exhausted and disappointed in the people. A servant was washing dishes in the stream next to him. She says hello and asks him where he is coming from. Frustratingly, he responds, "From Hell!"

She drops the dish she was washing and asks if he has seen her master there. He says hesitantly and with frustration, "Yes! Yes, I have."

She begs him to wait there for one moment as she runs to the house. "Bibi! Bibi!" she yells breathlessly. A lady hurries out, "Why are you yelling like this?" Bibi asks.

"But Bibi, there is a gentleman by the stream who says he has come from Hell. He has seen our master!"

"Oh my God. Really?!" her bibi says.

"Yes! It is true," the maid responds.

"Go get him. Beg him to come in." Bibi orders.

The maid returns and begs the man to come see her lady master.

He comes to the house and the lady asks him personally and confidentially, "How was my husband? Did he need anything?"

"He was fine," he answers with disbelief. "He said he needed some food and gold? I think?"

"Oh, yes, of course, by all means," the woman is flattered. "Please tell my husband we miss him and I am waiting for the day God chooses to take me there to be with him. Please wait here and I will get a bundle ready for him and for you as well."

He leaves the house with a bag of good food and a bag of gold pieces [*ashrafi*].

As he walks along the stream he thinks to himself, "I suppose the world is like this. People do get stuck in situations where they do not know what to do, where they become crippled and brainless. It might happen to me too." So he decides to return home and be with his wife and family.

Now let us hear from his family back home:

After the young man left, the family became very desperate. They decided to go find him and bring him back; no matter what it took.

So one day they close all the windows and the doors of their small house, they get a bowl of thick plaster and secure all the holes in the house. Then they open the faucets and let the water run until the house is filled with water. They take a door off and use it as a boat with shovels as their paddles. The wife, the mother, the father, and the goat sit on the floating door, rowing on top of their water-filled house to go and find the young man.

Soon the man turns into their alley, to head home.

"We found him! We found him! Hey! We are up here!" they shouted.

He stares up furiously at first, but he soon gives in and thinks, "Oh well. I have lots of money. I will fix the house and everything will be just fine."

❖ ❖ ❖

"Again! Again! Tell it again . . .," we demanded.

"*Yeki bood yeki nabood* [Once upon a time . . .] there was a young bride . . ." Kal Kokab repeated the story.

Thirty-One
A Kal Kokab Story: "Dayhadadoo"

Once upon a time there was a bad witch called Dayhadadoo—she was mean, bitter, and very unkind. She had once worked as a maid for her master, his wife, and their newborn daughter, Mahpishooni. Right after their daughter was born, the master and his wife died from a terrible disease. The baby orphan was left in the hands of the bad witch, Dayhadadoo.

Dayhadadoo, the baby girl, a few old servants, two large mean-looking dogs, a cow, several birds, and an old cat all lived in a large stone house on top of a remote hill. After the death of the masters, the old house had become almost abandoned—weeks and months went by before anyone visited them. Even the vendors who used to come around selling food and other necessities had stopped going near that house because when they went too close either someone threw rocks at them or the hungry dogs attacked their donkeys.

As a routine, the old maids put out some bones for the dogs, grass for the cow and the goats, water and seeds for the birds every morning, and left to doze off in the sun. Dayhadadoo woke up late; she came out when they were asleep and was in the habit of taking the bones from the dogs and putting them in front of the cow and the goats, and then she took the grass and gave it to the dogs before they had a chance to eat their food. She served the long-beaked birds in a flat dish, out of which they could hardly drink and put the water for the little birds with short beaks in tall jugs that they could not reach. Then she went around and kicked the "Open Door" first, then on to the "Closed Door" to make sure it was shut. She was very mean to the little girl as well and would not let her go out of the house, making her work very hard.

Mahpishooni was growing nicely in spite of Dayhadadoo's cruelty. She was kind and gentle and had a glow in her face. In fact that is why her parents had named her Mahpishooni, meaning a moon on the forehead. She worked all day and took care of the animals and the workers and everything else in that house. As soon as Dayhadadoo was done with her disservices, Mahpishooni went around and gave back to the dogs their bones and gave back to the cow and the goats their own grass. She exchanged the flat plate of water for the little birds and the deep jugs for the bird with a long beak, the pelican. When she was certain that Dayhadadoo had dozed off completely, she quietly climbed the stairs to close the "Open Door" which was banging and swinging in the wind—she closed it, lubricated and secured its hinges. Then she went to the "Closed Door" and left it open to get some air—she wiped the spider webs off and polished its wood. She talked to the animals and the doors and the plants. Their lives had changed since she had grown up and was capable of saving them from the harm of Dayhadadoo.

Not only did Mahpishooni spend hours taking care of her surroundings, she had found time to weave the most beautiful *gelim*s, something her mother had done when she was alive. The creatures in the stone house were all her friends. The "Closed Door" let her go inside the forbidden room where her mother's weaving equipment was kept, to have private time to weave. The "Open Door" slammed hard, the dogs barked, the goats baaed, the birds chirped and the cow mooed; all called out to warn Mahpishooni in case Dayhadadoo was approaching. The large bird and the little birds had the delicate mission of taking her artworks to the town's market to sell.

Her handmade *gelim*s had become popular in the market; people were paying good prices to own one. Curiously, no one knew where they were coming from or who had made them. The birds took them to the market and took the money in their beaks and flew back to the stone house. Without the knowledge of Dayhadadoo, Mahpishooni had managed to pay one of the maids some of the money to get food and supplies for her friends and for her art. Interestingly enough it had never occurred to the bad witch to wonder how everyone was fed and everything was in order. Mahpishooni's friends in the house had made a treasure box where they saved a portion of the money for the future of their savior; they knew that day would soon arrive.

The reputation of the beautiful *gelim*s had finally reached the Royal Courts. The King and the Queen wanted to own a *gelim* from the unknown artist. Eventually, they sent a messenger with a long message written on the skin of a deer in search of the unknown artist, with promises of a bright future for him or her.

One day, a young messenger named Kakol Zari (Golden Curls), having gone through the whole town, finally came to the door of the old stone house with the message from the courts announcing that the King and the Queen are looking for the artist who is creating the most amazing designs on *gelim*s.

Mahpishooni happened to be on the top terrace when she saw the messenger approach the hill.

It was a very exciting event when someone passed their old house. She had run down and sneaked out of the house to see the messenger. As soon as she appeared from the backyard and jumped in front of the horse to welcome the messenger, the horse bolted and threw the young man to the ground. The young messenger seemed to be in a lot of pain. Mahpishooni got very upset and started helping him off the ground with much care and compassion. They both looked at each other and . . . "Not one heart, but one hundred hearts," they fell in love.

When the boy fell off the horse, the rolled-up message also fell to the ground, rolling down the steep hill. Suddenly and before Mahpishooni helped the young man up to get on his horse, Dayhadadoo ran out of the house and saw the whole scene. She had been woken up by the sound of the horse's neigh followed by the dogs barking, the cows mooing, and the goats baaing. She was furious to see the young girl in touch with a man and outside of the house.

"How dare you go to the door?" she yelled. "Get back to the house and back to do your chores!" she was still screaming.

"But . . .," Mahpishooni said in disappointment and still hoping to soften her.

"No buts. These things are not for you. Don't even imagine it." She dismissed her. She also told Kakol Zari to get lost and never come back that way. "I will have you butchered if you come near this house," Dayhadadoo threatened him.

Mahpishooni went back inside in tears and went straight to her friends, the animals, the trees, the doors, etc. She cried and they listened to her story. All of them unanimously voted that she should find out what was in the message. Deep down they wanted her to see the young man once again.

"But how? I have no way of getting out of this prison," she said with so much envy. "Do not worry how. We will plan it. You just cheer up and make yourself pretty; we will take care of the rest," one of the old goats said and the rest of the objects and animals all nodded and looked at each other puzzled.

"The first thing we need to do is to go down the hill and find the rolled-up message!" said the old goat. At this time they all hushed each other because the cat was passing by. The only animal that was free to come and go near Dayhadadoo was an old Persian cat. Unfortunately the old cat was always in a bad mood and very hard to trust. She could tell Dayhadadoo about their secret. One of the dogs started to talk with frustration, "I am telling you, that cat is just as evil as Dayhadadoo herself. Do not trust her!" said the dog. The other dog who was younger suggested, "Maybe I can seduce her!" he said with a naughty smile. "I bet you could with all your charm!" said Mahpishooni. They all started to laugh.

"If we all start to make noises, the witch will come out to tell us off and then one of us could sneak outside, down the hill and grab the scroll," the cow said intelligently. "Look my friends, you are all in so much trouble as it is, I do not want to cause any more problems for you," said Mahpishooni. They all got quiet and started to think.

Many days passed and Mahpishooni was getting sadder and sadder. She had fallen in love and also was getting desperate to experience a new life as a free artist. Her friends in the house were noticing her unhappiness and wanted to help her.

Meanwhile the young messenger boy who had also fallen in love with Mahpishooni kept coming near her house trying to catch a glimpse of the beautiful girl one more time and to get the roll he had lost. The day of the ceremony of the artist introduction was approaching—artists from all over the country were claiming to be the producer of the magnificent *gelim*s in the hope of having the unique opportunity of working in the royal palace.

Finally, the messenger boy summoned the courage and went right up to the stone house. He started climbing the hill and looking for the lost scroll. Suddenly Dayhadadoo saw him and came running. The birds followed her outside and caught up with the boy who had found the scroll.

"Tell us what is in the message," the old pelican said. "Tell us before she gets you; we will deliver the message for you," said the little birds.

Kakol Zari looked up in desperation and said, "I know the magnificent *gelim*s come out of this house. I have seen you fly with them. I have seen you take them to the market. Tell me who makes them, the King and Queen want to know!" he said as he was running away from the house.

"It is Mahpishooni, the young girl you met, she makes them." They yelled out before Dayhadadoo took her slingshot and hit a couple of the little birds and the beak of the old pelican. They fell to the ground and the young man started to run. The boy seemed desperate and started yelling out, "Mahpishooni, come out! I am here to take you to the Royal Court." But it was all too late. Dayhadadoo was in charge.

He disappeared behind the winding hills. Mahpishooni and her friends were watching the whole thing and started to cry for their bird friends.

In the middle of the night, when it was all quiet and Dayhadadoo was busy with her hallucinations, the friends got together and planned to go save the injured birds. The dogs got the mission! Mahpishooni unchained them and quietly accompanied them to the gate and watched with apprehension as the dogs left the house, went down the hills, to each grab a bird in its mouth; not a peep from anyone.

Only the old cat purred and meowed, but Dayhadadoo got mad at her and told her to shut up!

Fortunately the birds were all still alive. Mahpishooni cleaned their wounds and put Mercurochrome on their wings. The goats pushed their food and water to the birds. No one slept that night.

The next morning, Kakol Zari went back to the royal palace and asked to be received by the Queen.

"My lady, I have found out who the artist is. She is a beautiful girl called Mahpishooni. She lives in an old house on top of the hill. She is imprisoned by a mean old witch, Dayhadadoo, who does not let her out of her sight. We have to help her," said Kakol Zari breathlessly.

"Calm down! Tell us more," said the Queen.

"My lady, please help her. She is imprisoned by the meanest witch who hurts her and everything else in that house. She has no chance of being free and happy," said the young messenger.

"Do not worry young man. Take a few soldiers with you tomorrow and free her!" said the Queen.

Kakol Zari was beside himself with excitement and love for the young girl. He got ready and delivered the Queen's message to the head of the Royal Guard. The head guard prepared a few of his soldiers to accompany him on the mission.

As soon as the sun was up, the small army prepared to leave the King's castle. Some on their horses and some on foot, they traveled for kilometers until they reached the grounds of the stone house.

They went straight to the gate and banged on the doors. "Dayhadadoo, we are here to take Mahpishooni from you; it is the Queen's order," the men hollered.

"Go away! You have no business trespassing," said Dayhadadoo.

"It is an order from the Queen, open up," the soldiers demanded.

"Order!? Order my foot! I order in my own house, not the Queen," Dayhadadoo said fearlessly.

The messengers waited a while and repeated the same message over and over. When they found out that there was no way through to the witch, they began calling out for Mahpishooni.

"Mahpishooni, dear girl, do not be afraid, come out, we will protect you," they said.

Dayhadadoo stood on top of the wall telling Mahpishooni, "Do not dare to leave, you naughty girl. I will not allow it." She forbade her.

"You can never leave," Dayhadadoo said confidently.

Mahpishooni was on the top terrace not knowing what to do. She did not want to lose her once in a lifetime chance but she was so afraid of Dayhadadoo.

Meanwhile her friends were encouraging her to take her chance. The cow brought her the box of treasure and said, "Mahpishooni, this is your own wealth. You have earned it with your own art and your kind heart. Take it and go."

Everyone else encouraged her to go, "Go . . . go . . . we will protect you."

So she got prepared, she said good-bye to all her friends one by one. She had tears in her eyes as she said good-bye. "What will happen to all of you now?" she said with tears. "We will be fine; go! Go now!" they yelled at her with a smile.

She looked at them and got ready to run.

Dayhadadoo was running around nervously when she saw Mahpishooni's shadow trying to run away.

"Hungry dogs, get her!" Dayhadadoo demanded.

"Why should we? She fed us and took care of us," the dogs said.

"No-good cow, noisy goats, get her! Dayhadadoo ordered.

"Why should we? She gave us grass and kept us clean, helped us give birth to our babies," said the cow and the goats.

"*Dar e Bazoo* (Open Door) get her!" Dayhadadoo screamed with anger.

"Why should I? She supported me, lubricated my hinges, and healed my cracks. I will never stop her!" said the Open Door.

"*Dar e baste* (Closed Door), get her!" she demanded.

"Why should I? She let me breathe, wiped the spiders off me, let me get air; she talked to me when I was lonely. I would never hold her!" said the Closed Door.

"Ugly birds, get her, do not let her get away!" Dayhadadoo said desperately.

"Why should we? If it were not for her, we would never have a drop of water or a bit of food. If it were not for her, our injured wings would never have healed!" said the birds.

Mahpishooni ran and ran. With the box of treasure and a heart filled with gratitude for her good friends, she ran into the arms of Kakol Zari. Free!

The following day, the Queen and the King held a celebration in honor of Mahpishooni. She became an artist of the court and taught many young students the art of weaving and the virtue of kindness.

The army returned to the old house and arrested Dayhadadoo and put her in a dungeon. Mahpishooni and Kakol Zari married and lived happily ever after.

◆ ◆ ◆

I wish I had the courage to tell you Kal Kokab's version of this story. For instance Dayhadadoo had something on her forehead, which I cannot tell you what!

She also had a lot to say about the maids and the way they spent their days! I cannot tell you that either. I can only go as far as telling you that we wet ourselves with laughter as she told the story.

Thirty-Two
Penmanship

"**G**uess what object this is?" I asked my brothers and sisters. "It's the size of a telephone receiver. It's made of metal. And you move it like a seesaw."

With the exception of my youngest brother (born in 1957), they knew what it was. Before I even finished giving them all the clues, they yelled out the answer with excitement, "*Johar khoshk kon* (ink absorber)! A device on our father's desk! He used it to dry the ink of his signature or the letters he wrote!"

Most of us had a similar device we took to school to dry the ink of our calligraphy practice. In fact many similar (almost extinct) objects and images, such as the small hexagonal bottles of ink (*davat*), the cotton loose fibers we put in the bottle to hold the ink, the wide-point reed pens, and the swollen ink-covered index fingers, were still very much alive in our minds.

As children none of us realized the importance of handwriting and the brain function involved in creating curves, lines and dots; the attributes of our language which offer a freedom to create. We should have trusted the wisdom of our ancient culture and its strict rules for graphical shapes of the letters, words, and compositions of whole calligraphy pieces; the ultimate spiritual art.

Many hours a week, we practiced handwriting and calligraphy as part of our curriculum in elementary and high school. We used to consider those hours as our time off—boring and a waste of time. During those hours, we played around and did not mind the teachers as much. We had a separate teacher for fine handwriting (*khat e riz*) and another for calligraphy (*khat e doroshti*); we called them *khanoom e riz* (petite lady) and *khanoom e dorosht* (hefty lady). We had, as part of our homework, page after page of writing from the books. On long holidays such as NoRouz, we were assigned to copy our Farsi textbook, without any errors, with a pen (*ketab nevisi*). The coziest sight from our childhood is the view of us lying down on our bellies, feet up, writing our homework, as we read out loud with a certain rhythm, so focused!

The less formal homework was done with wood-encased pencils. The cheaply made pencils (*shotor neshan*) were weak and broke all the time. The good kind of pencils was the Staedtler brand. Those came from abroad and were strong enough to withstand being chewed on to the lead and sharpened repeatedly. We kept our pencils until they were smaller than our fingers. Persian carpets were the best way of cleaning and refreshing the rubber erasers (Pelican brand), and the metal sharpeners with two sizes of holes were luxury items. Asking for an additional hard cover or the soft cover notebooks was always praised (an indication of having worked very hard)—a pleasure for our father to give them to us from the storage of school supplies in his home office.

Ballpoint pens (Bic) were introduced in Iran in the 1960s. Our father never bought them for us and insisted that we write with fountain pens. The teachers did not allow it either. We hand-wrote page after page of our assignments, as we kept filling up our pens with ink and drying up the smudged pages with the ink absorber device.

It was most prestigious to receive an expensive pen, such as a Parker, when earning good grades. The parents bought it (we now know), gave it to the principal, and the principal presented it to us during the school assembly.[1]

I began learning to type in my second year of college in America. The electric typewriters had just come out. My term papers were disastrous; I made too many mistakes. One of my fingers would involuntarily move and hit a key. Every mistake I made, which was on almost every letter, I had to put correction fluid over the letter, wait for it to dry, and retype it. Most of my papers weighed heavy, never flat, being saturated with liquid paper, and when held up to the light, the covered up letters still showed. Later on, special strips of papers were invented. We could put it under the hammer of the typewriter; it lifted the typed letter, or covered it with white ink, so we could type the correct letter over. It was better, it was at least dry; however, I used them so often that my papers were full of holes. Then we learned to make a copy of our messy papers and hand in the clean one; that miracle was introduced to us by the end of my graduate studies.

There has to be a difference between writing while the body and brain move in sync, and writing with minimum movement via a laptop. Our great-uncle Ali Dashti wrote all his books, more than twenty, by hand. He sat on a chair, held the paper on his lap, without putting a firm object under it for support, and wrote for hours. Sometimes, he held it up next to his heart, on the palm of his hand, and wrote. He always wrote with his fountain pen. Most of his handwritten materials were without any corrections or smudges on the paper. He must have danced with such harmony as he created his art on the paper.

"Respect brings eternal prosperity," a third-grade calligraphy worksheet. Photo: Sayeh Dashti.

Notes

1   I bought a set of pens for my son Shahaub and gave it to his principal to present to him. The principal told the assembly that his mother had brought the pens. Shahaub was about to kill me.

Thirty-Three
Why Talk?

We feared for the safety of our mother, even in the last days of her life. We feared that one of those days a mysterious car or the army would come to our door, handcuff our mother, and take her away.

It started every morning when she listened to the news on the radio. Without exception, she heard some official use an incorrect word, a word that did not actually express the meaning he or she was trying to communicate, or their sentences were grammatically incorrect or unsophisticated. My mother would get so disturbed that she had to intervene. Before the revolution, she called the palace of the Shah, and after the revolution, it was the head office of the Supreme Leader she tried to reach. She then insisted that she must talk to the Shah or Ayatollah Khomeini.

When Bibi visited us in the United States (1987), she insisted that she wanted to go to the United Nations. My cousin Mohammad Hossain (Abaj's son), who lived in New York at the time, and I accompanied her to the United Nations building. We sat with her in the U.N. General Assembly along with so many other visitors from all over the world. She demanded that we translate her every word. My cousin got up with her and addressed the General Assembly on her behalf:

Tell the Secretary-General (Javier Pérez de Cuéllar) that the United Nations started with a vision. I remember it clearly. It was towards the end of WWII. Its mission was to be a moderator for the nations of the world—its responsibility was to intervene whenever a country bullied another one. Now the United Nations is just sitting there and allowing Iraq and Iran to kill each other's youth. We are being bombed and no one is doing anything about it. I have to speak to him. When you say you do something, you must keep your word!

Bibi usually started with this statement: "I am a commoner woman! I need to speak to the king or the queen (or whoever happened to be the head of the government) to talk about something very, very important." Of course they did not allow that to happen, but she was persistent enough to make sure they connected her to someone who could communicate her message to the person in mind—some days, it took her hours to finally get through.

When she was reassured that her message would be delivered, she would demand firmly:

Tell the Shah (or the Ayatollah), you who have assumed the leadership of a country like Iran, must know better. The pride of our country has always been the men and women who not only were masters in the art of communication and expression, their words symbolized a deep meaning; it opened so many doors—our country is known for its powerful literature; for the masters who chose the most appropriate words for their meanings, their words were sharper than a sword.

Then she would refer to the date, the hour, and the exact words the person had misused in his or her public speech. "Why was such a word used in such and such context? How could a leader be so negligent and say something when he or she knows that it is not so?" she said as she was confronting their lack of accountability in the matter. "Tell him or her when our leader is using words to communicate with us, his words are instilling values and laws!" she insisted.

The poor person who was on the other end of the line had to commit to her in correct words before she would let him off the hook. "No! That is not what I said. Repeat after me . . ."

Anytime one of the leaders was due to make a speech on the radio or television, we knew there was going to be a reaction from our mother. She seemed like a caring mother, praying that the speech of one of her children goes flawlessly; she cared deeply for the speaker, the audience, and for the dignity of spoken words.

Bibi usually sat very close to the set to be able to hear it perfectly; none of us could make a sound. And then it happened! Coincidently, the speaker never failed to say something that was not the real meaning, the incorrect grammar, or even a poor choice of words. In her judgment, any one discrepancy was proof of injustice and she was there to detect it.. I can imagine when the inappropriate words showed up, she reacted as if she had been taken to see waste. The same sadness took a hold of her when she saw food being wasted. "Food is there to nourish the body of God's creatures; words are there to express the human soul," she proclaimed.

She went so far as objecting to the way prophets had talked in their holy books. "How could they talk to God as needy! And she would continue naming each one and the mistakes they had made in their books. "No, that is not right. God would never say such a thing!" Bibi would say with such confidence. Sometimes she would interrupt her own daily prayers, "No, I cannot say that. I cannot talk to God like this. God is beyond all this. I am sitting here telling God what to do!"

To her the inappropriate usage of words was an unforgivable sin; she expected eloquence. In her culture, in her family, when someone said something, that is what he meant—he knew the circumstances and was ready for the consequences. The words they used were an exchange of values; a principle. As her children, we could get away with a lot of mistakes; however, never with the usage of nonsense words. We were stopped and corrected each and every time. She insisted that we use the right words to express how we felt. For example, when we nagged and said that we were hungry, she checked, "Are you hungry, or are you tired and bored?" If we were not sure, she told us to go and hold our ears till we felt hunger.

Bibi always said precisely what she meant. Her words were so sincere that she never had to back them up with confirmation words such as, "I swear to God," "I swear on the life of my children," "I put my children in the grave," "May God punish me if I am not telling the truth," "To this piece of bread and salt we are eating," or "I mean it," in order to prove her sincerity. I hardly remember a time when she had to apologize

208

for what she had said. If she said it, that is what she meant to say and when she articulated words, she was ready to pay any price. This had led us to believe that people who were less committed had to cushion their words with higher powers' interventions. I remember how we exchanged glances when someone started a sentence with one of these terms, or when he tossed a piece of bread (which is considered holy in our culture), it meant that a lie was to follow!

Her words did not change based on the time of day or the conditions she was in, either. Her words in the morning had the same credibility as what she said in the afternoon, at night, when she was stressed, sick, or even when she was asleep. If she did not mean it, she would not say it.

In expressing her emotions, much like most cultured Iranians, Bibi recited an appropriate poem. She did not know many poems by heart; however, as she listened to someone who was reciting a poem she moved her head in affirmation and authentication of the poet's words, "Yes! That is how!"

There was equal action in her silence. When she was silent, it seemed as though she was digesting the realities of what was being presented to her. She lost patience with people chattering words of no usage and no meaning, no values. She was irritated when people bargained with realities of their lives. And when there was true meaning being expressed, she bowed to it. She could never get tired of hearing those words articulated over and over and over. She repeatedly asked people to tell her about such and such stories. It seemed like she found herself in the glorious world of the truth; like an audience in awe facing true art. At times she had the role of a mentor, correcting details, to make sure that the performer is reflecting the exact message. Likewise, she herself repeated her stories as if each word were showing a magnificent jewel, a key to the treasures in her chest. One could never get tired of hearing them.

My mother was so amused when she related to non-Farsi-speaking people. She communicated with body language and/or by saying the Farsi words in a more clear tone. However, when she really needed to communicate and people did not understand, she got aggravated. After trying to explain to the officers at the Los Angeles airport, in perfect Farsi, she decided to sit there quietly for hours waiting for them to figure out for themselves why she did not have the address of her daughter she was visiting. "Who are these people?" she wondered.

On the plane she kept asking for *chaii* and she finally found out that they call it tea. "Why Tea!?" she asked jokingly. "At least they could say chea! That would bring it closer to the meaning."

In her presence, we had to be careful not to contaminate the eloquent Farsi with any foreign words, "Either speak Farsi or speak another language!" she demanded.

Bibi did get into trouble once when she said something she did not mean:

It was a summer afternoon in the 1960s. The eight of us were home and in full swing of being destructive, loud, and naughty. Her voice was not reaching us. So she called my uncle's housekeeper and desperately demanded: "Mohammad, for God's sake. How could you sit there doing nothing while these children are killing me? Go get a policeman and bring him here!" In just a few minutes, the door to our living room opened and a policeman, in full uniform and with a gun, barged inside. We panicked and ran to different corners. Bibi got very pale. "Mohammad! Why would you bring a policeman into our house?"

Mohammad replied, "But, Bibi, you said!"

"I said, but I did not really mean it!" She slowed down as she knew she was saying something unusual.

Poor Mohammad was then completely confused. He kept repeating to himself, "But she said! But she said!"

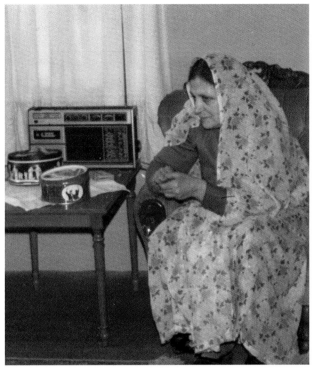

Bibi listening to the radio, about 1975. Photo: Dashti family album.

Bibi and me in the United Nations, 1987.

Thirty-Four
"I" Did That

By accident I broke a glass teacup in the kitchen. I then walked back to my room. It took only a few seconds to forget the incident. I had picked up the pieces and the broken glass had disappeared under piles of papers in the kitchen bin.

My father had gone into the kitchen a little later and while trying to remove the papers from the rest of the trash (recycling), he saw the broken teacup. He stood by the trash can, pointed to the glass pieces and quite unexpectedly insisted to know who was responsible for breaking the teacup. He then began to move back and forth from the kitchen to the living room while staring at the doors of our rooms, taking turns to stare at each room for a very long time. As each one of us walked out of our rooms to use the bathroom and to get ready for school, his long and intense stare followed us back and forth waiting for one of us to come forth with a confession.

◆ ◆ ◆

Having a formal relationship with our fathers was culturally required. We sat up when our father entered the room—we said hello and acknowledged his presence. We made sure we did not have our backs turned toward adults in the room, especially our father. If lack of space made it a necessity to have our backs to someone, we politely excused ourselves: "Sorry my back is to you," and the adult would say, "There is no reverse side to a flower (*gol posht o roo nadareh*).

During his retirement years, our father usually stayed in the living room for a short while and left to go to his study to write his journal or out in the garden to do gardening and watering the young trees until mealtime.

We were all required to wash our hands with soap and water, take our shoes off, and sit around the spread *sofreh* on the floor of Bibi's room. We sat around a spread on the floor cross-legged, our knees touching. When our father was present we made sure we used the utensils properly. He showed us how to hold the spoon and fork, how not to make noise with our mouths, how to chew our food for a long time, and never ever talk with our mouth full. In general, our meals were performed as a combination of traditionally formal and a European formal style all in peace and gratitude.

Our father was the most gentle, selfless, and ultimately undemanding man I have ever met. Aside from his extraordinary reaction to a couple of major events that had made history for such a gentle person, staring was our father's extreme way of showing his emotions.

One of those occasions was when he had punched the glass coffee table in the salon of *Khaneh ye Shahr* and the glass pieces had cut his right hand. Our father was enraged when a guest had bad-mouthed the Shah. He had kept the exaggerated bandage on his hand for a very long time and did not hesitate to talk about the incident with a true sense of duty. The glass on the coffee table was never replaced, not as long as he lived.

The second time was when all of us sisters had gone out with the car, taking along our little brother without notifying our mother.

Apparently all the while we were gone enjoying the ride one day, Bibi was paralyzed with fear; she could not find our brother! They had looked everywhere. Fezeh had not been able to convince her that we had taken our toddler brother along. She had not seen him leave with us and she could not lie to Bibi. Our father had come home a few minutes before we returned home. Those few minutes were enough time to make his blood boil. He had taken a branch of a tree (*tarkeh*) and had started swinging it in the air.

Once we saw Fezeh out on the street with bare feet and no headscarf, we knew something was terribly wrong. And when Bibi dismissed her cigarette by throwing it into the air from the window, we panicked. We raced out of the car, stumbling over each other and ran into our rooms, avoiding the swing of the stick. I do not know if in fact the thin stick touched any of us, but I did feel the blow. Our mother was obviously relieved once our overjoyed brother jumped out of the car into her arms. She immediately started scolding our father for overreacting, even though she was the one who had provoked him.

❖ ❖ ❖

Iran consists of many tribes, religions, languages, and customs. We have proudly and peacefully lived together as one nation for thousands of years. The only matter that occasionally divides us is our soccer. We have two major teams, Persepolis also referred to as Red (*qermezeteh*) and Taj (Blue). These names were changed after the Islamic Revolution, to Azadi and Esteqlal. Our family is a sincere red fan, has been, and will be forever. The two teams can easily disrespect one another during a match. It is allowed, in my view, for a husband and wife to be from two different religions, two completely different ideologies and interests, but still have a quality marriage and be respectful of each other's beliefs. However, a Persepolis fan and a Taj fan should not be married; the animosity is too deep! Only when our national team, which could consist of members of the two teams, plays against a foreign team, all differences vanish! That day the entire country was united.

Our Baba started walking fast, almost running breathlessly, from the Russian Embassy bridge and the corner store (Aqa Mostafa's) toward home, frustrated and charged up. He ran upstairs shouting, "Stop! You should be ashamed of yourselves! You could be heard from Aqa Mostafa's! Stop! Have you no manners?"

It was a moment of madness. The floor was almost collapsing. We were running around screaming from the bottom of our guts, jumping high; nothing could stop us. We continued to shout and jump up and down. He ran to Bibi, "What in the world is going on here?"

"We won! We won! We beat Israel!" Bibi and Fezeh were shouting and jumping with joy as well. Our Baba dropped his briefcase and shouted with joy, "What?" He started jumping up and down right along with us to the point we got worried about his asthma.

◆ ◆ ◆

In our house, accidental breakage had never mattered and had become a casual occurrence, especially during our teenage years when once in a while we helped ourselves to things in the kitchen. In our minds we never expected any consequences for breaking things. I was especially exempt not only because I was left-handed, but because my right hand was weak as well. They called me "*motchal*" meaning clumsy. I cannot figure out why hearing it felt like a compliment or even a sweet protective conspiracy between Bibi and me. Bibi said it in a kind way as she pointed out to others that they should not make me work hard. She used to say: "*In bad bakht e motchal ra velesh konid* (Leave her alone!)"

Except for the china set, which was never handled by anyone but Bibi, other china pieces and or glassware were not worthy of a fuss. The tray of teacups in our house never matched, neither did the set of plates or glasses—anything breakable was broken, in turn, by someone.

At one point, when hard melamine plates were introduced in Iran, we bought sets of plates hoping that now they are not going to break. When a plate fell to the ground in the kitchen, someone yelled, "Break it!" and the person would respond, "It is unbreakable; it is melamine." Just like the advertisement on TV. Those advertisements were soon proven wrong. In our house, they did break.

The main kitchen was on the lower level in Khazar house and the old, 1920 American made refrigerator (Philco) was in the hallway downstairs by the entrance. Unwilling to go up and down the stairs, we passed each other the dishes of china, melamine or metal, whatever they were made out of, straight from the top of the stairs, down. Many times, they either broke or were disfigured.

On the top floor we had a smaller kitchen for making tea and some light cooking by Bibi. The four bedrooms, the kitchenette, and the bathroom opened into the living room. A couple of us shared a room or had our own room once a sibling left the house to go abroad or get married. At one point I shared a room with my sisters Nafiseh and Sepideh.

That morning my father's stare followed each one of us from our rooms to the living room, to the bathroom, stared long at the bathroom door until we came out, continued to stare at us into our rooms, and then stared at our door, without exchanging a word; he was stuck. I was stuck too. I simply did not have what it took—the courage to singularly have the ownership of an act. "I" did that, required so much confidence.

That day finally Bibi came out and wondered why our father was doing that. "I just want someone to claim it," he said. "It does not matter that the cheap teacup is broken. My children should have more confidence. They should be able to say "I" did it. Our father kept saying that for a long time until we had all gotten ready, had breakfast, and left for school.

I will never know when and how he finally let go. I never said, "'I' did that" either.

Glorious moments in our soccer history. Photographer: Ali Kaveh.

214

Thirty-Five
Decisions, Decisions (*Estekhareh*)

The kings and queens of ancient Iran had strong support when faced with important decisions. The court's astrologers interpreted the positions of the celestial bodies, the dream interpreters analyzed their dreams, and other wisemen were consulted for their points of view.

As a nation we still enjoy the same support. We believe in supernatural powers and we deeply believe in the wise men of our literature. We call upon Molana, Sa'di, Omar Khayyam, Sepehri, and especially Hafez for their opinions. *Divan e Hafez* for instance has been a wise council for us for centuries. "Hafez knows everything," so we believe. We ask Hafez to guide us in making decisions. Sitting around in a circle, a learned person among our families or friends ceremoniously opens the *Divan* to call upon Hafez for help (*fal e Hafez*):

Ey, Khajeh Hafez e Shirazi (O' Hafez, the poet of Shiraz),
Tu kashef e har razi (you have the key to every secret),
Tu ra be shakh e nabatet qasam (for the sake of your beloved son, Shakheh Nabat),
Keh pardeh az in raz bardari (unveil this secret; show me a solution).

The book is opened to a random page, and there it is, every time. Hafez has the answer for each person in a gathering. How he knows is a mystery.

The businesses of our fortune-tellers and palm readers have flourished since the Islamic revolution in Iran. They mostly play the role of life coach for a variety of people, people from all walks of life. To make an appointment with a fortune-teller, one has to wait for weeks. There is a secretary and a long wait to get a fifteen-minute session. The fee is much higher than visiting a therapist or a professional life coach.

During the course of history, probably after the coming of Islam to Iran, major decisions, with costly consequences, are taken straight to God via the Koran. Koran, which is believed to be the words of God, has come to be the ultimate guide in decision-making. This is called *estekhareh*. There are people who know how to interpret the verses and guide people in decision-making. For lay people, the pages of some copies are labeled as Good or Bad. These days there are phone numbers you can call, a radio station and of course, now there are websites on the Internet where one can get a *fal e Hafez* or estekhareh from the Koran.

To more sophisticated people, not everyone is considered qualified to ask God sensitive and complex questions. Just like selecting an attorney, the best in the country, the person doing the estekhareh using the Koran has to be outstandingly holy. He has to know the Koran and know how to interpret it. Then it is final. The order is in; no questions asked, no second thoughts past that point. In case things do not work out, it is God's will, no blame on anyone. Imagine that!

A friend of my husband's from the village of Meigoon tells a story of God's executive management of a decision:

My sister was extremely beautiful and had many suitors. Can you believe that one of her suitors was a member of Parliament. Marrying him could have meant that our entire family would be rich. Our lives could have changed. We could have moved to Tehran and been prosperous (*aqebat be kheir bashim*).

My father asked the mullah in Meigoon to perform *estekhareh* with the Koran. The *estekhareh* was bad telling us that God was against this decision. So my father said no to the man and my sister was left single and alone for many years. For young men of Meigoon, I believe, it became a hard act to follow. We were all very sad; especially my mother who kept talking to God, not understanding why he had such a fate planned for her beautiful daughter.

Until one day a young man on a donkey (*kharak chi*) came around to carry some hay from our land to the mountains for his father who was a shepherd. My sister happened to be out washing clothes when they saw each other and fell in love.

The young *kharak chi* was hopelessly in love and dared to come to my father to ask for his daughter's hands. My father went to the mullah and asked him to do another *estekhareh*. This time the *estekhareh* was very good. The mullah showed the verse to my father who could not read or write. He said, "Here, the *estekhareh* says, have no fear; go ahead and do it; you have God's blessing."

My mother and the whole family, the neighbors, and the entire village of Meigoon were in awe of God's call. Nevertheless it was what God had decided and they had no choice but to go along with it and arranged a beautiful wedding.

I never forget the beautiful face of my sister as she happily jumped on the back of a donkey to go to the mountains to live with the sheep in a shack.

The young *kharak chi* happened to have a good business mind. He found out that in the north region of the country there was a good market for raisins. He started getting raisins from Meigoon, took them to the north and brought back rice to sell in Tehran. This was during a time of famine in the country and a high demand for rice. This transaction brought him great profit.

On one of his trips to the north, he happened to be sitting in a teahouse where he saw the sheriff put a flyer on the wooden post inside the teahouse. The flyer announced an order from Reza Shah that whoever develops lands in the north would get money and support from the government.

With the money he earned, he started buying lands in the north and developed them using the government loans. He became a very rich man. Reza Shah named him Mojarab, meaning skillful. To this day, the Mojarab family, his children, and grandchildren are living a prosperous life.

God knows better than us. The hard thing is that God has patience and we do not.

I remember Bibi's face when she got the approval of God for a decision she had already made on her own. Interestingly, she did not share with us that she had also made an *estekhareh* for a decision. The difference between her estekhareh and those of the others was that she made her own decisions first, and then wanted a confirmation from God! "*Ay benazam* (Right on!)" she would emphatically exclaim!

Smoking her cigarette, sitting on the edge of her bed waiting, she would get a phone call from Shiraz. Her contact, a most righteous man, would tell her: "*Estekhareh kheili khoob amadeh; anjam bedahid; kheir ast enshallah* (The will of God is a positive answer, go ahead and do it; you have his blessing)." Still having no idea what was going on with her, the sight of her anxiety-free face, the celebration afterwards by calling Fezeh to her room, followed by the tea ceremony, were the unmistakable signs telling us that she was secretly pleased with the wise God being on her side.

There were decisions she had made in her life which I am certain had cost her dearly. She did blame herself for not listening to the vote of God on some of the decisions. Apparently she had asked for an estekhareh then too. The vote had been negative, yet she had gone ahead and done what she had decided to do! Once in a while she would regretfully confess that she should have listened to the supernatural signs.

As children, we were hardly put in a position to make decisions. In fact as younger persons we were not presented with many choices; choices were made for us and we conveniently conformed. If one did not like certain foods, he would go hungry. The clothes were mostly picked for us. There was only one elementary school, one middle school, and one high school in the neighborhood we could go to. Inside the schools, there was one class for each grade and one teacher for that grade. All we had to do was to follow the rules of the school and those of the teachers. These were nonnegotiable facts, being obedient was a great virtue.

A tremendous opportunity by which we practiced choosing was when we played games. Even then, as a younger person, one would follow the rules of the game set by the older kids. The most liberating opportunities however were make-believe games. It took us hours to indulge in the decision-making involved in creating the most desirable image for ourselves.

As delicate as our make-believe games were, they had the magic of empowering us. Uniquely, the decisions we made in the virtual world had no real consequence. We did not have to pay a price for the choices we made! If things did not go the way we desired, the next day we simply changed them.

In our family there were many guidelines directing most individual choices: the firm principles of humanity, the welfare of Iran, the respect and the security of family members and the community. These were the order of priorities in making decisions. The word "*ab-e-roo*" meant guarding these principles at any cost, even death. Decisions were made to maintain the "*ab-e-roo.*"

Here is a *fal e Hafez* for you:

Than eternal life, union is better

O God, give me that, which is better.

Cut me with a sword, and I said no word,

From foe keeping friend's secret is better.

In this path to die enslaved to the Lord

Than all the world, that Soul is better.

Ask healer of my painful discord

Will this invalid ever get better?

In shade of the spruce, the rose that was floored

Than ruby red blood, its dust is better.

O pious ones, with heavens I'm bored

Than paradise, this garden is better.

O heart, always, in His alley beg and hoard

He, who commands eternity is better.

O youth, with the advice of the old be in accord

Than youthful luck, old wisdom is better.

No eye has seen a gem that soared

That of the pearl of my ear is better.

Though from "Zendeh Rood" (Zayandeh Rood) elixir of life poured

Than Isfahan, Our Shiraz is better.

Though friend's words sweetness stored

Than those words, Hafez's is better.[1]

Ghazal 419

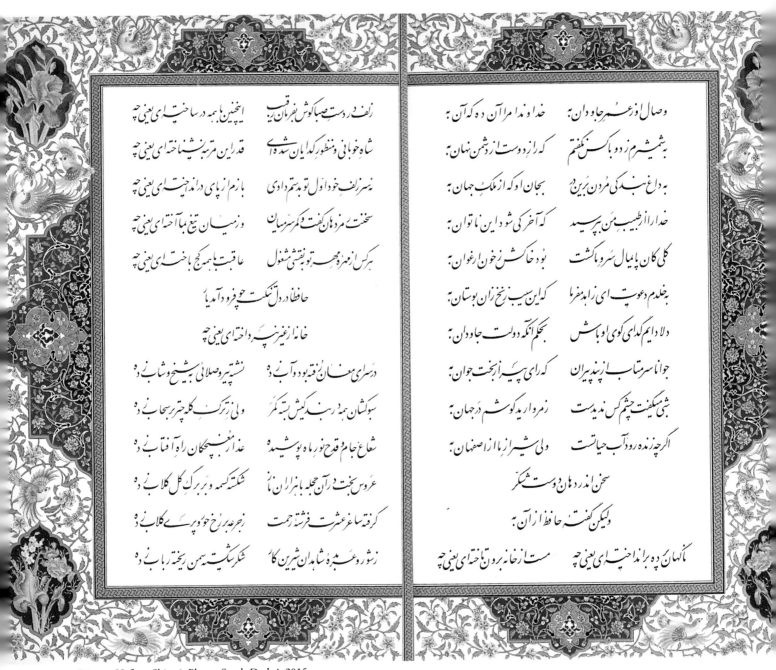

Divan e Hafez e Shirazi, Photo: Sayeh Dashti, 2015.

Notes

1   English translation: www.karoon.com

Thirty-Six
A Silver Soul

Our son Shahaub warned us: "If you die, I will lose myself the same way Fezeh did when Bibi died." What a weight on our shoulders; we were not allowed to die! We now have to seriously take care of our health—do anything we can, not to die before our time. I could not possibly allow my son go through the same pain Fezeh did.

The door to the Khazar house was open for people who were coming to pay respects to my mother's soul. My son Shahaub and I were standing by the stairs when a body, bundled up in a black wrap, was literally thrown into the hallway like a beheaded rooster. The body was hitting the walls completely unwillingly, many times, before a couple of people were able to get a hold of Fezeh and carry her upstairs.

She did not say a word; she sat next to Bibi's empty bed, staring into space. Her lips moved the same way they did when she was in Bibi's presence; confirming, meditating on each word as Bibi told stories. Now her eyes were avoiding any contact. What was going through her mind?

She sat there like a guardian to Bibi's soul; Fezeh was always Bibi's guardian. She was there as the advocate of my mother's rights and a servant to her own daughter, Banafsheh, who had lost her father early in life. To us, she was a symbol of strength and stability. She was like a female tiger protecting her cubs, our parents and her daughter, ready to tear apart any threat to them.

In Bibi's presence, her protection was soft and sweet: "*Bibi farmayesh ha mikonand* (what expectations do you have, Bibi?)" asking Bibi to be more realistic about her expectations of people or situations so as not to stress herself. She was most familiar with and shared the same values with our family.

Our father minded her more than anyone else in life. When he invited people that Bibi did not approve of, Fezeh made his life miserable. She would bang the pots and pants in the kitchen so loud to the point that Bibi laughingly objected to her daring rudeness, not being able to hide her joy. Our Baba could not or dared not be annoying; Fezeh was a strong filter.

As a child, I do not remember ever being corrected or disciplined by Fezeh, even though she had the authority to do so—unless of course when she helped Bibi by holding us!

The whole neighborhood, any neighborhood we moved to, minded this thin black lady. When we lived in *Khaneh ye Shahr*, she splashed large amounts of hot water out the window so the schoolchildren did not get close to the kitchen window! When we moved to the Khazar house, she showed the neighborhood who they were dealing with; she slapped the face of the rich landowner who had cheated and bullied our father.[1]

Fezeh wore her hair back in a brown or black lace, always dressed up in a dress and or a skirt, short heels, and knee-high nylons. She was very well groomed, clean and ready to serve her beloveds. She wore red lipstick and blush on her bony cheeks, *sormeh* (collyrium) in her sharp, small black eyes. When Bibi was not watching, or when situations got out of hand, she did things in her own semi-tribal way. She would tear her shirt and put mud on her head and chest sitting on the ground performing a ritual, rocking and moaning.

The door to her room was always open, presenting her perfectly orderly room. If Fezeh's door was closed, the world seemed doomed, the market shut.

In her room she had a portrait of Imam Ali holding a sword and a lion on his feet, an old black-and-white photograph of a random foreign woman with short hair up to her ears, wearing a dress. The picture was in black and white; however, a bright red color had been manually applied to her lips. A simple Persian carpet covered her room. She wrapped up hers and her daughter's bedding in a clean white cover, tucked them in the corner of her room where it could be used as cushions to lean on. There were a chest of drawers and a large wooden closet, neatly arranged with their personal belongings.

In wintertime, she had a small *korsi* in her room.[2] Most afternoons we took a nap under her neat white covers and were served tea before going back to school for the afternoon sessions. I still feel the battle of dragging myself from the comatose state of being so warm and secure in her room to the harsh cold and dryness of the winter afternoons of geometry, calligraphy, or algebra.

She seemed to always have been awake and alert. Whenever she was called upon, at any time of the day and night, she would say, "*Baleh* Bibi or *baleh* Aqa, and to us, Fezeh *joonom* (Yes, Bibi . . . Yes master. Yes my sweetheart)."

I cannot imagine how a burglar got past her constant wakefulness once. Nevertheless, she did run upstairs to Bibi and our Baba with a severe stutter reporting, "*Boz, boz, Aqa, boz*" instead of *dozd* (burglar).

Bibi talked about Fezeh's father, Sultan, as a saint. Sultan was the right-hand man of Aqa ye Bozorg. Fezeh's mother was Narges who was very beautiful and elegant, a black lady who was raised in the courts of a khan. Sultan was later employed by Aqa ye Bozorg as his personal assistant, his right-hand man. Our grandfather, our Baba's father, gave a house to Sultan and his family next to Aqa ye Bozorg's house (the house was still here in 2014). They had five children, two girls and three boys.

Fezeh means silver and her younger sister Zarafshan's name means spreading gold. Sa'id, Qanbar, and Jamshid were the three brothers: tall, handsome, well-mannered, and well-dressed. In my mother's eyes, the three young men were more than any black movie star, most specifically Sydney Poitier.

Whenever Sydney Poitier starred in a movie, Bibi sighed, "*Khak bar sar e Jamshid* (Damn Jamshid). Jamshid is more handsome than this guy. Why is he sitting here under the *korsi* with his hands on the heater next to him, doing nothing? Someone should have discovered him; he would have been just as famous as Sydney Poitier," Bibi said every time.

Bibi and Fezeh had both lost their mothers at a very young age and they both lost their young brothers. Bibi had lost her only brother and Fezeh had lost her oldest brother, Saiid. Fezeh had also lost her husband, Qasem, right after they had their only child, Banafsheh. Qasem was a white man and a driver; he was killed in an accident.

These losses were topics no one was ever allowed to bring up, discuss, share, or even accept. They were never brought up in front of Fezeh, or Banafsheh, and Fezeh made sure no one brought them up in front of Bibi.

In regards to us as children, Fezeh did the monitoring very quietly and behind the scenes, not allowing herself to parent us. For example, one of our sessions with our chemistry tutor was abruptly interrupted by Fezeh's innovative calculations.

My sister, Nafiseh, had a chemistry tutor when she was in ninth grade. He came to our house a couple of times a week. I was to attend the same sessions so that my sister would not be alone. This young man, a teenager himself, also played the guitar and was in love with classical music. One afternoon as he finished teaching us chemistry, he invited us to listen to a symphony. I do not remember which one, probably Tchaikovsky, for it had great, definite beats and it was extremely exhilarating. Our tutor was totally poised having won our awe. At this point he dared to raise the volume higher and higher not realizing that Fezeh had run upstairs to Bibi's room, breathlessly saying, "Bibi, Bibi, *che neshasti ke inha parking* (instead of party) *tashkeel dadand* (they are having a party)!" Bibi laughed so hard as she told us to try to respect Fezeh's idea of a party: boy+girl+music.

Fezeh left our house when her daughter married (Bibi was in her fifties). She lived with her daughter and her three grandchildren for the remainder of her life. She passed away in 1999, two years after Bibi died.

Fezeh. Photo: Dashti family album, Tehran, 1967.

Banafsheh and her uncle Jamshid at her engagement party at Elahieh house. Photo: Dashti family album.

Notes

[1]   Story 40, "A Precious Gift," in this volume.
[2]   Story 15, "Winter," in this volume.

Thirty-Seven
We Have Layers

Bibi came to life each time a good listener was added to her audience. A very close friend of Bibi's was visiting us one day. We were all sitting in her room, captivated by the stories she told for the thousandth time. She looked at us one by one—the look on her face was designed to order, to encourage, to teach etiquette, but at the same time, it revealed her expectation of her adult children to properly serve their guest, knowing that a guest will never reveal his or her true desire (*ta'arof*). We started to tease each other and secretly begged each other to go get the tea. The teasing escalated to pinching and begging for a favor from each other. Eventually one of us asked the guest, "Would you like some tea?" Bibi disclosed her disappointment by yelling at us, "Here we do not ask our guests if they want something, we just serve them."

❖ ❖ ❖

Bibi was an expert at making up words for what did not readily come to her mind. The words she created, however, conveyed meanings more appropriately than the original words.

As a southern woman, Bibi was accustomed to wearing many layers of clothing. As a woman living in Tehran, Bibi wore regular garments such as a suit, one-piece dress, and a skirt and blouse. Underneath the dresses, however, she wore layers and layers of undergarments, some with specific names, others with no particular names. It was for those self-created layers that she came up with labels uniquely hers:

Zirpoosh (slip), a long silk slip most women wear under their dress, was the first layer of clothing for Bibi. She realized that she did not have the proprietary right to its name, so she called it what everyone else did, zirpoosh. For the rest of the layers, she made up her own labels. The second layer she called *konfarans* (conference) a garment similar to a tight T-shirt that she wore to secure the silk slip and to secure her waist (*pak-o-pahloo*) from any possibility of exposure to air. To further shield the konfarans, she wore the *reportage*. Reportage was a soft, long underdress with long sleeves made out of a handmade cotton or wool for the winter. She usually hand-sewed this piece from the delicate cotton from the south called *malmal*. The final cushion was a *ganj e farakh* (loose treasure). Ganj e farakh was similar to a man's sweatshirt with long sleeves and a round tight neck. She then wore a pair of sweatpants she called *roshandel*. The word was associated with a middle-aged Jewish man, a neighbor we had when we lived in *Khaneh ye Shahr*. Roshandel, who was clearly a rich man at one time, had ended up living in a small attic of a small house in our neighborhood in downtown Tehran. Some of us got to see his room randomly on Saturdays (Sabbath) as we went to turn on the stove for him. We got to see the inside of many of our neighbors' houses because, being Orthodox Jews, they were forbidden to turn on the stove or touch electrical gadgets on Sabbath. They asked us Moslem kids to do it for them. His room was small with no windows yet he had many fancy items such as ski equipment lying around the room. He was always in his off-white long johns. In the evenings, he came out of his room wearing the same clothing and walked around the alley where we could see him from the windows of our living room. Bibi's underpants were the same color and shape as those of Roshandel.

Even though the main function of the layers served to safeguard Bibi's private body, her sensitivity to cold required layers as well. Taking a bath was a risk she seemed to take. After she took a bath, some of the layers were doubled up! We arranged them in three piles on two chairs, the way they were piled up in her closet (*doolabcheh*). We put them inside the bathroom in her bedroom for her to wear before she walked out of the bathroom. One of us stood there to hand her a layer at the time. She called out, "Konfarans, reportaje," and would laugh so hard with us at her creative labeling as she ran to her room with a big Rocky-style hooded bathrobe. On top of these layers she wore her regular dress.

She did the same thing to us when we were small kids. After a bath, she would dress us with layer after layer of clothing, put a fistful of Vaseline on our faces, and tuck us under the blanket under the *korsi*. No vinegar for a week after a bath! (We have no idea where she got that idea.)

The dresses women wore in the south were ceremonial. From the top, a lady wore a flat, thin bonnet called *lachak* or *kolakhcheh*. *Lachak* is a flat rectangular cloth made of cotton with lace on either side to tie under the chin. Most of them are embroidered with colorful beads and shiny lace (*qaitoon e shab nama*) to show underneath the *maynaar*. Its function is to hold the *maynaar* in place.

Maynaar or *maghnaeh* is a lightweight, see-through lace worn as a scarf under the *chador*. It is usually in black or in white. Some wear their maynaar with both wings in front (*maynaar e do bali*) and some wear it with one short wing in front and the longer wing thrown to the back, covering one shoulder (*yek bali*). Our bibis wore it yek bali. The fancy maynaars were made with very delicate lace called *toor e khashkhashi*. Both the lachak and maynaar symbolically represented the honor and the power of the southern families. If a woman throws a maynaar or a lachak, they create a refuge. Abdollah Dashti (my father) in his journal, *Az Jam/Riz ta Tabriz* (From Jam/Riz to Tabriz)[1] describes one such occasion:

In 1921, the British army was replaced by the S.P.R [South Persia Rifles]. In an attempt to overcome the khans of Dalaki, the S.P.R force attacks the fort of Nour Mohammad Khan, khan of Dalaki. Nour Mohammad Khan does not open the door, but he was shot in both of his legs. It was at that moment that the wife of Nour Mohammad Khan throws her *lachak* at the feet of the S.P.R. lieutenant [*maynaar andakht*]. He was man enough not to kill their son, Ahmad Khan, and did not ravage their house. But all of Dalaki was looted.

On top of the maynaar they wore a chado*r*. The chadors of the bibis were never black and were not meant to cover their faces; they were made of colorful, lightweight fabric (*val*) with silk flowers embroidered on them. Some of the patterns had large flowers and some had flowers with branches and leaves. The chador is longer than the maynaar, but not all the way to the ground—usually above the knee and hung loose on the back.

The tunic is called *joomeh e do bar chak*. This is a long tunic, below knee length with a round collar, buttoned to the waist with hidden buttons or hooks (*dokmeh qablemeii* or *qazan qofli*). It opened on both sides of the waist, allowing the much-elaborated pleated skirt to pop out on both sides.

Underneath the joomeh e do bar chak, they wore a straight long shirt with hidden pockets made of very soft handwoven fabric called *malmal* (similar to Bibi's reportage).

Joomeh is topped with *arkholak* (short coat). The short coat is usually made of fabrics such as velvet, Banares, or Gujarat (padded cotton). Its underarm is left open for better movement. The sleeves are long and finish up with a triangle on the back of the hand. Most of the decoration on the arkholak is done with gold or silver embroidery (*sermeh doozi*).

From the waist down, they wore very loose pants called *shalvar* (similar to *shalwar kameez*) fastened with a band at the waist. On top of these pants they wore the very fancy skirts made of pleated material, yards and yards of delicate fabrics. The skirts are called shalvar (pants) as well, yet they do not separate in the middle like pants do; they are skirts.

The pleated shalvar is tightened to fit the waist by a band running through the waistband (*lifeh*); elasticized bands came later. All kinds of very fancy fabrics came through the port of Bushehr from India, China, Europe, and Africa.

The most popular fabrics were *val e gol abrishami*, *sondos*, *estabraq*, *halata*, velvet, silk, cottons, etc.

Many women workers such as Zarafshoon got good money from the khans' wives and daughters to embroider yards and yards of fabrics. Bibi had learned to do *sermeh doozi* (embroidery with silver yarn) when she was a child. She had pieces of the silver yarn in her closet all those years. Many times she took them out, expressing regret that none of her daughters showed interest in learning the craft. We are not sure if she ever actually learned it herself!

Bibi wearing her chador in yek bali style. Photo: Dashti family album.

As a bibi, one did not promiscuously reveal anything personal; her physical needs, her emotions, or opinions were never exposed (*ta'arof*). No one ever verbally expressed, "I am in love," "I hate," "I am hungry," "I am tired," or "I need a break," etc.—never. As a bibi, you had a reserved manner. That is probably why poetry has been our most acceptable way of relating to others emotionally. In this formal way, men and women tamed their emotional lives. If one's emotion was not expressed through poetry, if there was eye-to-eye confrontation, the person was considered shameless (*vaqih*): "*eva! rast too roy e adam voy miseteh vo migeh!*" (Do you believe this? She stands there, in your face, looking you in the eye and says it!) was what one usually heard when expressing feelings without layers.

In the south, everyone across generations knows many of the poems of our grandmasters by heart, despite the fact that most may not even know how to read or write.

We arrived at the door of a resident—a minibus full of travelers, deep in the plains of Asalooyeh near Borazjan. A middle-aged woman opened the door and stood there. It was three o'clock in the afternoon. That hour in the afternoon is like three o'clock in the morning elsewhere. The towns are asleep.

We asked if we could come in for some food, intending to pay them handsomely for their favor. She stood back, avoiding eye contact. She moved to the side of the door graciously, making way, unblocking our entrance. The door to her house was wide open then. With a smooth and clear voice, she started reciting a page of poetry by Hafez. Her head moved along with her hands, bowing and bending, making gestures according to the poem. The long poem was to welcome a beloved guest. She performed like an opera singer and moved her body like a tai chi master:

> In the hope of union, my very life, I'll give up
> As a bird of Paradise, this worldly trap I will hop.
> In the hope of one day, being your worthy servant
> Mastery of both worlds I'll gladly drop.
> May the cloud of guidance unload its rain
> Before I am back to dust, into the air I rise up.
> Beside my tomb bring minstrels and wine
> My spirit will then dance to music and scent of the cup.
> Show me your beauty, O graceful beloved of mine
> To my life and the world, with ovation I put a stop.
> On my deathbed give me a glimpse of your face
> So like Hafez, I too, will reach the top.
> —Ghazal # 336

She then left for the kitchen as soon as the other members of the family, mostly men, rushed to welcome us to their home. They prepared the most exquisite meal for about twenty of us in less than an hour. They refused to accept any money or anything in return, instead, as we said good-bye, the head of the family, an elderly man, walked us to the door (*badraqeh*). With tears in his eyes, he murmured another poem while the entire family politely stood in silence:

When sorrows upon seekers' hearts settle, will not rattle
When beauty with comfort starts battle, will unsettle.

When to fate they submit their mind, themselves will bind
Finally, when Beloved's beautiful curls find, put egos behind.

If they come to us a moment, and sit near, disappear
Yet when joy in their hearts will appear, becomes clear.

If they understand that a lonely tear is but a gem that is dear
With a love so sincere, face early-risers they fear.

When laughter like red rubies to my eyes cling, my tears bring
From my face, when hidden secrets spring, joyously they sing.

The healing balm of the pain of love is not easy for sure, and is pure
Those who use their mind to find such a cure, many failures will endure.

Those who climbed fortune's ladder wrung after wrung, were strung and hung
And the ones who in praise sing Hafez's song, are thought wrong.

Those favored by this spirit, noble and pure, tempt and allure
For love's pain if a cure they must secure, then failure will endure.[2]
—Hafez, ghazal number 194

A southern woman's dress. Photo by Nasrollah Kasraian.

Notes

1   Abdollah Dashti, *Az Jam/Reez ta Tabriz* (From Jam/Reez to Tabriz). Compiled and edited by Badieh Dashti. (Tehran: Farhang e Hezareh e Sevom, 1385 [2006]): 14.

2   Ghazals number 194 and 336: Translated by Shahriar Shahriari, Los Angeles, CA, 1999. www.shahriari.com/

Thirty-Eight
Khaloo's Presents
(*Parcheh ye Khaloo*)

Khaloo's new wife (*zan e no-o*) committed two unforgivable sins in the beginning of her marriage. First, she had dared to remove the portrait of Khaloo from the mantelshelf (*taqcheh*) and worst yet, on a trip to Tehran, she had failed to please Bibi's daughters. For the second sin, the old wife (*zan e Khaloo*) was also to blame.

Khaloo had two wives. Both wives lived in peace under the same roof. Their mission was to serve their husband. Being a fair man, Khaloo took turns spending nights with each wife and was morally bound to provide for them equally. The first wife had seniority over the new one and was to be respected and obeyed by the new wife. Her duty was to train the new wife well in how to best serve their husband. One of the firm orders given by Khaloo was that the mantelshelf (*taqcheh*) of every room in the house was to be decorated with a large framed portrait of himself.

Most traditional houses in Iran have rooms with shelves built into the plaster walls where decorative pieces are displayed. The centerpiece, mantelshelf, is the place for the most precious (presentable) possessions.

In our house (*Khaneh ye Shahr*), no object was really considered too precious. On the mantelshelf of the main room, there was a dark purple velvet spread with silver handwoven stitches in the shape of teardrops and two Chinese metal vases (*ja cheraghi*). The two vases had eventually become receptacles for *mohr* (prayer stone), *tasbih* (prayer beads), pacifiers, bra paddings, keys, etc. In general, miscellaneous objects that had a use yet had no designated places ended up in those vases.

Things were different in Khaloo's house. The most valuable object was Khaloo's portrait. The portraits were initially in black and white; as technology advanced, so did his portraits. From black and white, they advanced to a sepia tone then to the state of the art once they were injected with bright red color on his lips and cheeks.

The naïve young new wife had brought some of her belongings (*jahizieh*) to her husband's house and had assumed she could decorate the one room that belonged to her and Khaloo with her own valuables. In doing so, the new wife had removed Khaloo's portrait in order to replace them with her wedding mirror and candleholders. Khaloo was in a rage when he arrived home that night. He blamed his old wife for not teaching the new wife the proper respect for her husband. The news of such a catastrophe travelled all over the country!

Khaloo was a fair man though. He wanted the best for his family. First and foremost, he had ordered his wives to observe what the daughters of Aqa ye Bozorg did and wanted them to do the same. He also expected his sons to follow the path of the *aqa zadeh*s (the sons of the Bibis).

When our cousin was sent to America to study, Khaloo prepared to send his son to America as well. He got a ticket for his son and told him, "You go to America and do what Bibi's son did." That was about all the preparatory instructions the young eighteen-year-old boy from Borazjan got. He arrived at New York's JFK airport in the summer of 1969 with a phone number and some cash in his pocket, not a word of English, not having a clue about what he was facing.

Our cousin, of course, followed the family tradition of hospitality and service. He went to New York to receive Khaloo's son and took him along to his state and enrolled him in the university. The capable young man did very well and continued his education on to graduate school and a PhD degree.

Khaloo was a textile merchant from a small region near Borazjan. He bought the cheapest fabrics from the bazaar in Tehran and sold them in the south and made a decent income, enough to run a two-women and six-children household comfortably and with pride. In fact, when one of the Bibis asked him why he got the second wife, he responded, "Khaloo, *pulom ziad avideh*" (I have too much money).

Each time he came to visit us in Tehran, he would come with one of the wives and bring yards of fabric as presents for Bibi's daughters.

Bibi would usually have them made into covers for mattresses or blankets before we even laid eyes on them. Even then, they were so unattractive that we could not help but make fun of them. This had become a source of guilt and anxiety for Bibi. What if on one of his visits, one of the servants brought them the bedding made out of his gift to us? What if one of her daughters made fun of the weird-looking fabrics and hurt Khaloo's feelings or embarrassed him in front of his wives?

Time and again, as soon as Khaloo, one of his wives, and a large package appeared at the bend of the alley, someone would run to the house exclaiming, "Put away the beddings, Khaloo is here!" Rapid movements followed the sudden announcement in our house. Each person took part in the action by hiding the mattresses or the blankets made out of Khaloo's fabrics.

Compulsively, Bibi made sure that Khaloo and his wife got the best and the most special bedding in the house. Her anxiety had eventually developed into a superstition. "What if not valuing this simple, well-intentioned, ambitious man's feelings brought bad luck to my children?" She had to make sure that they never saw where the fabrics had ended up. Bibi would warn us, "Make sure we do not hurt their feelings" (*Pedar saga mikoshametoon agar bekhandid*).

That day, we were prepared. We knew about the disaster in Khaloo's house and the embarrassment the new wife had created for herself by removing her husband's portrait. We were determined to empower her.

It was the new wife's first visit to Tehran. As usual, they had brought us yards of fabrics. Bibi opened the package confidently while all her girls were sitting in the room. We were shocked to see the distasteful fabrics. However, in order to please Khaloo, we pretended to be overjoyed. Pulling and pushing, we staged a fight over the fabrics. We overdid it to the point of giving them the wrong message. Khaloo was disappointed in his new wife one more time and also blamed the first wife. "You should have told her to tell me to bring more fabrics for the young bibies," he scolded the wives irritably. This was an even bigger mistake the new wife had made!

Ja cheraghi. Photo: Mohsen Jazayeri, Tehran, 2014.

Ja cheraghi on mantelpiece in Khaneh ye Shahr, about 1948. From left to right: Badieh, Bibi, Nafiseh, Talieh, and our father.

Thirty-Nine
Warp and Weft

When I was about thirteen years old (1962), my family moved to our great-uncle's house and stayed for one year while he was serving as ambassador to Beirut. Living in his home was a special treat; we were introduced to many luxuries that came with the house as well. We saw a gramophone for the first time. The wind-up gramophone was installed in a fine wooden cabinet with shelves full of records. Many symphonies, operas, Iranian classics, and American singers' albums were part of his collection of music. We sat in the salon and listened to those albums for hours as we flew on the wings of music. We were mesmerized by all of them, especially by the music of Nat King Cole, Johnny Mathis, and Frank Sinatra. We played those records over and over to the point that some of the records turned white from the scratches of the needle.

Our great-uncle Ali Dashti was also known for having one of the richest libraries in the country. His collections of books connected us to the world of ideas. My sisters and I went through the books shelf by shelf and began reading the books we thought were important to read. In that year, we read many classics such as *The Hunchback of Notre Dame* and *Les Miserables* by Victor Hugo, *War and Peace* by Leo Tolstoy, The *Three Musketeers* and *Le Conte de Monte-Cristo* by Alexandre Dumas, *Gadfly* by Ethel Lilian Voynich and more, all translated into Farsi.

The only book I do remember almost word for word is *Gone with the Wind*, a novel by Margaret Mitchell. Nafiseh had started to read the three-volume book first. She looked so absorbed in the book. As soon as she put the book down, I took it and hid in the bathroom to read it. Sepideh had also noticed our fascination and could not be left out. So she started reading it as soon as she found the book not in our possession. The spacious European bathroom next to our uncle's master bedroom with a carpet inside, two toilet bowls (one regular bowl and the other a bidet), and a comfortable bathtub became the most private and peaceful place to read.

The three of us, after many fights, hiding, and locking the bathroom door to read just a few more pages, agreed on some kind of arrangement. We agreed to take turns, two hours each. My older sister had priority no doubt, then it was my turn, and then my younger sister's. The challenge was to discipline ourselves to not only respect each other's turns but not to share what we had already read before we all caught up. The photos from the movie incorporated inside the three large volumes had become a prize for our thirsty eyes. Amazingly, we never looked at the pictures before we got to the page. When one by one we finished the book, we shared the photos, and we shared the moments of tears to mourn the end of such an incredible period of reading. The chance to give our souls so much joy was over, so it seemed. But we owned it; the story was ours. We played the roles of the characters as we read the book. We compared the characters of the novel with the people we knew and with ourselves. Some days we were Scarlett O'Hara and another day Melanie Hamilton. We fell in love with Ashley Wilkes and then with Rhett Butler. We adored Mammy and thought of our own nannies. We suffered with the O'Haras through the war and famine and mourned alongside Rhett Butler when his daughter, Bonnie Blue, died. Our favorite color became dark green; we made a vow that our future curtains would be dark green velvet just like the ones Scarlett had turned into a dress. Everything else in Tara Plantation was what we were going to have when we had our own houses.[1]

With the exception of the chapters about the Civil War, which were too painful and distasteful for our hopeful souls, we read each chapter over and over again.

It was a few months after that summer that we heard the news: *Gone with the Wind* was on the screen in Tehran!

Overwhelmed by the thrill, the same afternoon that we heard the news, the three of us, completely unprepared yet entitled, ran out of the house empty-handed. We grabbed a taxi and hurriedly told him to just take us to Kasra Theater! Listening to us on the way, the taxi driver started asking questions and gently reminded us that we cannot convince the theater employees that this movie belonged to us. "You have to pay!" he carefully reminded us.

Was it possible that others were not aware how important it was that we see the movie right away? In our immature minds, we could not convert such wild levels of passion and devotion into the wisdom of patience and planning. *How ignorant can people be?* we thought. The gentleman turned the car around halfway to the theater and brought us back home.

I cannot rightly describe what it felt like to be separated from the texture of the real world; we were like three drunken children forced to sober up. A profound silence, as well as fear, took over us on the way back. In our hearts, we knew he was right; we were so thankful that we got home safely.

The next day, we got the money, and our older sisters took us to the movie. Once we sat in the theater, the walls separating us from our dream world vanished again; the movie was even more magnificent than the book.

During that one year in what was the most ideal environment, we became good readers. Throughout our junior and senior high school years, we continued to read most of the classics and many new books that were translated into Persian as well as books by new Iranian writers. American books were not very popular in Iran yet—most of the books translated were from Europe (especially East Europe), Latin America, and Russia.

A brilliant and mind-boggling book we read was from one of the masters of fiction, Gabriel García Márquez, *One Hundred Years of Solitude.* The lifestyle of the Buendía family in that book resembled ours in so many ways; their days were also so full of life beyond the capacity of any other family. In our family, like the Buendías, there was no wasted time, no time for transition; we also had to notice everything in the moment we lived it. The repetition of generations portrayed in *One Hundred Years of Solitude* seemed to be what our family was trying to achieve.

We had fallen in love with that book. I made a vow to learn the Spanish language fluently so that some day I could read the books by Gabriel García Márquez in his original language and to get to know him personally to see for myself how it was possible that he knew our family so well![2]

Even though I hardly remember the details of the stories, those books were telling—only a few characters' names and a general idea—I do not doubt that the warp and weft of our makeup is made partly by all that we read so diligently.

◆ ◆ ◆

The most astounding news was out! *Zan e rooz* (Modern Woman magazine) had this breaking news in one of its 1967 issues: Lieutenant Gerard and Dr. Kimble, the main characters of the *Fugitive* television series, had a friendly lunch together! There was no questioning it; the magazine did have proof. It had a picture of the two of them sitting in a café, having lunch like two friends would! Who could believe that? The whole school was talking about it, and I had seen the picture with my own eyes. The article in the magazine was condescending. I ran home that day to tell everyone.

Iranian families sat around their television sets with so much sympathy for the good doctor. Even though the episodes took only a half-hour, the intensity of our compassion lasted a week and then again was renewed with the next episode. Every Tuesday evening, the streets of Tehran became empty; everyone rushed home to see the television series *The Fugitive*. The innocent Dr. Kimble had captured our justice-seeking hearts. At the same time, we were charmed by the decent and committed nature of the lieutenant whose obsession was to capture the fugitive. Hollywood had managed to take over our minds and our hearts: from across the globe, the humanistic acts of Dr. Kimble and the chase had turned into the focus of our lives. I remember dreaming of it and waking up in a sweat. "But Dr. Kimble is innocent!" I would panic at the thought of a decent man being misjudged.

The viewers in our home included Bibi, our Baba, eight of us children, Fezeh and her family—all mesmerized by the events and the characters in the film, believing it all to be reality.

Fezeh and Banafsheh were the most serious viewers. Zarafshoon and Jamshid (Fezeh's sister and brother) added to the authenticity of every scene by chanting once in a while, "*Astakhforollah, panah bar khoda* (God, give mercy. We resort to your goodness God; help him)."

The best part of the event was when once in a while, this *Fugitive* Night turned into a feast. This was when our father arrived home early to watch the program and treated us to the most luxurious dinner. The very special treats were mortadella cold cuts (*kalbas*), baguettes, pickles, Pepsi Cola, and Canada Dry. The sandwiches were made before the program started.

◆ ◆ ◆

Most American and European politicians and Hollywood actors and actresses had become our role models, our heroes. We followed their news and the details of their lives. We were being convinced that Westerners were also human and that they understood things. In fact, in some tricky ways, they were replacing our own heroes such as Rostam, Esfandiar, and so many more.

We were being overwhelmed by Western influence—art and culture, books, movies, music, fashion, politics, social issues—ignoring our own. All that we were exposed to as young people were coming from the West, yet deep down, we felt we knew them, and we were the only ones who really understood them!

President Eisenhower visited Iran in December 1959, and we all went to cheer his arrival. There were about a million people in the streets. We were given small paper American flags to wave for the president. It was magnificent to see his bald head and face all the same color, light pink. It was a cold winter day, but the excitement kept us warm.

We came back home all very excited and told Bibi about all that we had seen. That was a mistake because Bibi got really mad when she heard that the president's motorcade ran over Persian carpets spread on the streets. Before we finished telling her all of the story, she ran to the phone and started calling the Shah's palace. Finally, she got through and told the man on the phone, "Tell the Shah to control himself. We are losing face this way. Do we have to be so extravagant in front of the world when we are still trying to build our country? For God's sake, this is so childish. What is the world going to think of us now?" She went on and on. Any sound on the street for hours after that made us think, this time for sure they are going to take her away.

When the Shah and the Empress Farah went to visit John F. Kennedy and Jacqueline Kennedy, Ali Dashti had a word with the Shah when he returned. "The queen who is representing Iran should not be wearing so much jewelry." "You were there to persuade America to help build Iran, not to show off fake wealth!" our great-uncle told him.

Queen Elizabeth passed by our house to go to the British Embassy one day the same year. Kilometer after kilometer of the walls along her route to the embassy were splashed with fresh paint overnight. We were walking home, and we saw her in the back of a Rolls Royce, and she waved at us; she looked a little like Bibi!

And who among us did not feel the devastation, the pain, on the day President Kennedy was assassinated? The despair I personally felt that day coming home from school was so deep. I must admit it was close to the devastation I felt when my own father died, only then I had been stricken by a private calamity. This was a public pain shared by everyone. I could hardly walk home. At home, there was a deathly silence. The news was too bitter to tolerate. The tradition in our family was to keep the most vulnerable protected from facing the hostile reality. However the magnitude of that tragedy had shaken our nation, making it impossible for the protective adults to hide the bitter reality from their families. Each one of us arrived home with a pale face and hid in a corner to mourn in silence. The fact that a savage could do a thing like that, to kill a man like that, confused us.

Jacqueline's sorrow was kind of familiar to us, a woman with young children who lost her husband. Of course we thought Jacqueline would be there to raise them with the love of the whole world—her extended family. But that expectation was not met either! How could she possibly marry a rich old man so soon? It was disgusting how she had betrayed us.

What now? What do we tell ourselves? Hollywood was better entertainment, we decided. They knew what we liked and the stories ended the way we could digest—happy endings.

Notes

1   Who remembers the green velvet curtains of our Beverly Glen house in Los Angeles (1985–1992)?
2   Oh no! Gabriel García Márquez just passed away (April 2014). I missed the opportunity and I have not learned Spanish yet.

Forty
A Precious Gift

Elahieh House
178 Khazar Street
Elahieh, Shemiran, Tehran
Tel: 26697

Two donkeys were running away with our carpets, their owners trying to catch up with them. The donkeys' long blue-bead necklaces decorated with brass bells were flying from side to side, creating a nostalgic rhythm. They ran, the robbers ran, and my brother Abbas's friend, Reza, and couple of other young men of the neighborhood who had suspected them were chasing them. Finally, past the Russian Embassy they were caught. The donkeys, the robbers, and the carpets were brought to our house in Elahieh and into the salon.

When the construction of Elahieh House was completed, Bibi had the Persian carpets washed in the creek (*roudkhooneh*) that ran next to the house. There were still no walls and no boundaries between our house, the creek, and the street. The carpets had been washed and laid flat on the pebbles to dry in the sun. During the quiet hours of an afternoon, two workers who were passing by in the creek had loaded their donkeys with our carpets and had taken off. Once they were brought inside the guest room (salon), they intended to leave the carpets, hoping to get away, but Fezeh made them wait in the salon until Bibi woke up from her afternoon nap to settle the matter. Bibi woke up, had her tea, and came downstairs. She stood by the donkeys and asked the two workers what they had to say in defense of their action. They told Bibi that the carpets looked so old, they had assumed someone had thrown them away. It seemed logical to Bibi. They were pardoned, fed, and were allowed to leave. "For god's sake, Fezeh, you brought the donkeys into the salon?" Bibi was so amused.

During the last months of construction, my sisters and I were sent to Shiraz to stay with our aunt (Abaj), my father and our brothers stayed in the tent, and a room was made ready for Bibi and Fezeh inside the unfinished house. The tent was completely furnished and piled up with rugs, beds, barrels of tar, cement debris, dugout boulders, and boxes of clothes, dishes, blankets, etc. A telephone landline was the very first thing set up in the tent; it was hooked up with a long wire from the house. Our father truly enjoyed picking up the phone and loudly responding, "Hello, this is the tent, may I help you? (*Allo, chador, befarmaid*).

A few of the objects were stored in the nomadic tent set up by our father as the construction trailer made it back to the house safely; the rest were damaged. For instance, a wheelbarrow filled with bricks was put on top of a metal cylinder full of antique Chinese pieces (*Zarfha ye gole morghi*)—those were cracked all the way to the bottom, not one had survived.

The carpets had been through rough times as well; they were spread on the ground in the tent.

Before the 1979 revolution in Iran, the name of our street was Heravi, named after the family who owned the entire lot extending from the Turkish Embassy to the

Photo: Our brother Abbas and his friend Kayhan, 1965. Our house is in the background to the right.
Source: Abbas's photo album.

243

Russian Embassy (about four acres). Our parents had managed to purchase a piece of that lot. Bibi had sold a piece of land she had inherited, and our Baba had sold what he owned, and they borrowed the rest from a woman who came to our door at the first of each month to receive her interest. The transaction, however, was not a smooth one; they had sold our parents two thousand square meters at fifty *tuman*s per square meter, which was reasonable at the time; however, part of the land was inside the creek, sold illegally. There were daily discussions and arguments between our family and the owner. The owner could have compensated for the illegal land with the extra piece of the land to the south, but instead, he made a deal with the real estate agent who built a small house on the disputed land overnight—literally! Our father was never able to recover the lost land; instead, Fezeh made the owner pay for his greed.

We were home on a quiet Friday morning. We began hearing a commotion on the street and ran to the windows to see. Like a faithful guard, Fezeh was always alert and ready to protect us. She had immediately detected the approach of the proprietor who was harassing our father out on the street. She ran out to the street with bare feet and a bare head. Our brother, Dadashi, had noticed and ran after her to defend our father. She dragged the man out of his car, pushed him to the sidewalk, and slapped him hard across the face over and over. Our father and brother were eventually able to hold her and let the old man go before he got more. Fezeh was brought inside, and we all ran downstairs cheering her. Our parents, satisfied with the revenge, nevertheless scolded her for hitting an elderly man.

The architect of the house was a friend of our family, Mohandes Dabbagh. He built a simple yet efficient rectangular house on about two hundred and fifty square meters on the northwest corner of the property. He brought the final architectural plan to us one evening. The blueprint seemed too abstract, except the drawing of the large French window alongside the stairway, which showed the picture of a woman's head sticking out of the window. That face gave us a tangible lead as to what that house was going to look like.

The floor plans materialized to an actual house shortly. The main entrance was on Heravi (Khazar) Street, entering a large foyer. To the south of the entry was our father's office, with a bathroom under the stairs, a large door opening to the salon, and the dining room with a coatroom in front. To the left of the smaller hallway were a full bath and an entrance into the kitchen. On the east of the kitchen was Fezeh's room with a glass door to the yard and the creek. The kitchen had a small service window into the dining room, which was open to the salon. (Initially, there was no wall between the dining room and the salon.) The salon had large glass windows and doors to a terrace with small stairs into the garden and a basement underneath our father's office.

The stairway led to a large hallway with a small window on top of the front door on Khazar Street; to the north of the entire stairway was a large French window, which opened to Homayoon *Koucheh*. One or two of the smaller windows opened; the rest were fixed glass—some tinted and some clear. The view from the top of the French window was the Alborz Mountains, with all the details visible to the eyes.

The foyer on the second floor opened to a hall or a den with four rooms, a full bath, and a storage room for bedding. The folded mattresses, blankets, and pillows stacked up from the floor to the ceiling for as many guests that arrived in our house. There were three large rooms on the right, plus a master bedroom to the left. From the east, the den opened to a small balcony facing the creek. In front of the three bedrooms was a long, narrow terrace as wide as the width of a twin mattress.

On summer nights, we took our mattresses and slept outside on the narrow terrace, one's feet touching the head of the other. The sound of the water running by the house and the vast starry sky made us sleep deeply during our teenage years, making it difficult to wake up as our father touched our faces with his toes, creating a kind shadow over our faces—time to wake up!

Some days I woke up with the pull of a string I attached to my wrist. The string reached the terrace downstairs, and my friend Afsaneh and her grandmother walked right to it and pulled the string to wake me. I joined them for early morning walks.

A few houses had already been built on the street before we began building ours. Our father visited all the neighbors and reassured them that he will build his house in such a way so as not to invade their privacy. "For that reason," our neighbor Mrs. Kambiz told us, "your father had these windows tinted, and most of the north side windows were raised in order to give us privacy."

The yard was vast enough to plant all kinds of fruits and decorative trees brought from nurseries outside of Tehran (Karaj). There was room for a garage and space for our father to have his own beehives. The construction of a wall around the property stayed pending for a couple of years due to the illegal sale by the owner. The bedrooms were assigned to us either individually or shared, and our parents had their own bathroom opening into the master bedroom. Bibi had a window overlooking the mountains and another window to the yard and the creek. She had her own private door opening to her balcony and a space that opened to the roof and to the starry sky. We thought of this opening as a meeting place for Bibi and God! The kitchen downstairs, with its blue tiles and modern cabinets, was spacious and accommodating. Fezeh had her room and her own entrance from the side door to the yard.

The glass chandelier in the salon shed light on the bright new gray Persian carpets and new furniture in the salon to welcome our guests. Our proud parents were hosting families and friends with open arms.

The first guest sat down with a certain buoyancy to criticize the plan, and our father firmly objected, "I have respectfully shared the plan with everyone I knew, asking for opinions and guidance. Whoever saw the plan, including you, sir, said that it was fine and flawless. I will not tolerate criticism at this point, now that the house is completed."

Our parents had expended all their resources in order to build a house for their family. In the process, they had encountered others' greed and lack of camaraderie. In their tribal culture, friends celebrated each other's moments of glory. In their culture, the community showed solidarity. As a tribesman, our father was now defending his territory against pointless criticism.

When our family purchased that property in Elahieh in 1963, it unknowingly influenced the culture of that neighborhood. The livelihood and the tribal background of our parents, Fezeh and her family, and all of us children drew people from the two very diverse sides of the neighborhood. Our home became a meeting point between the very poor, working class of the east side of Elahieh (*mahaleh ye sopoorha* [street cleaners]) and the very elite society of the west side of the Old Shemiran Road, home to the dignitaries of the time.[1] Both classes felt at home in our house, and to us, there were no differences.

The house in Elahieh withstood the intense forces generated by our transition from childhood to adulthood. The house served as a launch platform as we took off to our own establishments.[2] It also became a safe haven for all of us whenever we sought refuge. Each one of us who returned home and lived in that house added something to its structure and or function: a stairway here, a wall there, a swimming pool, a kitchenette upstairs, or a guest room (office) out in the yard. A few years after our father had passed away and Fezeh had left, Bibi rented out the downstairs suite, and the tenants became part of the history of that property.

Every day, we joined Bibi in her room for lunch. From left to right: Sepideh, Abbas, Mohammad Hassan (Dadashi), Mohammad Hossain, Bibi, Talieh, Sayeh, Badieh, Nafiseh. Photo: Dashti family album.

Every day, we joined Bibi in her room for lunch. From left to right: Sepideh, Abbas, Dadashi, Mohammad Hossain, Bibi, Talieh, Sayeh, Badieh, Nafiseh.

Our father died in that house; his office became his last resting place before he passed away in 1971.

Fezeh stayed in that house with Bibi until she moved in with her daughter and her daughter's husband when they had their first baby.

Bibi lived in Elahieh House until the last hours of her life in 1997. She became known as "*salar e Elahieh*" (the king of Elahieh).

We waited many years before we faced the reality of having to demolish our childhood home. Following years of disputes, conflicts, frictions, and dissension among the eight of us, the majority of us voted to choose a partner (Reza Davari) to build a five-story building where we could each independently own an apartment on our family's property. Sharing our space with people completely alien and at times even resentful of our tribal culture ultimately tested our territorial instincts; however, that remained our only choice. Our youngest brother, Mohammad Hossain, was chosen as the family's representative to deal with all the legal and other hassles of that construction. He sacrificed many years of his life to see it through to the finish line.

The ultramodern five-story building was completed in 2011 and now stands tall in place of the original house in Elahieh, Khazar Street. The view of the Alborz Mountains and the starry sky is hidden by many high-rises, and the sound of traffic overwhelms the rhythm of the running water in the creek. The spirit of being home, which continues to live on in our hearts, is a never-ending gift from our parents to us.

Notes

1   Shariati Street was called Jadeh ye Qadim e Shemiran. The bus stop for our neighborhood was called Dar e Dovom e Sefarat e Englis; colloquially referred to as: *doyyom*.

2   Except for Talieh, we all got married while living at the house in Elahieh. Also, Banafsheh, Jamshid (Fezeh's brother), our cousins' children Elham, Yousef, Zahra, and Amin had their weddings in that house as well.

Forty-One
A History of Elahieh

The value system of the West and the spiritual values of the East owe it to the history of mankind to perform yet another duty: they are obliged to complete and perfect each other. What they could give to one another will impact humanity. This is that "beyond reach opportunity," which will lead mankind to prosperity: A man dedicated to truth and dedicated to morality [*haqiqat va manaviat*].

Tagore, Tehran 1934[1]

Before the Qajar Dynasty, the Elahieh area was called Khor Azin. *Khor* or *khorshid* means the sun or a great light. The verb *azin bastan* means to beautify, to decorate, or ornament—*Khor Azin* therefore means decorated by the sun.[2]

Afzal al Molk, a historian of Mozaffar al Din Shah Qajar's era (1853–1907), and most other historians who have written about the history of Shemiran agree that the name Elahieh is attributed to Mirza Mohammad Ja'far Hakim Elahi Lavasani.[3] Elahi bought a portion of Khor Azin lands in 1866, and gradually the whole area was referred to as Elahieh. Years later, Ali Khan Amin al Dowleh, the prime minister of Mozaffar al Din Shah (February 1897–June 1898), bought another large portion of Elahieh and built a vacation house for himself. He lived most of the summer months in his property in Elahieh and entertained his guests there. According to Afzal al Molk, Mozaffar al Din Shah, his children, and other princes and princesses, the dignitaries of the court and its servants were regular guests in this garden.[4]

In 1891, Ali Khan Amin al Dowleh started a wooden match factory in Zargandeh, the southern part of Khor Azin. Mostoufi writes:

Amin al Dowleh believed that our economy was too dependent on imported products. He believed that essential products should be produced inside our own country by Iranian factories. He understood perfectly that the import of all kinds of products had exceeded the exported goods. Continuation of that situation, where even our horses are coming from Russia, could mean that soon all the gold and the riches of Iran, including what Nader Shah brought from India, would be owned by the Imperial Bank of England or the Pawn Bank of Russia.[5]

Unfortunately, due to the scarcity of wood in that area, the factory could not compete with the Austrian and Swedish matches in Iran and was forced to close.[6] Local residents report that the match factory gave its grounds to a paint factory, then to a glue factory, and at the present time (2014), it is the campus of Azad University Medical School, Elahieh Branch.

The district of Elahieh consisted of many large gardens, some belonging to European embassies and the homes of many politicians and dignitaries. The famous gardens of Elahieh included the German embassy (north side of Elahieh), the garden of the Turkish embassy in the center of Elahieh (Pol e Rumi), and the Russian embassy (south of Elahieh and north of Zargandeh). Many other embassies—Danish, Swiss, Belgian, Icelandic, Cuban, Indian, and Finnish—are also situated in Elahieh. The British Embassy compound borders Elahieh on the east.

Wipert von Blücher was the ambassador of Germany in Iran during the first years of Reza Shah's reign. He has written extensively about his experience on a trip to the German embassy's summer garden in Elahieh:

We were supposed to travel to the summer villa of the German Embassy that was certainly more beautiful than the building downtown. After a short stay in Tehran we continued on our journey. We travelled on a wide road that went straight from Tehran to the north of the city [Pahlavi Street, now called *Vali ye asr*] and ended up in the pleasant Shemiran district located in the foothills of the Alborz Mountains. Shah's summer palace and the villas of ambassadors and many well-off Iranians are located there. Undoubtedly, Shemiran is one of the most beautiful places in the world. At an elevation of 1,500 meters, resting on the slopes of the 4,000-meter-high Touchal Peak and surrounded by a range of mountains, it is breathtaking. In the south there is a valley with Tehran in its center at 300 meters less height and behind it there are still more ranges of mountains. This area is truly rich with water and glorious ancient trees.

The garden of the German Embassy is five acres with fabulous trees, mostly sycamore, poplar, willow, and walnut trees; it goes all the way close to the mountains and has the most beautiful view of Touchal Peak. More than twelve *qanat*s are used to irrigate this garden.[7]

Besides the numerous *qanat*s and wells, most of the gardens were irrigated by the creek that comes from the Ja'far Abad River off the Alborz Mountains. All the gardens and the streets are decorated with old sycamore, mulberry, walnut, and willow trees. Honeysuckles (*peech e Amin al Dowleh*) climb most of the trees in Elahieh, filling the air with heavenly perfume and the sound of streamlets running along those trees on each and every alley.

One of the large gardens of Elahieh was inherited by Dr. Ali Amini who was prime minister under Mohammad Reza Shah (May 6, 1961 to July 19, 1962). Another large garden belonged to Amin Daftar, one of the dignitaries of Nasser al Din Shah's court. After his death, his wife Fatemeh (daughter of Asef al Dowleh, the reverend chief custodian of Imam Reza Mausoleum) inherited the garden. In her lifetime, the garden was divided into small and large plots and was sold to different people. That garden continued from the western part of Elahieh to the river (creek) and bordered the bridge of the Russian embassy (presently the southern boundary of Khazar Street). In 1924, the Anglo-Iranian Oil Company bought the main part of this land from Fatemeh, including the main house (furnished), at the price of 7,500 *tumans*.[8] This property continued to be the residence of the CEOs of the British company and host of important conferences. A part of this property still belongs to the Iranian Oil Company. The structure of the building has not changed; only some repairs inside the building still continue.

At Dashti intersection, in the east of Elahieh, the four houses on each of the four corners belonged to Senator Ali Dashti (southwest corner); Siasi, a Tehran University professor (northeast corner); Prime Minister Dr. Mosaddeq (northwest corner); and MP Majd, a member of the parliament (southeast corner).

Elahieh was so beautiful, cozy, and quiet. Next to our house was the creek, and around it, there were fields of wheat and hills filled with yellow flowers. Elahieh was the secret place of lovers and students who wanted a peaceful place to study. All you heard were the music of birds and streams of water running through. In the afternoons a pair of well-groomed horses walked out of the gate of our neighbors (Mr. and Mrs. Kiani) as they went around the neighborhood, adding yet more rhythm to the serenity of Elahieh.

Elahieh is still a posh neighborhood in Shemiran. It is bordered by Tajrish and the Alborz Mountains on the north, Mahmoudieh in the west, Qeitarieh to the east, and Zargandeh from the south. There are entrances to two metro stations in Elahieh bringing people from all over the city to the neighborhood. Two gigantic bases of the two major double-decked freeways, Ayatollah Sadr and Shahid Modares freeways, have completely swallowed our old house in Tighestan (Soltani's). There are now more high-rises in Elahieh than anywhere else in Tehran and yet more to come by the hour!

The face of Elahieh is disfigured much like a divine punishment or maybe a divine mockery.

Rabindranath Tagore meeting with members of the Literary Society of Iran (Anjoman e Adabi) in 1932. Seated from left: Ali Dashti, Tagore, Mohammad Taqi Bahar, and Dinshah Irani. Standing at center: Sa'id Nafisy. Photo: Dashti family album.

اگر پرش فکر آزاد حافظ در سعدی نیست ، یا جذبه‌های عرفانی
و یرا بمدار جلال الدین بالا نبرده است ، در عوض شاهکاری چون بوستان
آفریده و زبان وی در خیر انسانیت و تشویق بعدل و انصاف بکار افتاده
حتی از نصیحت و انذار خداوندان زور باز نایستاده است .

مادر سعدی افکار فلسفی خیام را جستجو نمیکنیم تا از نیافتن آن به
ملامت برخیزیم ، ولی هنگامی که صحبت از افکار خیام یا جهش روحی جلال
الدین بمیان میاید بگویم که این دو نوع فکر در سعدی وجود نداشته
اما در عوض غزلهائی از نوک خامه او جاری شده است که تا فرزندان این
مرز و بوم عشق میورزند و تا وقتی که آرزو دلمارابه تپش میاندازد اشعار
ترسعدی زبان حال همه ما خواهد بود .

و هرگز فراموش نمیکنیم که سعدی آن قوت روح و نیروی ایمان
را دارا بوده است که به پادشاه مستبدی بگوید :

بنو بتند ملوک اندرین سپنج سرای
کنون که نوبت تست ای ملک بعدل گرای

تیغستان ــ ۲۰ اردیبهشت ۱۳۳۹

Ali Dashti's book: The Realm of Sa'di.
Signed Tighestan, 20 Ordibehesht 1339.

Khazar Street from our rooftop.
Photo: Mohsen Jazayeri, 2015.

Notes

[1] Rabindranath Tagore (1861–1941), the Indian poet and philosopher and recipient of the 1913 Nobel Prize for literature, visited Iran in 1934 and met with Ali Dashti.

[2] S. Hayyem, *Persian-English Dictionary* (Tehran: Farhang-e Mansour Publishing, December 31, 2003): 5 and 367.

[3] Mansoureh Etehadieh and Cyrous Sadvandian, *Gholamhossain Afzalalmolk, Afzalaltavarikh* (Tehran: Nashr e Tarikh e Iran, 1361 [1982]).

[4] Manouchehr Sotoodeh, *Joghrafia ye tarikhi e Shemiran* (Tehran: Moasseseh ye motaleat va tahqiqat e farhangi, 1371 [1992]): 113–14.

[5] Abdollah Mostoufi, *Sharh e zendegani e man*, 4th ed. (Tehran: Dayereh e sefid, 1388 [2009]): 2:25.

[6] Mohammad Ali Jamalzadeh, *Ganj e shaygan: oza e eqtesadi e Iran* (Tehran: Sokhan, 1384).

[7] Wipert von Blücher, *Safarnameh e Blocher* (Blocher's travel journal) Trans. Kaykavoos Jahandari, 2nd ed. (Tehran: Kharazmi, 1369 [1990]): 179.

[8] In 2014, the range of prices for properties in this area was between twelve million, residential, to one hundred and thirty million *tuman*s, commercial, per square meter. The exchange rate was 3400 *tuman*s per dollar.

Forty-Two

The Generous Have No Money— The Rich, No Generosity

Karam daran e aalam ra deram nist, Deram daran e aalam ra karam nist!
—Sa'di, *Golestan*, Chapter 7[1]

Bibi chanted this poem by Sa'di every time she reached into her thin flat black leather purse. She would return the purse to the wall closet in her room with disappointment and start walking around and chanting, "The generous have no money—the rich, no generosity!" Then she would laugh wholeheartedly and share a story with the recipient of her generosity. As she walked around the room, her voice gained momentum, and she looked more certain of the meaning of the poem. She stood tall and seemed more confident for the encore, this time stronger, as if she were leading the national anthem.

No one left empty-handed after coming to Bibi. She felt obliged to donate something she believed the person might need or want. She gave dates, rice, cooking oil, extra clothes, shoes, notebooks, pots and pants, and money (she humbly told the person it was for the bus fare), etc. Therefore there was never anything extra left in our closets or in the house. She gave what she had to whoever had come to ask for help or just to visit. Whenever we looked for something we had not used for a while, we knew right away she had given it away. Besides her very personal items such as a comb, slippers, a purse, and a few clothes, she kept nothing else she could call hers.

❖ ❖ ❖

Bibi was in her fifties when she lost her husband. She was left with a large household, three young boys, and a daughter still at home, heavy expenses of mortgage, running her own family and the families depending on her, all with very limited assets, questioning whether the men of the family had done the right thing refusing all the opportunities to receive well-deserved rewards—even though she herself believed that they were like captains leading their ships to shore, putting the lives of the people ahead of themselves, not expecting gifts for what they considered their patriotic duties as well as their humanistic responsibilities.

Their good name was alive for sure, yet the values of the times were changing; money was talking now. Her generous and ambitious upbringing was demanding so much more. Besides, the good name of her family had inevitably created a reputation; people expected wealth to follow their fame and grandeur.

Bibi's thin purse was like her pot of rice—a bottomless pit. With one pot of rice, she fed so many people. Somehow she managed to run the household and give some to the needy and save her face (*ab-e-roo*). She never asked for money from anyone and believed that if it is something that needs be done, the money will come. She truly believed that God had her back. Very seldom did she go to her balcony and to the special place she met with God for money. She told us this story about one of those occasions:

A bill for the amount of 4,500 *tuman*s was due. I was struggling to figure out how to pay it. It was important to pay it on time, and I did not want to ask anyone for help. There were no gold coins nor anything else I could sell or put up as collateral to borrow from the bank. That was one of the occasions when I had no choice but to ask God. So I did. The next morning after I had a good talk with God, a man came to our door and brought a bag of money from the farm we had in Shah Abdol Azim. There were 4,500 *tuman*s in there![2]

Sepideh said:

It was about noontime when the doorbell to Khazar House rang. It was just a few months after our Baba had passed away. Our farm keeper had brought a bag of herbs and another small bundle. He was ashamed because he never brought the money he earned from that land and sold the produce for himself. In fact, he took over the land years later. Bibi went to receive him in our father's office that had been turned to a small salon after he passed away. He handed Bibi a small bundle of money and put his head down, asking for Bibi's forgiveness. Bibi opened the bundle and started crying. It was the exact amount Bibi had asked God for.

The man went to the kitchen to talk to Fezeh and to tell her that things had been hard and he had not had a chance to get more money all those months and years!

Fezeh told him, "You don't realize that God hit you on the back of your head to come today and deliver this money. Bibi is crying with God, not because of you."

Bibi sympathized with a disappointed burglar who left our house empty-handed and had only found some dates to eat. She believed the burglar should have left a letter like this:

Dear lady, it took me so much planning to come to this neighborhood and to this house thinking that there are going to be locks and dead bolts on each door and treasure inside. Alas, I found no walls separating your house from the street—no locks on any doors, nothing valuable in the house worth stealing. I pray for you, lady . . . Sorry I took some dates with me.[3]

Signed by The Burglar

A similar situation occurred after the revolution of 1978. The revolutionary guards came to search our house expecting to confiscate mountains of jewelry, valuables, and so on. According to Bibi, it took them hours to search the whole house. Of course they could not find anything of monetary value. The agent told our mother, "Lady, you are either very sneaky or very dumb."

Bibi laughed with them and asked them if they have had lunch. Then she recited the same poem, "Karam daran e aalam ra deram nist, Deram daran e aalam ra karam nist."

The gradual increase in the volume of her voice, along with the mesmerized look on her face, and an apparent pride, was a reminder of what she indeed stood for: humility!

Aqa ye Bozorg had said that none of us will ever be wealthy. "Money will come our way many times, however we will never be enslaved by it," he had firmly ordered. "God will not bless you, my children, if you ever say, I do not care." He wrote this in his will.

This inheritance has cost us! None of us have a normal relationship with money. For generations, there has not been a businessman (a successful businessman, that is) in our family. Most of us struggle with the management of money, having a hard time believing that we could have high morality and still be wealthy. The poem continues:

Become rich! once your heart and your body prospers,

You can eat, you can give and flourish in this world and eternity.

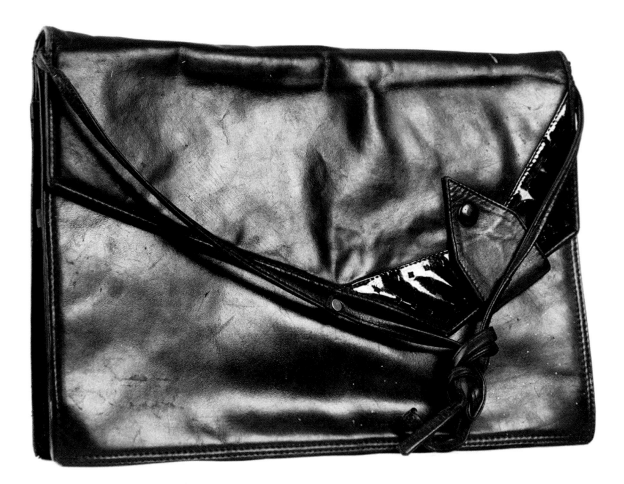

Bibi's purse. Photo: Mohsen Jazayeri, 2014.

Notes

1   Saʿdi's *Golestan*, Chapter 7: On effect of education, Story 19: Contention of Saʿdi with a disputant concerning wealth and poverty.

2   There were many eyewitnesses to this incredible incident (coincidence?), Fezeh, our neighbors, Khanoom e Kambiz and Foroogh Khanoom Kafaʾi, Sepideh, and more. They talked about it for years.

3   Our house on Khazar Street was without a wall for many years. The mailing address for our house was Elahieh, Khazar, No. 178, the house with no walls (*khooneh ye bi divar*).

Forty-Three
May I Take Your Broom, Sir?

A t almost every stage of human history, man has looked for support from magic and the supernatural. To help our wishes come true, we make vows to God, either directly or via the assistance of a mediator. In times of suffering, we plead to the highest spirits to intervene.

Deaths, illnesses, accidents, final exams, and love affairs are mostly observed in the name of an imam or a saint with the hope to further bless the soul of the deceased, to cure the sick, to make the youth pass their exams, the lovers to join their beloveds, etc.

There are saints who specialize in different matters, so we believe. We also feel that the saints who have suffered the most are purer and closer to God; we choose them because they know what it means to be so desperate. I cannot believe that I once helplessly searched my mind for the name of Her Holiness Zeinab's children, when Nargol, my grandniece was in the hospital. We have assigned a saint for travelers, one who cures the sick, one who helps empower people, one who blesses the soul of the innocent, and one who protects our goods against thieves, and during football matches, we resort to all of them.

His Holiness Imam Abbas, who had lost his arms during a *jihad*, is one of the most trusted imams and was highly respected by Fezeh. When Fezeh left something somewhere and wanted to make sure it was safe, she would declare that the arms of Imam Abbas are on it, protecting it.

We had a male worker, Rajab, who did the daily shopping. Fezeh suspected that he was not being truthful about the money he was spending. She reported her suspicion to Bibi, and together they confronted Rajab. Rajab swore that he had never taken any money and would never do such a thing. Fezeh said, "I believe you. From now on, I will ask Imam Abbas to accompany you when you go shopping." Bibi agreed, and they both waited for Rajab to react. Rajab said, "I am not going. Send someone else."

The name of Ali, our first imam, has always assisted men in doing things they normally cannot do. Two wheels of my Volvo fell into a narrow waterway as I tried to make a U-turn in a narrow street in Tehran. Four men ran to help me. They each grabbed a corner of the heavy car and tried to lift it. The car did not move. Then as if they knew when, all four of them, along with the people on the street, in one voice called out, "Ali," and the car was lifted like a feather up in the air. My baby was asleep in her seat in the back. She opened her eyes and said, "*Ya* Ali," and went back to sleep.

Lazy men joke about that and say, "When you hear Ali, stay away, hard work is in progress Go where you hear Hossain, there will be free food!"

In Iran, hospitality, spirituality, and compassion drive us to give money and food and offer services generously. In honor of the divine, in order to defy the harm caused by the evil eye or simply to welcome a person to our homes, we use any excuse to give and share.

Hardly anyone goes hungry during the months of religious ceremonies. Tens of humongous pots, each filling up the back of a pickup truck, are cooking everywhere. In small alleys, inside homes, in the mosques, hospitals, shops, or on the sides of the roads, people most generously donate a variety of foods and drinks (*nazri*). The lines to get the blessed food are long in every neighborhood, rich or poor.

Ash reshteh (noodle soup), *sholleh zard* (rice pudding), *halva, sharbat* (a traditional Middle Eastern beverage of sweetened, diluted fruit syrup or juice), and *polo va khoresht e qeimeh* (rice and split pea stew) used to be the most common nazri foods. These days, however, other foods have been added. There are *baqeleh polo* (rice and lima beans), *fesenjoon* (pomegranate and walnut stew), *qormeh sabzi* (vegetable stew), *adas polo* (rice and lentils), and other gourmet foods. Last Moharram, the new fast-food shop on Zafar Street in Tehran, donated pizza and orange juice; the money exchange business near Tajrish, North Tehran, donated *chelo kabob* to offer appreciation for the incredible rise of the dollar against the *rial* that had made them very rich. On our prophet's birthday in June 2012, we were served Danish and chocolate milk on the highway to Meigoon.

For every new car, a sheep is sacrificed. For every new house, a new baby, a loved one coming from abroad, the arrival of an honorable guest—any time one avoids a potentially dangerous situation or receives any really good news calls for the sacrifice of a lamb, a cow, or even a chicken; blood must be spilled. The food thenceforth is donated to the poor. The butcher's share is usually the skin and the intestines of the animal.

My friend Jila in Los Angeles put four eggs (would-be blood) in four Ziploc bags and ran over them with her new car for a spiritual car insurance.

❖ ❖ ❖

In 2004, a European ambassador was our guest when we hiked trails deep into the glorious Zagros Mountains. It took us eleven hours to get to Daryacheh ye Gahar, the highest lake in the Middle East.

We set off early in the morning from a nearby village. We were told that it would be a two-hour walk to the lake from the village. Every two hours, we passed by a black tent and asked how far the lake was; we were told only two more hours. Sure enough, it took us about five two-hour walks and a mule ride to finally get to the lake.

At each stop, a lamb was sacrificed to welcome us. The meat was quickly barbecued on wooden skewers cut from fig trees. For the first time we watched how they wrapped the intestine of the lamb tightly around the skewer to make sausage, the best we had ever tasted.

The skins were preserved and salted to be used for making a tent, clothing, or an area rug. Every part of the sheep had a use. Even the manure and or the food left in the intestines were saved for fertilizer. We were truly flattered by the hospitality of the tribes we visited.

The ambassador whispered in my ear, "If one more lamb is slaughtered, I will kill myself." It made me sad that he could not see how the people were giving us everything they had and even things they could not normally afford, such as a whole lamb. But I sort of understood him not wanting to watch the bloody scenes before he has his daily steak, wondering if he had assumed the meat he eats grows on a tree.

The son of the ambassador who had never walked on dirt in his entire life of twenty-some years uttered in disappointment, "I have a feeling this is the last day of my life."

He had completely lost his self-confidence. His father was letting him know how very disappointed he was in him. At 65, he himself was walking ahead of all of us, marveling at the last of the tent people and the glorious mountains, the mudbrick buildings, and the black tents. My sons crossed the streams by balancing with their arms like gymnasts; my husband felt at home, being a mountain man himself. Even my sister Nafiseh and I were walking with ease, ignoring the blisters on our feet thanks to our enthusiasm.

The son of the ambassador (nicknamed Qoli) was so pale and so exhausted from walking and taking his shoes and socks off and putting them back on every time we crossed a winding stream. He gobbled the kebabs each time as if it would be his last opportunity for a meal. He ate the most kebab when another lamb was barbecued following a snake alert in the tent.

We were offered tea as we sat in the tent with the chief of a tribe and the male members of his family. (Rhe women were watching us from their own tents.) Qoli had panicked when two men carrying large rifles led us to a large black tent made from sheepskin. He and I were led to the tent to wait for our group to catch up with us.

"Why are they armed?" He had completely given up on his life when he asked me that. I reassured him by repeating that we were going to be fine. "Most tribal people are still armed to protect their tribe like old times," I said. However, I was worried about the way they might think of us, an Iranian woman with a young European man in the middle of remote mountains of Lorestan. However, knowing that I was among my countrymen made me feel safe.

Trusting my judgment, the lad started to wind down and was drinking his tea with a forced smile. Alas, unexpectedly, the whole crowd sitting on the ground, leaning against the majestic carpet-covered beddings (*rakhtekhab peech*), jumped out of the tent shouting, "Snake! Snake!" We all ran out of the tent. In no time, as if nothing had happened, they invited us back in. "It is a homie!" they said. Qoli started to cry.

Fortunately, my husband and the rest of our team—the ambassador, my children, and my sister—arrived on mules, and the celebration started with yet another most delicious lamb kebab. Rice and everything else they had was put on the *sofreh* for us. All that they had to eat was offered, only to welcome us, no charges, nothing expected in return (*dar tabaq e ekhlas gozashtand*).

We reached our destination late at night. The majestic lake was like a clear bowl of water. (The water in Gahar Lake comes into it from the streams underneath the lake.) We just knelt down and drank straight from it. All the men jumped in there swimming the vast lake (except Qoli!).

◈ ◈ ◈

In urban settings, Thanksgiving is performed rather differently, very formal and remarkably fancy.

Sofreh ye nazr is a large cloth spread on the carpet with place settings for a sizable number of people. Many statements are made during these ceremonies. For instance, the top of the *sofreh* is usually away from the entrance and is reserved for the eldest and the more important guests. The bottom of the *sofreh* is by the door, where the younger and not so important guests or the servants sit. This creates a huge dilemma when one invites too many important or too many sensitive people.

Harsh and merciless critiques usually follow each of these *sofreh*s, comments about the place they were seated, the serving dishes and the type of service, the food, and of course gossip about the guests and the hosts.

Comments were of this nature: "The rice was not done properly" (*vali berenjesh dam nakeshideh bood*), "She had worked hard, wouldn't you say she should have put more cooked yogurt on the soup?" (*In keh inqadr zahmat keshideh bood, hala chi mishod agar kashkesh ra bishtar mirikht?*), or "Had we not been invited? Why would she sit us next to the door?" (*Magar ma davat nakardeh amedeh boodim ke bayad nazdik e dar beshinim?*)

Later, after eating a lot more than one should, most guests experience indigestion, but they blame it on the food or the intention of the host: "I don't know what was in the food that made me sick. Whatever did she put in there? Was the fruit not washed properly?" (*Nemidoonam chi to ghazahash bood; marizemoon kard. Shayad miveh ash nashosteh bood!*) [I am being sarcastic here!]

Thus absolute perfection is required to dare host a *sofreh*. It also takes a lot of faith and community cooperation to volunteer for such feasts.

There are more casual *sofreh*s such as *Bibi Se Shambeh* or *Sham e Ghariboon,* but those are usually for smaller favors the divine had bestowed upon people. Regardless, deals are constantly made with God: "If you do this, I will do that."

Sofreh ye Abul Fazl (*Hazrat e Abbas*) is the most elaborate. This *sofreh* is a feast for women only. A woman preacher is invited to chant a verse or two from the Koran and some hadith—women shed tears and hands go to the sky in pleas.

No one can touch the food until the end of the prayers that sometimes goes on for over an hour.

Fancier and more elaborate than *sofreh e aqd* (marriage ceremony), this *sofreh*, with colorful foods, candles, and fresh flowers, has become a work of art. Guests take home *sofreh* favors of blessed food. No matter how rich you are, you want to take the *nazri* food home to your loved ones for blessing.

At one of the outdoor sofrehs I had gone to with Bibi, there were lit candles and fresh lilies floating on the swimming pool, and the sofreh was spread on Persian carpets all around the large pool. The most fashionable ladies were walking around and on the surface of the sofreh like models on the catwalk.

Modern women, as well as the more traditional, share the same ceremony when it comes to observing the sofreh. They wear a delicate lace chador at the time of prayer, and they all love and respect the imams, especially Abbas and Ali. Perfect nails, brand-new sheer nylons, and pedicured toes get the chance to present themselves. The very young girls who serve the guests with their bare feet on the sofreh show off their art of operating smoothly, knowing that the mothers of some suitors will be among the guests watching.

I have had two *sofreh Abol Fazl* of my own in Los Angeles. One was when I passed the qualification exam and one for the funeral of Ammeh Simin, my husband's sister. The first one was very casual, and my guests were boys and girls of different religious backgrounds. One of the students who read the Koran for us (our preacher) was a Communist! The second one was a perfect Tehrani-style sofreh with my china and a hired woman preacher.

Being designated as the person who gives the nazri on important days such as *Ashoora* or *Tasooa* requires a level of social status, dignity, and trust in the more traditional neighborhoods such as Meigoon. My husband has been qualified for this privilege; he has been promoted from *Tasooa* to *Ashoora*'s lunch in Meigoon for the last four years. He is sacrificing cows now instead of lambs. His nazri feeds about seven hundred people.

Bibi had a couple of nazris that sustained her to the last days of her life. She had a lemonade and halva (*angosht peech*) *nazr* every Ashoora for her son Dadashi's health. Every year on the twenty-eighth of Safar she had a *nazr* of *sholl e zard* for Abaj's health.

Fezeh had an *ash e sholleh qalamkar* (vegetable soup with lamb) for her daughter's health. Every year without exception, these vows were renewed. If they made a vow to God, which meant that if God gave the health of their loved one, they would give to the poor every year in honor of a sacred prophet, that vow could never be broken.

Being a helper at these ceremonies is not only a reward accompanying you to the other world, it is a spiritual experience in this world as well. We were told if we stirred the food in the pot while cooking and made a wish, it would certainly come true. (I have to check and see if all that I wished for from God, I received.)

❖ ❖ ❖

"Bibi was sitting on the floor of her room next to the wall closet (*doolabcheh*) where she kept her valuables. She took the silverware out of the blue wooden box and handed them to me. Packs of serving sets, knives and forks, all sizes of spoons were carefully put out of the cloth cover to be taken downstairs," my sister Sepideh said, remembering.

"You know how to set these. Put the small spoons next to quince jam and the large knives and forks next to the fish and chicken dishes. The spatulas go next to the rice dishes. Make sure you put the knife and the spoon to the right and the fork to the left of each plate. The sharp side of the knife should be towards the plate. Do it the way we do when my friends come to lunch," Sepideh quoted Bibi. "Bibi was completely in charge," she continued.

"She had already placed the order with Fezeh and Mohammad. Jamshid, Mehdi Khan (the driver), and everyone else had taken their orders to shop and to prepare food for more than eighty guests for the nazri lunch," Sepideh said.

I see the image of Bibi as she spread the white cotton sofreh on the floor of the salon downstairs. The cotton spread had light orange embroidery at the edges. There were matching napkins too.

"All the pieces of china, silverware, candles, and incredible food made by the male chef were coming to decorate the sofreh," Sepideh said. "There were no preachers, no band, no books, simply a feast, no reference to any specific saint. However, it was a true celebration of our Baba's soul, the first anniversary of his passing, the way he would have wanted it. Everything was prepared and the guests were about to arrive," Sepideh said.

◆ ◆ ◆

Tehran may not look clean to some people; however, our city has in place the will to stay clean. A lot of effort has always gone into keeping it that way.

The street sweepers (*soopoor*) are more than just government employees; they are neighborhood watchmen, handymen when you need extra help in the house to lift something or to bring the groceries inside the house; they are there to assist you. They start very early in the morning and at times sleep under a tree with their brooms under their heads.

The scratching sound of the handmade broom (made out of *jarro* plant tied to a stick) on the streets sweeping the dry leaves or dust was always the first sound we heard in the mornings; the same workers shoveled the snow in the winters.

Tehran had not had that much snow in years. There was more than a meter of snow that winter (1971–72). Most of the street sweepers and the simple workers had made a wooden shovel (*paroo*) to clear the snow off the roofs of the houses and also to clean the streets.

Even though family members and friends expected their invitations to the first anniversary of my father's passing, none were invited. During the first month after a person's death, the homes are open, day and night, to all people who come to pay respects to the deceased. Lunch, dinner, tea, fruit, and sweets are served around the clock to all who come in. However, the ceremony of the fortieth day after the burial and the first year anniversary is by invitation only.

Bibi's guest list was distinctive. The invitations were delivered by Bibi's agents as they went around the neighborhood, shouting out to the rooftops, asking the street sweepers and the snow cleaners to make sure they come to lunch.

Nafiseh remembers clearly:

You know how there is silence when it is snowing heavily? There were no cars passing by on Khazar Street. Every once in a while you would hear a car with chains on its tires pulling itself up our street or the sound of "*Ya* Ali" as men helped a car out of a ditch. The *soopoor*s passed our house calling out, "*Barf paroo mikonim. Barfi eh. Barfi*" [snow cleaner; we shovel the snow!]

When Bibi was taking a break, she went to the window upstairs to smoke her cigarette. She told them, "No thank you. There are workers on the roof already cleaning, but make sure you come back here for lunch."

Our mother sent us off to the streets to call them all. I personally walked on Khazar and the small alleys and called the workers on the roof, "*Ahay, Aqa*. When your work is done, come to the brick house for lunch."

Nafiseh had tears in her eyes as she described the scene:

Fezeh was like a king that day. Do you remember when we had guests? No matter how important they were, if Fezeh did not like them or was tired, she would let them know by banging the pots and pans in the kitchen! That day, she was most respectful of our guests. Bibi's male helpers were most obedient. There was one hundred percent cooperation from everyone. An honorable system was in place. The entrance of the house in Khazar was packed up to the ceiling with wooden shovels, brooms, soaking wet socks, and hats. The sound of utensils was being heard in silence.

Finally, the guests walked out of the dining room content and warm, their souls fed.

They stood in front of Bibi and her crew, blessing my father's soul. Reaching to the rooftops, past the snowy skies to heaven, they performed the flashiest, the most sincere, and the holiest, "Allah ma sal e Alla Mohammad va aal e Mohammad." (May God bless Mohammad and his family. May God bless the soul of Mr. Abdollah Dashti.)

Street cleaners at the back of the British Embassy, Tehran, 1340 (1961). Photo: Daryoush Tahami.

Forty-Four
The Evil Eye

The white Arabian stallion belonging to Aqa ye Bozorg died suddenly. That morning, my father had dared to ride the pampered animal around the neighborhood in Borazjan. As he approached a palm grove belonging to a certain woman, the horse shied, reared up on its hind legs, then crashed down on its knees and died. My father panicked, frozen with fear and confusion. He knew the horse did not like to be ridden by anyone other than his own master, but my father was an experienced rider and was confident he could handle the horse. He had no explanation for what had happened.

"Quite unexpectedly and violently, jumping first one way and then the other, he exhibited fear of something he felt come in to his surroundings—something no one else could see" is all my father could say. Later on that day, that certain woman walked to the house of Aqa ye Bozorg begging for forgiveness! "Aqa, it was my evil eye that killed your horse. Please forgive me. I should have peed on your horse before I heard his neigh. That is when I glared at him. *Arreh*, this must be Sheikh Ma Sain's horse.'"

◆ ◆ ◆

People around us were most enthusiastic about life—they made sure the cosmic signs were interpreted in a nonthreatening manner so as not to add any anxiety to a very busy life in progress. As the siren of an ambulance approached, for instance, the immediate response from the adults in our household was, "Oh, look, someone is giving birth."

The large cypress tree in the backyard hosted the nests of many crows and other birds. There was always a chance that we would receive the droppings of those birds on our heads or faces as we played outdoors. Again, as soon as a bird relieved itself and before a feeling of repugnance could take over, we heard, "Wow, how lucky you are. Did you know that this is the greatest sign of luck? The closer to your face, the luckier you are."

This is what it was like when someone accidentally dropped and or broke something. The person would hear right away from near or far, upstairs or downstairs, a couple of adults shouting in relief, "Thank God. Whoever you are, you just broke the curse of the evil eye." It was never asked what broke, how valuable that thing was, and never ever interpreted as clumsiness. Then some caring person showed up with a broom and a dustpan to release us from the scene, to protect us from any threat to our body or soul. We were never to be reminded or scolded about the incident. In fact, if the piece was valuable, it gave a heroic feeling to the person who broke it by accident.

A teacup with a large tea leaf in it was never returned for a more proper serving with a strainer. It was announced, "This means we are soon having a dear guest." "Look how tall the guest is!" We then cheerfully anticipated the event. When the guest showed up, there was no doubt in our minds that it was the work of the tea leaf! If by any chance guests did not respond to the sign, a pair of shoes left on top of one another by the door would certainly engage the angels to help bring the favorite guest.

An itch in the palm of our hands meant money was coming our way. The person next to you would say, "Here, let me scratch your hand, I want a share of that money too."

When the smoke of a cigarette or *qalyan* was blown into our faces, before we reacted, we were told that we were going to get rich. The hopeful message redirected the cough into a big smile, welcoming the smoke.

Lucky were the ones who by chance showed up at a time of good fortune. These people are called *khosh qadam* (blessed footsteps) or blessed hands (*dast e ba barekat*) if what they gave brought more. They were welcomed to any house or any shop at any time; without having made any special efforts, they got all the credit.[1]

There were always a few people around, however, who were known for their "evil eye" (*cheshm e shoor*) or "heavy steps" (*qadam e sangin*); they caused the red alarm of negativity to go on. "They bring bad energy to us every time they visit" was a firm assumption. They were never rejected however. No matter how negative those people were, they had to be welcomed because in an Iranian home, no one should be denied respectful hospitality.

As soon as the guest left, however, our caretakers were ready to burn *esfand* (peganum harmala seeds) on burning charcoal. The popping seeds and the thick smoke coming from the seeds of wild rue mixed with other ingredients such as *golpar* (cow parsnip) were taken all over the house and circled around the heads of those afflicted by or exposed to the gaze of the visitor's bad eye. As this was being done, a slogan was recited several times to make sure we were safe from the evil eye, "*Esfand o Esfand dooneh, Esfand si o se dooneh, cheshm e hasood beterekeh.*" (Wild rue seeds, the thirty-three seeds, may the eyes of the jealous burst.) A house could survive without some essentials, but never without an *esfand* burner and an endless supply of *esfand*.

Some people's evil eye was believed to be so overwhelmingly destructive that other means had to be utilized to ward it off, such as peeing or spitting on the person prone to be stricken by the evil eye, burning a strand of hair from the suspected predator, or setting on fire a piece of their clothing. Only after all of the above were performed was everyone able to relaxe confidently; the evil eye was warded off.

The most susceptible to the evil eye were babies, beautiful people, and also those showing signs of extreme joy and prosperity. Khaleh Robabeh told us not to tell how old our babies were in case the babies looked too healthy or too big for their age; six-month-old babies were said to be about two years old! Typically a warning was issued following an incredible success or achievement. "Oh do not tell anyone!"

❖ ❖ ❖

My sister Sepideh was about seventeen years old then. She was all dressed up to go to a party when the evil eye of our neighbor hit her. She came out of our room into the living room where Bibi and her friend and neighbor were sitting and having tea. The woman looked at her and said, "Look at her! Look how incredible she looks! Look at her narrow ankles. Mrs. Dashti, she has your legs, she is so lucky." No one said anything, yet faces turned white with fear. Sepideh left, and before she turned to the corner, she twisted her ankle and returned home in pain. Fezeh ran to the neighbor's house to spread some anticurse substance on her doorstep and returned to burn *esfand*. The *esfand* burner was swung around Sepideh's head many times. Alas, it was too late. To this date, her ankle swells for no reason.

For years following that day when our neighbor was about to visit us, Bibi would warn us not to show off in front of her and not to say anything about ourselves. Fezeh took the necessary precautions of getting a thread from the neighbor's dress and started the *esfand* ahead of time. She believed that the smoke of *esfand* creates a barrier, an invisible shield, within which the loved ones could be safe.

◆ ◆ ◆

We had moved back to Iran in 1992, and our oversized furniture had filled up the suite downstairs in the Elahieh house. Even though many of the pieces seemed out of place, they were eye-catching. I had hung a large antique mirror by the entrance (in the old coatroom). The glass tables were new and a little too flashy for a house that was shaken by an Iraqi bomb just a few months earlier. All our friends and relatives were coming to visit us and to welcome us home. A family member and her husband were the last guests that evening. The moment they arrived, the husband looked at the mirror by the entrance and said, "Wow! This is too good for here, you should take it inside the room." They sat down, and we served them tea. He picked up his cup of tea and commented, "Wow! These cups are too expensive, you should put them away and use regular cups for here." Then he touched the glass coffee table and commented, "Wow! Have you specially ordered these? This is not a regular size, is it? Look how thick the glass is." I said, "Yes! I am so glad you noticed. I had them specially made with round edges so my babies do not cut their faces as they run around. I myself love my eight-seat glass dining room set. It is all new," I said innocently. As I was saying all that, a hesitation did cross my mind, *Was I showing off?*

When they finally left, my husband and I went to the back room (formerly Fezeh's) to watch a video on our "oversized" television set. This is when we heard the loudest bang. We ran to the coatroom and saw the mirror on the ground. We both ran into the salon expecting the two large glass tables to have been broken to pieces; they were not. Nothing was broken! Bibi had run downstairs to see what had happened. "Of course!" she said as she was leaving us to go back to bed. "Burn some *esfand* right away and stop showing off! This was his evil eye!"

"Why would anyone have so many things anyways? People are going to wonder," she was complaining all the way back up the stairs.

Talking to my children in America and sending them blessing via Skype. Photo: Sayeh Dashti, Tehran 2015.

267

Notes

1   We got credit for the termination of the Iran/Iraq war. It ended the day we arrived in Tehran in August 1988. People thanked us and we felt like heroes.

Forty-Five
Dogless in Tehran

Bibi stood next to Shanzoo who was resting on a towel, giving birth to twelve puppies ever so gently. Bibi seemed amazed by the power of nature and the grace of the mother dog in labor. She stood there in reverence as my husband and children helped Shanzoo deliver her puppies. Repeatedly she articulated, "Wow, the power of God. See how dignified this female is."

At first it seemed unimaginable to bring dogs to where Bibi lived. We had a pair of Doberman dogs staying in Bibi's house when we moved back to Iran. I was truly embarrassed each time the dogs barked. The dogs did run upstairs occasionally and ended up on Bibi's balcony or in her bedroom; I wanted to die each time.

On their backs, all four feet up in the air, loving the struggle and the attention much like human babies, our dogs refused to cooperate when they saw me so desperate. I would drag them on the ground harshly, lift them on their two legs, and stand them up much taller than myself, trying to take them downstairs to the yard. Guess who stopped me each time? "Let go of these creatures of God, they are helpless animals (*heivoon e zaboon basteh*)." Bibi came to their rescue!

She saved food for our dogs, "these creatures of God," and came to a certain realization daily: "Who says we are any dearer in the eyes of God than a dog or any other creature for that matter?" Then she told us about a dog in the story "People of the Cave (Seven Sleepers)" in the Koran (surah 18, verse 9–26).

A dog accompanied the youths into the cave and was also asleep for three hundred years, but when people passed by the cave, it looked as if the dog was just keeping watch at the entrance, making them afraid of seeking what is in the cave once they saw the dog.

❖ ❖ ❖

Having a pet was simply not a part of our culture. Oddly enough, cats were free to come and go in all neighborhoods, in and out of any house, any room at any hour they chose; they lived among people. Some houses were the residence of so many cats. In those houses, someone always put a bowl of water or milk or the leftover food outside for the cats to eat and drink. The gangs of cats walked around the neighborhoods either quietly or got into terrible fights. Some evenings, the sound of a cat giving birth to her kittens broke the silence as everyone waited it out. If a catfight was anywhere near where people were sitting, someone threw a shoe at them to break up the fight. The bad boys on the street demonstrated their antisocial tendencies by killing a cat for no apparent reason or probably with the background our literature had defined: "Cats are ungrateful and manipulative. They leave you to go wherever there is better food no matter how much you have served them (*gorbeh sefat*)."

At one point in time, the first floor suite of Khazar house was rented out to a Swedish family with a gorgeous young teenage girl. The Swedish girl had asked our teenage brother if he could bring her a Persian cat. My brother gladly told his friend Reza from across the street (*Mahaleh ye Sopoorha*) to bring a nice Persian cat for the girl. His friend's first response was "Dead or alive?"

On the other hand, even though dogs are known in our literature as being the most faithful, Moslems consider them to be unsanitary; the immediate reaction of people sitting around out on the streets was to look for a stone to throw at an approaching dog. During our childhood, the only dogs we chanced to encounter were stray dogs: hungry, dirty, and maybe even sick.

The neighborhood of Elahieh was characterized by its vast gardens, abundance of large trees, and fresh streams on the sides of the narrow streets—a lush green paradise. There were still many vacant lots where the young boys used to play soccer and or wander around. Other than that, the area was a place for gangs of street dogs. These dogs and the watchdogs of the gardens, particularly the dogs of the Russian embassy, had become a threat preventing us from leisurely walking and or playing in that paradise.

Rumors had it that the Communist Russians were keeping dogs whose fathers were wolves and mothers were dogs. Whenever we passed the embassy in our family car, we all shouted, "Khrushchev, Khrushchev!" We waited for the dogs to bark, and then we drove away. In my life, nothing quite matched that excitement. Not only had we challenged the Communists, we had dared the wolf dogs.

We had been warned many times not to take the shortcut by the Russian embassy, especially not in the afternoons. The afternoons in Tehran used to be like midnights in a remote city—shops were closed and people took a nap right after lunch. The streets were empty, making it a dangerous place for young girls to be out. We walked fast and were advised to take the main street sidewalk or the bus coming home from school. Alas, we did not listen.

On a Thursday afternoon, my younger sister Sepideh and I treated ourselves to two giant-size cream puffs (*noon e khame'i*). We got the pastries in two separate brown bags and took the shortcut to the vacant land facing the Russian embassy. We chose that spot because it was the most beautiful place overlooking the creek and the forestlike garden of the embassy, away from any car or any stranger. We climbed the hill and climbed on top of a boulder. We put our books and notebooks underneath us (no backpacks then) and began pulling the precious pastries out of the bags.

Suddenly, the gate across the hill slid open to let out a car. The two wolf dogs dashed out of gate, ran up to the hilltop, and began sniffing our cream puffs!

We dropped the pastries and stayed there, immobile, terrified. No, in fact the word *terrified* is not all it was. I personally had a severe sensation of loss. Loss of faith in the universe and loss of dignity, for I was making strange noises out of fear, loss of power, and control over my knees. My legs were so weak and wobbly, almost paralyzed. We both sat there, completely motionless for more than a half-hour after the dogs were called back in through the gate. Worst yet, we could not tell anyone about the event. How many times had we been warned not to walk that way?

Eventually, we crawled down the hill, leaving our muddy cream puffs behind, defeated, ashamed, and shaken up. The Russians had won!

The Russian Embassy next to our house. Photo: Sayeh Dashti, 2014.

Such were my encounters with dogs before I moved to America. In America, of course, I met many dogs that were dear pets to their owners, members of their families. I was respectful of them but never petted them. I realized that it is customary for people to compliment the dog owner by acknowledging the cuteness of their pets. I never paid attention to them and usually tried to avoid passing by too closely. Then years later my husband walked in the house with a Doberman dog. I was furious and did not talk to him for a week. It was of no use, of course; our children loved him and promised he would only stay outside in the yard, and he did. I began appreciating Dobbie for the feeling of safety he brought to our life. In fact, I felt so safe that I once told a friend who stayed with me when my husband was away that she was no longer needed. "We have a dog now, you don't have to come anymore!" Needless to say, she was extremely offended, and I almost lost her as a friend.

My children lived with their dogs; they considered themselves to be related to dogs, while we parented them all. Through these "creatures of God," my children experienced true love, true hurt, and the harsh reality of loss. These dogs helped us adjust to incredible changes we experienced: moving from one country to another and from one house to another, separations, and loss of our dear ones.

Dobbie bit my son on the head once. Everyone said he wanted to kiss the baby! Another dog in our house bit my son on the nerve in the back of his hand. He almost fainted and my husband risked all our lives driving to Tehran from the mountains on a Friday afternoon to take him to a doctor. He drove like a madman. We were in shock, not knowing whether we should fear the possibility of rabies or a deadly car accident.

He managed to get us to the clinic in twelve minutes, a drive that should have taken over an hour. When all was safe, the dog lovers had this to say about the incident: "Farid was trying to protect his owner!" We had named him Farid because Farid, our Afghani housekeeper in Meigoon, had brought him for us. The word *Farid* means alone, and when the dog started biting everyone, we put him in solitary confinement and called him *Monfared* (really alone).

The gentle Shanzoo had an allergic reaction to donkeys. As she was gently checking out the herbs and insects in the backyard, suddenly, with the speed of lightning she ran into the road, bit the stomach of a passing donkey, and ran back. Her speed and calm manner could fool anyone. The only thing that gave her away was a mustache on the sides of her mouth from the fur of the poor donkey's belly and the painful "Arrrrarrr" of the donkey in the distance. Other than that, I could have sworn that Shanzoo was right there next to me in the yard the whole time.

Adaptation was a profound process. I could never look into our dogs' eyes. Sometimes Dobbie, Shanzoo, or Lazloe (my favorite dogs) would stretch their bodies next to the kitchen window and stare at me for a long, long time. I could see that their eyes were talking to me. I was shy wanting to ask them not to talk to me like that. I lost focus of my humanness for a moment and felt like I was encountering another world of beings, and of course, I could not afford to do that. I was in the midst of my human responsibilities as a mother. When my children were small, some days, about four in the afternoon, when my energy was at its lowest and my children were tired and got into fights with each other, the phone ringing constantly and Dobbie barking breathlessly. I could smash the phone, yell at my children, or run into my room and lock the door, but I never knew what to do with the dog. I feared being mad at her was like being angry with God. Maybe she was one of the creatures we read about in the holy book—an intelligent spirit able to appear in human and animal forms and to possess humans, a *jinn*. There are good jinns and bad jinns. Dobbie was definitely a good jinn; nevertheless, she was a jinn. *Who would want a jinn in the backyard?* I constantly thought.

So the gates to our home and to our hearts opened up to dogs, dogs of all kinds. We had a variety of dogs that included Doberman, greyhound, Chihuahua, and unknown breeds picked up by our van off the streets, dogs that just resided in our backyard on the mountain who came to socialize with our dogs and also because we provided food and shelter. We got tons of chicken feet and boiled them in humongous pots for all the dogs. The house, the clothes, the hills, and the trees smelled like something I cannot describe.

Naming our dogs remained a challenge. After all, we believed that a name is a serious matter. We called them "dog" for a while, and then we got more creative. From Dog to Hey Doggy to Dobbie, Michael Jackson, Blondie, and Jazz, the names got more distinguished when our children started to choose. The Greek gods and goddesses now were walking in our backyards, left, right, and center.

When we moved to Iran in early nineties, there was no packaged dog food. Many animals were sacrificed to feed these mythical gods. On the birthday of Isis and her twin brother (my son Shawhin's dogs), we treated them to two whole barbecued chickens.In spite of these fancy names, they were usually called Doggy by most of our workers at home. The one person who was more used to dogs, an Afghani man, called all of them Kamal. He had picked up the name Kamal from hearing my children telling their dogs, "Come on!"

Jazz was the first dog we kept inside the house. We had to keep her inside because our beautiful greyhound was killed by the coyotes on the hills of Los Angeles.

Jazz was also the worst dog we ever had. She was the size of a rat and as hard to discipline as a rat. We even had to seek professional help; she was untreatable. She had no principles. She kept leaving the yard through small cracks in the gate and ran across the street to get attention from the obnoxious dogs and their owners sitting in the cafés. Many times the restaurant owners brought her back to our house with such arrogance. "How could you leave this precious doll unattended? How?"

I hated Jazz!

We lost many dogs. Michael Jackson left the house and never returned. (Was it because my husband told him to get out and get lost?) Greyhound was killed by coyotes. Isis was killed by a pack of wolves in the mountains of Meigoon. My husband got into a battle with the wolves for Isis's sake. He threw a knife at one and injured one. The wolf died and was hung in our basement for weeks until I returned home from my trip and raised hell.

Lazlo died of bone cancer, and Shanzoo was stolen. Goffie, my brother's family dog, the sweetest and most loving dog, died of old age. Blondie got sick and was put to death, Monfared died of guilt (!). Many puppies did not survive the harsh weather of the mountains near Tehran. Dobbie was given to a friend when we left America. Hittit and Pajaro were given to nice people who cared about dogs.

We have no dogs now!

Dobbie in our house in Los Angeles. Photo: Sayeh Dashti, 1985.

Baran belongs to my son Shawhin and his
wife Shideh. Photo: Shawhin Roudbari,
Boulder, Colorado, 2014.

Forty Six

We Intoxicate the Wine, Not the Other Way Around

Badeh az ma mast shod, ney ma az oo
Qaleb az ma hast shod, ney ma az oo!

[We intoxicate the wine,
not the other way around!
Our bodies came to be, because we gave them life,
not the other way around!]
—Molana[1]

"Reza Khan wanted to be a president at first, but he was advised not to." Bibi was telling us the introduction to the story of the horror they experienced when Reza Shah ordered an overnight decree of no *hijab* for Iranian women (1936). She continued, "He became a Shah instead in 1925. Even Ali Dashti told him that Iran was not ready for a president. So he started the Pahlavi Dynasty. It was like death." Bibi could not find a better word. "We could not imagine how we could go outside of the house without our head coverings. Fezeh was panicking. Now she had to depend on men to buy our personal things."

"Reza Khan was a very intelligent man," Bibi continued. "He brought discipline, central authority, modern life for the people, schools for boys and girls, trains, cinema, the telephone, roads, bridges, tunnels, etc.

"You know, when he built a bridge in the North [Pol e Veresk], he made the engineers and their families stay under the bridge as a train ran over it for the first time!" Bibi said. "It sounds cruel, but Reza Shah's message to the engineers was that if you ignore the safety of the bridge, you and your family will be the first ones to go!"

Most Iranians of our parents' generation have many stories about Reza Shah's unprecedented way of disciplining. I have usually heard the narrators tell those stories with an admiration for him as a vigilante who had taken the law and justice in his own hands. "In order to shape up, that is what we need as a nation," they claimed. One of these stories goes:

Once during a visit to Hamadan, he was told that the people were going hungry because the bakers were hoarding wheat in order to raise the price of bread. He ordered one of the bakers thrown in the oven alive. By the next day, every bakery was filled with low-priced bread!

Bibi continued, "We respected Reza Shah, but he did it all too quickly. He wanted to make Iran as modern as Europe, like Turkey was trying to do. Aqda'i told him many times that our people are religious and the religious traditions must be respected. But Reza Khan was in a hurry to change everything. He certainly did not want to fall behind Atatürk, the leader of Turkey, who was his close friend and had the same philosophy."

Traditionally speaking, Iranian women never wore the kind of Islamic hijab that we see after the revolution. Each region of Iran had its own custom and dress both for men and women. The women of the south wore what they called a maynaar, a very light lace they twisted around their head in a feminine way, with all their face and the front of their hair showing. The maynaar is long enough to cover their chest with semicircular folds and hangs in the back like a tail of a peacock. Underneath it, the women wore incredible skirts in wild and rich colors, layer on top of another layer.

There are many stories and songs about the maynaar. One of those, Bibi had told us once, was when a woman threatened that she would take off her maynaar, a gesture of protesting an atrocity, all men backed off. "When that happened, laws would change," Bibi said firmly.

At home, Bibi usually wore her maynaar or a colorful chador when someone visited; around the house, though, she wore no head coverings.

She had straight light brown hair, which parted in the middle (a little more to the left). She hated white hair and dyed her hair a light brunette.[2]

It was Bibi who gave character to what she wore. The way she wore her head coverings—when she flipped over the side of her chador over her left shoulder, it was as if a general were putting on the last piece of the uniform, ready to command.

Her chadors were usually in bright flowery fabrics. She wore them when she did her daily prayers and also when she had a visitor. She never wore the formal black chador like some religious Tehrani women do. I believe her hair covering was to distinguish herself as a woman and not a religious obligation. It seemed certain that no man had ever dared to look at her in an indecent way; she was above and beyond it all.

In 1993, in the Islamic Republic of Iran, when Bibi and the three of us sisters were entering a mosque to attend the funeral of a friend of the family, we were stopped. The woman usher would not let Bibi go in because her hijab was not proper. Bibi was wearing her *aba*, a black dress, and black sheer nylons; we anticipated a huge problem.

Bibi, forthrightly, told the young woman, "First of all, you are ignorant and illiterate. Second of all, you are not a true Moslem because you don't know what is in the Koran. Go bring the Koran, and I will teach you. Have you not read surah number sixty-five, verse number four where the Koran talks about women who have reached menopause? Did you know that not only do I not have to have your hijab, I do not have to wear any clothing, period!" And then she ordered us, her daughters, to follow her inside the hall as she pushed the woman out of the way.

The young girl was dumbfounded, and we were proudly stunned. We got to go in, yet all through the time we were sitting there, we could see how the ushers were pointing out Bibi to each other. We were expecting at any moment to be escorted out and face trouble.

◆ ◆ ◆

I followed Bibi to England when she left America after her very short visit in 1987, as I thought those were my last chances to be with her. She seemed much more comfortable in Europe than in America.

She allowed us to take her around London and Manchester. She even took the double-decker bus with us. (We used to have the same buses in Tehran). During one of these trips to central London, we encountered an Iranian family on the bus whose women and female children were wearing strict Islamic hijab.

First, Bibi called their little girl and smiled at her. Then she told her, "Do not let your parents do this to you!" And then she turned to the girl's mother and scolded her, "How could you do this to this innocent child?"

The mother got very pale and turned to her husband who was wearing a very modest white shirt hanging loose on top of his trousers and had an unshaven chubby face. The man could not say anything. Obviously, they were new in the country and did not have the confidence to defend themselves; however, Bibi was not willing to let it go.

All the way, I was begging Bibi to please not say anything. We could all be in trouble, I feared. "No! Wait one minute (*eiy veis bebinam*)." She just continued lecturing the whole bus about all that was going on in our country and asked me to translate! She stood up in the bus and pointed at that family with rage.

Thank God we reached our destination safely. Before I could relax, however, she walked up to the man and told him, "You got what you wanted in our country. Why are you here now looking so ridiculous? And that poor child? Go! Go back. Do not embarrass us any longer."

"Mother, please," I was begging.

By now, the bus conductor was helping her out of the bus as though he were assisting Her Majesty the Queen herself; he was siding with her. Even though I was proud of her courage, I kept glancing back all day waiting for the Iranian embassy agents to find us.

When Bibi went out, she wore a magnificent formal *aba bishte*, which she wore on the crown of her head, where her face and the front of her elegant dress were showing as she proudly walked. Aqda'i had brought her those abas from Egypt where he served as ambassador.

Dinner with her uncle Ali Dashti at Darband Hotel, north of Tehran. Bibi is wearing an aba (her dress was white chiffon with purple flowers).

For very formal occasions, she wore a fancy black aba with golden embroidery and golden tassels. The most magnificent scene was when she got all dressed up with gloves, high heels and the aba and wore lipstick.

She usually did not wear makeup or jewelry. What she did wear was a watch with a large face; I think it was an Omega. She had a gold bracelet and a pearl pin in the shape of a grapevine pinned on the fold of her jacket and that was it, no other ornaments. Her makeup was lipstick and a brown pencil for her sparse eyebrows. When our father was invited to a formal dinner to which men were required to wear a tuxedo and ladies were obliged to wear a soiree dress with long white gloves, our oldest sister Talieh accompanied him instead of Bibi. I assume Bibi's modesty did not allow her to go.

Following the decision of Reza Khan to unveil women, many women stayed home. One day, however, Bibi decided to go out to visit a friend. Fezeh of course accompanied her.

Bibi put on her suit and wore a European hat. Our aunts, Abaj and Khaleh Zakieh, wrapped Fezeh in a large piece of cloth and put a Western hat on her head, and out they went.

Notes

1   Molana Jalal al-Din Rumi, *Mathnavi*, book one, *Bazargan va tooti*, verse #1812.

2   I used to send her hair colors (Nice and Easy brand) from America when Iran was at war with Iraq.

Forty Seven
Seyyed Behzad

It looked like a landscape from the American Wild West that had long since been abandoned. Other than thorn bushes, the only vegetation in sight was palm trees. In the heat of the afternoon, the silhouettes of the palm trees standing scattered in the distance shimmered with heat. A mudbrick house, the only sign of life in the middle of the plain between Bushehr and Borazjan, was the residence of a shaman. When we arrived there, his family let us in, served us tea, and asked us to wait for Seyyed Behzad to wake up from his afternoon nap.

The modest room was carpeted with area rugs made of the dry leaves of palm trees [*pang*] and leaning against the walls were many cushions. At first, it seemed unlikely that so many people might ever show up there to lean against them. In the middle of the room, there was a bookstand and a small cushion for the shaman to sit on. Next to his sitting place lay a thin dry branch of a fig tree, a calculator, and couple of spare printing paper rolls.

The spiritual atmosphere had impressed my young children, as they were unusually quiet. Our guides (my cousin's wife, her maid, along with her husband, our driver, and his wife) had already taken advantage of the opportunity and had begun meditating and praying in silence.

An hour later, a thin middle-aged man in white clothing, a wide green shawl around his waist and wearing a green turban[1] walked in and sat cross-legged at his place. He put his prayer book on the bookstand, and one by one, he pointed to us to approach his seat. My cousin's housekeeper was the first one to go. She walked on her knees and halfway across the room, she shyly asked her husband to join her. "Seyyed Behzad, the last time my lady's body was invaded by the jinns for six months, we came to you," the husband said as he was looking at his wife respectfully. Seyyed Behzad asked, "Are they back?" The husband started talking with great speed, "No, Seyyed, they are not. My wife is herself now. They were making her do unusual things. They made her shout and scream and hit her own children. She even cursed at me! That is when we came to you and you made them go away."

Seyyed stared at them and asked, "And you are back because?" The young woman dared to talk now. "Oh, Seyyed, please give me a couple more whips with your lash, just to make them stay away," my cousin's maid was begging. Seyyed waved for the next person to approach, "Go! Don't be ridiculous." Seyyed Behzad dismissed them. The husband wanted to kiss his hand, but he did not allow it. The very joyous couple walked backward on their knees, feeling blessed.

It was my turn. He pointed to me. As I got up to go sit by him, I heard the sound of many cars approaching. I looked out of the window and saw a large bus and a couple of minibuses loaded with people parking by the house.

The door opened, a large group of people walked in: men, women, and children. They had come from all over the country to get his blessings. Some came in and filled up the room, row after row, and the rest stayed outside waiting for their turn.

I took a chance and whispered to Seyyed Behzad if I could see him alone for a moment. I did realize that this was a daring request; however, I could not talk about my problems publicly. To my surprise, he accepted it. He got up and walked with me to the side door of the room and listened most attentively as I talked briefly about my dilemma.[2]

I followed him back into the room and sat by his bookstand as he turned the portable calculator on. He cut off a long tape and started to scribble on it. He folded the paper into a one-by-one inch square and gave it to me. His instructions were that I keep it on my body and never ever separate from it, not until my problem is resolved. I took the folded paper and said, "Merci, Seyyed Behzad."

"Merci? Merci!" He was teasing me. As moody as he was known to be, he seemed to like us. When I asked if we could stay inside because my daughter was doing research on traditional medicine, he made an exception and allowed us to stay.

The woman who had come from the north of the country was next. "Greetings, Seyyed Behzad, I have come a long distance to—" The woman was ready to perform all kinds of formalities; however, Seyyed cut her off impatiently and waved for her to start talking about her problem. She started crying and said, "My daughter is obsessed with cleanliness. She compulsively washes her hands many hours a day and refuses to milk the cow. She insists it is not sanitary! She says her compulsion is out of her control."

"Sit her down and have the cow pee on her"[3] was all Seyyed Behzad said and waved to have her dismissed. She thanked him properly. "I am so grateful, o' my Divine Seyyed, my Divine Saviour."

A young woman asked others if she could be next and people allowed her. "Sir Seyyed, I have come from Tehran. I realize that I am a very fortunate person. I have everything that I want. I have been suffering for four years now. I keep thinking that I am going to get sick and I will die soon. I shiver for days before I go to the doctor for a checkup. I shiver badly. People tell me that I am spoiled and unthankful, but I am not. I am so thankful for all that God has given me. My mind tells me these things. My mind is ruining my life. What should I do? Please help me."

She kept talking and repeating the same thing. Seyyed interrupted her and eventually raised his voice, "Your mind is talking too much. You do not have to listen to your brain every time it talks. You are a human, not a parrot."

Then he wrote a similar scribble for her on the roll of paper and instructed her, "Any time your brain talks nonsense, squeeze this paper on your forehead and tell it to shut up."

One by one the people approached his seat, got the most sensible and convincing replies, brief and right to the point—no witchcraft, no trance, no money in return, and not accepting any gifts or favors.

I was so incredibly impressed by him. I whispered into the ear of my cousin's wife, "Is this not a chance for you? Have you told him about your infertility?" She knew that infertility was a physical reality for her and her husband; a condition no divinity could change. She said, "I do not want to lose my faith in him. I will never ask him."

We returned to Tehran. I went to the bazaar and bought a small leather locket to hold my folded prayer in. I was amazed to see that most shops carried the same lockets: necklaces, bracelets, belts; all kinds of accessories to keep the tokens of the holy messages on the body.

A few weeks later, Nafiseh told me that Seyyed Behzad had sent a message to say hello to Merci"for him and to see if her problem had been solved. "Yes! I do not believe it actually happened that way. This was an impossible situation. How could something so complicated be solved in just a few weeks?" I said while I felt truly honored by his attention and sense of humor. I also told my sister that I had thought to myself, if this complicated dilemma was actually resolved, I would have no choice but to start believing in the supernatural. "Now, do you believe that there is really something out there?" she said triumphantly. Instead, I reasoned, "Believing is the key here. The man is full of common sense. The folded paper on our bodies is a constant reminder of the priority of our problems. He also knows that whenever we stay focused, our problems will be solved."

"You are so naïve!" Nafiseh said. "The very wisdom leading you to believe that you are the one who has figured out this whole thing on your own is the work of that magic," she lectured me.

I still have the prayer Seyyed Behzad gave me in 1988. Photo: Sayeh Dashti, Ra'is Coffee Shop, Shemiran, 2014.

Prayer lockets. Photo: Sayeh Dashti, Tajrish, Tehran, 2015.

Notes

1   The green shawl and turban are the clothes of the *seyyed*s who are descendants of the Prophet Mohammad.

3   I am not telling you!

4   Similar to flooding or saturation techniques of therapy for patients with obsessive-compulsive disorder.

Forty-Eight
Chocolate from Heaven

Chocolate from heaven is what my children named the fresh dates (*rotab*) from Dashtestan. The only way to taste them is to be near there or to have a mother smuggle them into the country you live in, if not Iran.

We were lucky—we had our own palm groves (*nakhlestan*) in Borazjan. Every summer, many sealed tin containers of dates at different stages of ripening were delivered to us in Tehran. First we got *kharak* in clusters—hard, yellow fruit with a somewhat acrid taste. Some of the kharaks were wrinkled, hard as a rock, but they were still sweet, and we ate them like hard candies. Then in the middle of summer, about mid-August, when the temperature of Borazjan goes as high as forty-five degrees Centigrade and the humidity gets to about 90 percent, we got the rotab. It takes that heat to ripen the rock hard kharak into fresh sweet rotab, ready to burst out of its thin skin. That high temperature is called *khorma pazoon* (cooking dates). The hard kharak starts getting soft and brown from the bottom and eventually turns into fresh sweet rotab, "chocolate from heaven." That was a delicacy we owned and a novelty other families in Tehran did not have. So Bibi got large soup tureens from her china and made portions for all her friends. First, our male workers brought the dates into the kitchen and ripped open the tops of the tin containers with a sharp knife with the help of the metal handle of the grinder. Then they emptied the metal containers into the *majmaeh* (a large and round copper tray) to loosen up the rotabs and to spread the syrup evenly on top. Fezeh brought the china bowls and lay them on the kitchen floor. The round trays were arranged around the china, and the children were sent out of the kitchen. Bibi was called in to perform the delicate task. She sat on the ground, and with both hands, she filled up the large china soup tureens with the delicate rotabs and put syrup on top for a further glow. A trusted adult, usually one of the aunts, cleaned around the tureens, put the lids on, and handed them to the driver to deliver to the houses of family and friends. It was a solemn occasion.

Before disposable containers were introduced, the dishes that were used to present food to friends were the best china people had. Tehranis had a pleasant custom of filling up the dish of food they received with something special in return. They usually put cookies or candies or something homemade (in Shiraz, they put jasmine or rose petals) when they returned the dish.

To avoid going sour, the rest of the rotabs were kept in their large tin containers and at the bottom of our shelfless Philco refrigerator. Our father celebrated the arrival of his precious product of the south by eating a whole dish of rotab in one sitting.

In the palm groves, the rest of the rotabs are left on the date palms to fully ripen while the syrup is collected at the base of the palm tree. In a few weeks, the rotabs turn into dates (*khorma*). The dates are still soft and unbelievably sweet, but they lose some of their juice and are safe to keep for a year. The dates came to us a month later and were kept in the metal containers with ripped-open lids. Since they should not be refrigerated, they were kept in a cabinet in the kitchen. It was hard to get the khorma out as they were packed tight and the edges of the containers were sharp. No matter how difficult, there was always a plate of dates on the tablecloth (*sofreh*). Our best quality dates were Kabkab and Khanizi. Dates generate hot energy in the body. We ate them to balance the energy property of the food we ate, dipping it into yogurt or *kashk* (cooked yogurt) for a cooler energy, and if we happened to have fish for our meal, which has a cold energy property, we dipped it in sesame butter (*ardeh*), which is warm by nature.

We hardly heard about food being evaluated by the amount of protein, calories, vitamins, or other contents. In our home, there was always the talk of the nature of the energy of each food, whether it was hot or cold or its relation to the function of the body's four humors. All foods were prepared in accordance with a harmonious balance and interworking of the four humors: blood, phlegm, yellow bile, and black bile.

It was an absolute sin to mix some foods together. For instance, fish and yogurt or honey and Persian melon. If we had too much cold-natured food such as pomegranate, melon or citrus fruits, we got stomachaches, and the remedy was to have a cup of boiling water and crystal sugar (*nabat dagh*), and in case we had too many dates, we topped it up with yogurt or a cup of water mixed with hedge-mustard seeds (*khak e shir*).

You might not be able to get Kabkab or Khanizi where you are; however, you can dare to create the rich, spicy, wild taste of hot Dashtestan's most common foods. Here are the recipes for *lalak*, *qalyeh mahi*, and *ranginak* for desert provided by my cousin Attieh:

Lalak

Lalak is ground wheat. For each cup of lalak, use two cups of water
Lots of fried onions, very oily
A bit of salt
A little sugar (more than salt)

Put the water in the frying onion and let it boil. Then add the lalak and stir until water covers the lalak and until it boils again. Keep stirring. Bring the flame down to low. You can use chicken broth instead of water.

Cook the whole thing in a pot and not a pan. Wrap the lid with a towel or a rag and let the lalak cook like rice until soft. Serve lalak with date syrup and *ghalieh mahi*.

Qalieh Mahi

Different kinds of fish or shrimp may be used. The most common fish of the Persian Gulf are *qobad* (trout), *halva*, *shir* (lionfish), *sangesar* (otolith), *shoorideh* (salty fish).

Lightly fry the onion and the garlic. Garlic and red chili pepper should be smashed together to bring tears to your eyes.

Herbs: cilantro, *shanbelileh* [fenugreek], and a little bit of dill.

Chop up very finely and lightly fry. Add water as if you are making a soup. Add tamarind. (Soak the tamarind in hot water and use the pulp without the seeds and roots; the amount is optional). Think of it as tomato sauce. Add the fish or shrimp last and let the whole thing boil until tender. The fish for *qalieh* is usually lionfish, otolith fish, or trout. Wash the filets of fish; put some turmeric and salt on it to take the bad smell away. Do not forget the salt.

Serve lalak in a flat plate, put heated date syrup on it, and add the qalieh on the side.

Ranginak

Ranginak is made of dates, walnuts, flour, oil, powdered sugar, and cinnamon for decoration.

First, we take the seeds out of the dates. Then we put the walnut chunks inside the date and roll the date between the palms of our hands to make a ball. We arrange the balls around a flat dish to cover the entire surface of the dish.

In a saucepan, we put about two cups of flour and stir it on the stove to get brown. We need to stir it constantly in order not to burn it. Then we gently add a cup of oil and stir again until the paste becomes brown and the aroma of halva fills the house. We pour the paste on top of the dates on the plate when it is still very hot.

With a sifter, we scatter powdered sugar on the top and all over evenly.

Cut out a piece of paper with a design of your choice and lay it on top of the powdered sugar and fill up the carved design with cinnamon. We put it away to cool down.

If you started to sweat, are about to choke to death, and do not know when you had enough, then you have gotten it right.

Enjoy! Survive!

Dates on a palm tree. Photo: Sayeh Dashti, Borazjan, 1997.

Ranginak. Photo: Sayeh Dashti, at Attieh's house, Qeitarieh, Tehran, 2014.

Forty-Nine
Homemade Delivery

D riving daily on the narrow and winding roads in West Los Angeles had almost become an automatic act. Many times it felt as if the car knew where it was going, allowing me to do my own things, i.e., putting on mascara, changing a sweater, eating, etc. The only thing that suddenly distracted me was a scent or rather a memory of a scent. The most familiar yet mysterious aroma from the past followed by a nostalgic feeling would become irresistible. Somehow on a curve on the road, the sensation of an aroma that mysteriously took me to the vague, distant past was retrieved in my memory.

I had been away from home for so long, I avoided such vivid images of the past. This association, however, took me home with it despite my subconscious effort to stay in denial; not facing the reality that I missed home so badly. It inevitably invited me to search in my mind for its source. Was it a certain food? Was it a perfume? What was it? I was not succeeding. The more I thought, the less I could find; it remained a mystery for a couple of years. There were times when I stopped the car and sniffed. I would feel dizzy with a certain rapture; a divine sensation, yet I could not find out where it came from.

One random day, while having millions of things on my mind, it suddenly occurred to me. The secret was revealed. What a tremendous discovery it was.

I wanted to applaud my brain for functioning properly. I felt as complete as holding a beloved after a long, long separation.

It came to me, it enveloped me:

It was the aroma of dried figs inside my nursery school lunch box.

The image of the yellow-checkered leather lunch box became so vivid I could touch it. I used to embrace the joy of having in my possession a piece of home in the strange environment of the nursery school. As a child, those small round dried figs in my lunch box had become like magic marbles in my pocket.

I could imagine myself holding on to the lunch box. I must have peeked in there, in search of the security of home, too many times a day.

Is it the same mechanism that drives me and most of my fellow countrymen who have been torn from our homeland to carry astonishing amounts of food items from Iran to our families all over the world? Do we want them to smell and taste the warmth of home?

Traveling to different parts of the world, I have never seen other nationalities have so many suitcases.

The airport Customs employees in California seem to be aware of this fact. If one has been to Iran, the red alarm is on. "Behold! Search this sentimental creature!"

They all know we have food items. They all know we lie about it. The reason they do not stop us all to search and take away our pistachios, dried herbs, couple of fresh green plums, walnuts, sour cherries, etc., is probably because they do not have enough staff members and or adequate time to do so. Randomly, they let some of us go without a search. What a relief!

Leaving Customs at California airports feels like being a champion coming out of the tunnel entrance into the stadium packed with fans. The children waiting anxiously at the airport cheering their heroes; as if welcoming their champions to the field. The first thing they want to know is, did you do it? Did you bring us the fruit rolls, pickles, the nuts, the fresh fruit? Caviar?

My husband put five baby sour cherry trees in his coat pockets and smuggled them into San Francisco Airport. Hooray!!!!!!!!!

I am proud to say that on one of my trips to visit my children, I smuggled seventy pounds of fruit rolls I had personally made, including a table cover of one and a half meters in diameter that I had managed to create out of fruit for my son's wedding. It was made of seven summer fruits: sour cherries, apricots, wild sour plums [*hali*], nectarines, peaches, *rotab*s [fresh dates], and giant blackberries.

The round golden table cover had been cooked by the sun on the roof of our home in the mountains. Before it completely dried, I wrote a message on it to my son and his bride, congratulating them. The message was written in ruby red made of sweet cherries.

I usually guard the fruit rolls as they dry in the sun to make sure no insects or particles of dirt alight on them. When I returned after a few minutes to check on the spread I noticed that the writing had turned to bright yellow! The honeybees were indulging in the sweet syrup! I know how disappointed they usually are as they come around and try the fresh spread of fruits. Unfortunately for them, they are usually so nastily sour that they leave disappointed. I was secretly happy for them. I gently picked up the round sour table spread. It had turned out perfectly; only the message, completely legible was left hollow. The yellow calligraphy, *CONGRATULATIONS*, remained on the roof; alive and busy.

On that trip I was stopped at the airport in San Francisco by the Customs. The agent took a piece of it to the office of the Department of Agriculture at the airport for inspection. He came back in 20 minutes or so and told me that it was okay to bring processed food into the country, "But lady! This much?!!!" He hated me for that. I had so much to tell him, but I simply said, "You don't know my children."

I wanted to tell him that you do not know that my children have seen the young trees being planted, they have seen them grow, they have waited for the blossoms to give birth to fruits. They have followed their growth via the Internet and by pictures we send them. They have asked us to tell them exactly how many inches each tree has grown since they were away from the trees and from their family. I wanted to tell him that now the trees are tall, the sour cherry trees are like beautiful young girls, full of coquetry. I wanted to tell him that after the rain, when the sunshine hits the young trees, the whole ground lights up like a Christmas tree, filled with shiny red ornaments. The cherries are sweet and sour and delicate, filled with heavenly wine. My children, who were told not to eat the cherries unwashed, came home looking guilty. You see, they were mostly drunk with its juice; the purple stain around their mouths gave them away every time.

I wonder if he realized how proud I was to have been able to magically squeeze the essence of home into thin layers of fruit rolls. I had come to present to them the accomplishment of a holy mission; not allowing even a single piece of fruit to go to waste. My children and grandchildren owned it; it belonged to them and they must have it.

If he only knew that my adult children fight over their share of the fruit rolls. If he had only seen the sparkle in my daughter's bright eyes as she felt the connection with home. If he only knew that my son-in-law hides his share in a safe. My grandchildren agreed to exchange their pacifiers for a promise of pieces of these rolls. If he only knew that my older son meditates as he keeps the roll in his mouth and my younger son's girlfriend bashfully eats away roll after roll like a little mouse. If he only knew that the tallest member of the Chinese National Wushu team performed a whole ceremony in front of us and in honor of the rolls, testifying that they are unlike anything he ever tasted in his life. If he only knew!

Left: Sour cherries and wild plums. Right: Fruit roll (*lavashak*) made from sour cherries and wild plums. Photo: Sayeh Dashti, Meigoon, 2015.

Note from my grandson Kea, Berkeley, California, 2012.

Fifty
Enshallah (God Willing)

I get caught every time I say *Enshallah*! My granddaughter, Darya, jumps out of her seat every time she hears me say *"Enshallah!"*

"Bibi, you said *Enshallah*," she catches me every time.

How alert could she be? She was still a baby when I admitted how as children we resented hearing our mother say that word. My grandchildren were very curious to know why that was. I tried explaining my feelings and at the same time I wanted to protect the image of my mother, the real Bibi, in the minds of her great-grandchildren.

"You see, kids, it must have been very difficult for our mother to arrange for an outing with eight children and so many other responsibilities," I said, trying to find an excuse for Bibi. Then quietly I revealed, "My mother was just not an outdoors person. Her children, on the other hand, would have loved to go out for a picnic every holiday." They wanted to know more.

"In the beginning, we trusted our mother and we trusted God. The word *Enshallah* means if God wills it. So we started begging God to will it. God seldom willed it; once or twice a year, if we were lucky," I said. "Was God on your mother's side?" six-year-old Kea asked. "I am sure God wanted what was best for all of us," I said and continued:

Thanks be to God, one day a year, *sizdeh be dar*, the thirteenth day of NoRouz (Persian picnic) was set aside for a picnic in nature, and perhaps, once more in the summer when we forced our mother to take us for a picnic in a great park called Manzarieh in the north of Tehran. The rest of the time she dismissed all our nagging by saying *Enshallah*.

Again Darya jumped up and yelled, "Bibi, you said *Enshallah!*"

◆ ◆ ◆

The *sizdeh be dar* outings were so magical, of course we wanted more of them. Our family rented a big bus from a company called TBT, the kind of bus that travelled between cities. All of us ran inside taking the large airplane-style seats covered with white cloth. Our heads could hardly reach the top of the seat in front of us, nevertheless we were each given a seat. Usually another family (Zohi and her family) accompanied

292

us. The entire bus was filled up with little and big people. We sang all the way to our destination. Most of what we were letting out of our throats with such intensity was not just songs; we mostly improvised screams of joy."[1]

My grandchildren Kea and Darya. Photo: Sayeh Dashti, Berkeley, California, 2012.

We told my youngest grandchild Kayhan, born 2013, about Enshallah, and his re-sponse was "Bandydoonda. Dadadooda. Ice cream." Photo: Kayhan Morshed (at age two): Sayeh Dashti, Berkeley, California, 2014.

Ironically, as much as I resented hearing this word as a child, I had become conditioned to using the same excuse as a mother, but it was not working! What a useful tool our mother had to dismiss any inconvenient or unwanted activity; it was the age of parents' will and parents were God.

During motherhood of young children, however, my generation had turned out to be much less dependent on God's will. We had claimed the power of being able to change things on our own. Consequently, in order to dismiss the uncomfortable, the undesirable, or to have the luxury of indecisiveness, we said, "I will try" but that was not working either. Well, maybe there was a different kind of God now on the job. Or maybe the old God was not being on our side as mothers! It was the age of children's will.

This same God had now led my son to read the entire collection of *Star Wars* at the age of 12. He knew every quotation by heart. He read them like a holy book. He kissed the book before he went to sleep and laid it on the chair next to his pillow.

When I came to his room to tuck him in, he would jump with panic making sure I did not sit on his holy *Star Wars*.

He was being Luke, the Skywalker and his mentor was Jedi Master, Yoda.

Yoda had revealed the fact to him that if one says, I will try, one is allowing a leeway not to commit to a decision.

Mothers of my generation did not have the grandeur of our own mothers. At the same time, we had already lost the support of God. Now our children were more important; they had a voice and had learned to challenge us. This was the age of reason. Every child wanted to know "Why?" "Just tell me why!"

So the challenge started. I was being defeated and would get mad at my son for not buying my "I will try" way of not committing. My son would pause, look up with a pale and calm face and a mystified smile saying, "Do or do not! There is no try."

I feared Yoda's wisdom. He was more powerful and more knowledgeable than me, in every way. Now his apprentice, my son, was not even letting me feel the fear. "Fear is the path to the dark side. Fear leads to anger, anger leads to hate, hate leads to suffering."

My three children, Shawhin, Shahaub, Nooshin. Photo: Tehran, August 1999.

Notes

1   Story 25, "NoRouz," in this volume.

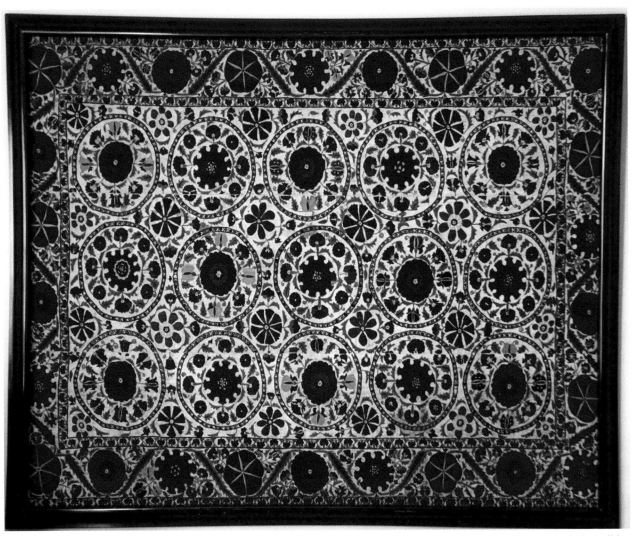

This hand-crocheted kingsize bedspread (*Rashti-doozi*) was given by our father to Bibi as a gift. It was used as a tablecloth at all her children's weddings. Bibi brought this for me when she came to visit us in Los Angeles. Photo: Mohsen Jazayeri, 2015.

Edwards Brothers Malloy
Thorofare, NJ USA
November 28, 2016